Arresting Development

WORLD COMICS AND GRAPHIC NONFICTION SERIES
FREDERICK LUIS ALDAMA AND CHRISTOPHER GONZALEZ, EDITORS

The World Comics and Graphic Nonfiction series includes monographs and edited volumes that focus on the analysis and interpretation of comic books and graphic nonfiction from around the world. The books published in the series use analytical approaches from literature, art history, cultural studies, communication studies, media studies, and film studies, among other fields, to help define the comic book studies field at a time of great vitality and growth.

[CHRISTOPHER PIZZINO]

Arresting Development

COMICS AT THE BOUNDARIES OF LITERATURE

University of Texas Press 〰 AUSTIN

Requests for permission to reproduce material from this work should be sent to:
Permissions
University of Texas Press
P.O. Box 7819
Austin, TX 78713-7819
http://utpress.utexas.edu/index.php/rp-form

♾ The paper used in this book meets the minimum requirements of ANSI/NISO Z39.48-1992 (R1997) (Permanence of Paper).

LIBRARY OF CONGRESS CATALOGING-IN-PUBLICATION DATA

Names: Pizzino, Christopher, author.
Title: Arresting development : comics at the boundaries of literature / Christopher Pizzino.
Description: First edition. Austin : University of Texas Press, 2016. Includes bibliographical references and index.
Series: The world comics and graphic nonfiction series
Identifiers: LCCN 2016003031 (print) LCCN 2016005501 (ebook)
   ISBN 9781477309773 (cloth : alk. paper)
   ISBN 9781477310687 (pbk. : alk. paper)
   ISBN 9781477309780 (library e-book)
   ISBN 9781477309797 (non-library e-book)
Subjects: LCSH: Comic books, strips, etc.—History and criticism.
Classification: LCC PN6714 .P59 2016 (print) LCC PN6714 (ebook)
   DDC 741.5/9—dc23
   LC record available at http://LCCN.loc.gov/2016003031

doi: 10.7560/309773

For Michael McKeon

Contents

Acknowledgments

I think it fitting to begin by thanking my students at the University of Georgia, whose sharp eyes and critical skills have shaped my own perceptions. I would be remiss not to recognize the following individuals by name: Elizabeth Beck, Caitlin Belton, Lauren Berg, Katelyn Binder, Philip Brettschneider, Justin Burnley, Tiffany Chu, Andrew Cole, Parker Couch, Nikki Curry, Ben DeCorso, Wes Fenlon, Ariel Garrett, Sean Gorman, Josh Johns, Jacob Karle, Zach Keepers, Christine Lee, Jamie Lewis, Joey Lynn, Jasmine Morrissette, Patrick Najjar, Miranda Nelson, Erin O'Quinn, Lian Peters, Emma Powers, Emily Shaw, Mike Smith, Ty Stewart, MacKenzie Turner and Tom Webster. I am indebted to students in my 2014 graduate seminar, Image Theory and Visual Narrative, for stimulating discussion that influenced the final shape of the book. I also thank the members of UGA's Comics Reading Group, especially Miriam Brown-Spiers, Laurie Norris and group founder Casey Westerman, for being great interlocutors in the early stages of my research. I also offer thanks to UGA's Comics Creators Association, particularly group founder Megan Nelson, whose enthusiasm, wisdom and goodwill exemplify what's best in the comics community.

Time and resources for the completion of key portions of this book were generously supplied by a research fellowship from the Willson Center for the Humanities and Arts at UGA and by the university's Sarah Moss Research Grant. Not all comics scholars receive such pronounced support from their home institutions, and I feel my debt to the university keenly.

It takes a village to complete a book—at least it does when the book is mine—and this work has benefited from not one but two strong villages. My colleagues in UGA's English Department welcomed the arrival of a comics scholar in their midst and have provided unstinting professional and intellectual support. Doug Anderson, Adam Parkes and Aidan Wasley have been trustworthy guides and mentors throughout the process of writing and publication. Michelle Baliff, Chris Eaket, Roxanne Eberle, LeAnne Howe, Miriam Jacobson, Barbara McCaskill, Richard Menke, Jed Rasula, Susan Rosenbaum, Esra Santesso, Fran Teague and Andrew Zawacki all deserve thanks for being there, as readers, interlocutors or cheerleaders, as this book coalesced. Thanks also to Ed Pavlić, whom I had the pleasure of working with before we arrived by separate routes at UGA. Ed has remained a valued colleague and adviser through bad times and good.

The second village is the field of comics studies, which has offered intellectual sustenance and solidarity despite its being scattered across so many disciplines. While grateful to colleagues I've met at countless conference centers, restaurants and hotel lobbies and lounges over the years when this book was written, I have special debts to those with whom I've worked in the Modern Language Association's Discussion Group on Comics and Graphic Narratives, including Jonathan Gray, Susan Kirtley, Martha Kuhlman and Nhora Lucía Serrano. I also thank Tim Caron, with whom I've had the pleasure of crossing paths at conferences since before the Discussion Group existed, and Hilda Chacón, who was good enough to include my paper on Gilbert Hernandez on a panel at MLA 2013. I am indebted to Qiana Whitted for great conversations on mid-century comics during a visit she made to UGA in 2014. Donald Ault at the University of Florida, along with Mel Loucks and the other organizers of the university's Conference on Comics Studies, deserves special mention; I appreciate the opportunity to present my work, and I thank the conference participants for the stimulating discussion that influenced some of this book's key concepts. William Kuskin has been a great editor, mentor and friend, and my interactions with him have fortified my critical resolve and sharpened this book's purpose again and again. I must especially thank Charles Hatfield and Hillary Chute; I owe great personal and intellectual debts to both of them, not least for serving as insightful readers of the manuscript. Charles has been an exemplary senior colleague, and his wisdom is surpassed only by his graciousness. Hillary, whom I've had the privilege of knowing since graduate school, remains a deeply valued friend and interlocutor.

My oldest scholarly and personal debts, which I can never hope to repay, are the greatest pleasure to acknowledge here. Anthony Lioi has been as wonderful a friend and fellow nerd as I could hope to have, and I feel keenly how inadequate any words of thanks to him could be. I'm grateful for his faith in this project, which not infrequently surpassed my own. It is also a delight to thank Channette Romero, whose years of encouragement, advice and friendship have been invaluable beyond measure. Without her support, not least her reading of portions of this manuscript and her patience in listening to many halting expositions of half-finished ideas, this book would never have been completed.

Any responsible fan-addict should not neglect to thank his or her dealers, and thus I must pay tribute to Rob Brown and Devlin Thompson at Bizarro-WUXTRY, a comix shop worthy of the name. I am also thankful for superb research assistance from Eric Aubuchon, Rajesh Reddy and especially Kaitlyn Smith, who tackled a number of complex tasks with great skill and insight.

Working with the University of Texas Press has been a true pleasure. The support provided by Jim Burr has made all the difference, and I am grateful for the chance to thank him in print for the key role he has played in making this book a reality. Frederick Luis Aldama and Christopher Gonzalez, editors of UTP's World Comics and Graphic Nonfiction series, likewise deserve greater thanks than I can easily articulate. It's been a privilege to get to know Frederick and to reconnect with Christopher, who has long had my respect as a colleague and as my editor for the special issue of *ImageTexT* (7.1, 2013), in which portions of chapter 6 first appeared as "Autoclastic Icons: Bloodletting and Burning in Gilbert Hernandez's Palomar." My thanks to *ImageTexT* for granting reprint permissions. Portions of chapters 1 and 2 originally appeared in *PMLA* 130.3 (May 2015), published by the Modern Language Association of America.

Despite their vocations being grounded in the printed and spoken word—my mother as an English teacher, my father as a minister—both my parents accepted my childhood comics reading without reproach. Perhaps the blame for such a foolhardy venture as this book should ultimately be laid at their doorstep. In all seriousness, I wish to thank my parents, my brother, and my sister and her family for their love and support, especially during seasons when this book was an all-consuming task.

Deeply grateful thanks are due to Christine M. Nicklin, the most perceptive, patient, thorough and tireless reader of *Arresting Development*. Her enthusiasm for this project, and her confounding tolerance of its author, are things neither words nor pictures can readily capture.

I offer final thanks to Michael McKeon, whose work on questions of legitimation has been a permanent influence on my own. I dedicate this book to him both for his mentoring, which profoundly guided my growth as a young scholar, and for the rare quality of his personal and professional example.

Arresting Development

Introduction

FROM THE BASEMENT

Comics Not Just for Kids Anymore, Reports 85,000th Mainstream News Story

HEADLINE FROM *THE ONION*, 2012

I n an era when journalism is not always distinguishable from fake news, a scholarly book that begins by citing *The Onion* is not, I suppose, very shocking. What may surprise the reader is how far I will take the hint contained in this epigraph: to wit, I claim that the story mainstream US culture tells itself about comics is deeply flawed. Once upon a time—so the story goes—comics were disposable and juvenile, fit only for children or for culturally stunted adults unable to leave their adolescence behind. Then the medium awakened from its long period of arrested development, thanks to the rise of graphic novels—book-length comics of high literary quality. This two-part narrative of comics' coming of age could hardly be neater, but it is odd that such a simple story should need to be continuously repeated.

The Onion's claim to 85,000 articles about how comics are "not just for kids anymore" is typically exaggerated, but it is true that such articles have been published for about thirty years. This is a suspiciously long coming of age, and it suggests complications that do not fit the official narrative of comics' upward mobility. In fact, comics are not on equal footing with most other print or visual media in the United States, and this inequality has had a profound influence on comics, both on the medium as a whole and on individual comics makers. I have written this book to show how the medium's status struggles affect even the most respected contemporary creators, and how the signs of these struggles can be read on the comics page.

The simplest way to summarize the problems comics face is to say that the medium is still considered illegitimate, despite the rise of the graphic novel; usually, the latter is treated as a special case. In the article that follows the typically hyperbolic *Onion* headline, we learn exactly what this "85,000th mainstream news story" claims about comics today:

> "Exchanging lighthearted fare for darker subject matter, films like 'The Dark Knight Rises' and graphic novels by authors such as Chris Ware show that comics can have immense appeal for adults," read the groundbreaking article, making an astute and truly mind-blowing observation that had only been made 84,999 times before. "You may think adult-oriented comic books are merely the province of Archie and Jughead, but if the current trend is any indication, one thing remains clear: Comics are growing up." The incredibly perceptive and original article also specifically mentioned the work of writer Alan Moore, an obscure reference point that has only been used in every single article like this ever written. (1)

Anyone acquainted with mainstream journalism on comics will recognize these familiar patterns: the association of comics with blockbuster films derived from them (as if the success of the films necessarily means the elevation of the comics), the developmental language ("growing up") used in conjunction with claims about adult content ("darker subject matter"), the mention of well-known comics creators long since granted a measure of respect in mainstream culture (Ware and Moore), and the implicit contrast between the work of such creators and comics fit for young readers ("lighthearted fare" such as Archie comics). Numerical exaggeration aside, this article gives an accurate sketch of the unstable ground on which comics are currently situated. There seems to be an agreement that comics were once fit only for young readers, and that the medium has matured so that it is worthy of some adult attention. Yet this claim to legitimacy is proclaimed again and again without being established once and for all. The repetition indicates a deep cultural unease with comics, as does the phrase "not just for kids anymore," praise so faint that it verges on condemnation. The kind of article *The Onion* is mocking implies that comics have fitfully extended their reach into the realm of adult literature without having left behind their default role as juvenile reading ("the province of Archie and Jughead"). It would seem that adult comics readers *might* not be overgrown children, despite evidence to the contrary; after all, they do read comics.

In the face of such a negligible gain in status, it is natural for comics readers and scholars to feel divided about the mainstream story of comics' coming of age. It is a convenient elevator pitch, to use business parlance, for comics reading. It explains in the space of a sound bite why adult audiences should read graphic novels today—and, not to exempt myself, why the reader holding this book should give comics serious attention. But such an utterly false history cannot show us what is actually interesting about comics, of whatever kind. The medium's story is not one of natural development from pulp infancy to literary adulthood. It is a history of conflict in which comics have continuously been read by adults, but have been banned, threatened with censorship, excluded from or subordinated to other media in educational settings, and otherwise pushed to the margins of culture.

Many comics readers are aware of this fraught history, and the cultural memory of the worst days of censorship, if not always accurate, remains vivid. Yet there is also awareness that the medium is less severely marginalized today, even if current conditions are not ideal. The category of graphic novel does not signal the end of comics' status struggles, but it might at least point the way to a more level cultural playing field. Thus we see "a new convention of . . . bemoaning the need to justify the medium" along with a tacit understanding that the mainstream story is of some value, even if its repetition only reminds us of all it leaves out (Williams and Lyons xiii). The article in *The Onion*, which seems both to mock journalistic accounts of the status quo and to accept that it is, in fact, the status quo, exemplifies this state of affairs.

In this study, I refuse even a grudging acceptance of the mainstream narrative, understandable though acceptance might be. Seeking a clearer understanding of how comics are marginalized today, I argue that focusing on the problem of status greatly enriches our reading of the graphic novel and our understanding of how marginalized media work. I begin with the proposition that while comics are less reviled now than they were in the worst years of censorship, the medium is still designated illegitimate by default. Working from this proposition, which is unfolded at length in the first chapter, I show that contemporary comics creators, despite the measure of respect some have been accorded, know quite well where their medium stands in culture at large and display this awareness frequently in their work. The stories comics creators tell about their own status, the dynamic and intricate pictures they make of it and of their medium's struggle with illegitimacy, are the central concern of this study.

More broadly, this is also a book about how cultural status, and the separation of high and low culture, art and pulp, sophisticated appreciation and vulgar consumption—all the old divisions that have supposedly faded away—still influence not only the status of the books we read, but also the value of the act of reading, and the cultural and social standing of readers. One scholar observes that "in an increasingly postmodern world in which the distinction between high and low culture is often assumed to have been eroded, outmoded biases continue to persist in the shaping of how we understand culture broadly," and that comics are often marked as culturally illegitimate despite the supposed collapse of the old cultural hierarchy (Beaty, *Comics Versus Art* 7). My own view is that high-low cultural distinctions are not at all "outmoded" or obsolete (though one wishes they were). Ideas of what counts as respectable culture have softened considerably since the middle of the twentieth century, but they are not essentially different—not, at least, when it comes to comics. The myth of the high-low collapse has only made ongoing status problems more difficult to notice and articulate. Yet the illegitimacy of the medium should call for sustained attention, not least because the very act of reading comics can alter readers' status by regulating what, and who, can be designated respectably "adult."

Thus I pursue a way of reading comics that works against the narrative of respectability and remains fascinated with the problem of status—especially with how it is visible, and readable, on the comics page. Contemporary comics are marked again and again by the stigma of illegitimacy, and this marking is active, complex, and deeply fraught. The four creators I examine in my case studies are all acclaimed as graphic novelists, yet they do not consider themselves exempt from the status problems affecting comics as a whole. Instead, they dwell on the medium's illegitimacy as something they cannot avoid. As we will see, they address status problems with extraordinary creative energy, but it is a divided and self-opposed energy, split by the pressure of the very problem it confronts. The term I give this dynamic is "autoclasm," or self-breaking, and it is the hallmark of the comics considered here.

"Autoclasm" expresses the illegitimacy of comics not as a theme that can be safely contained, but as a reality inside which the comics creator must struggle. What motivates the self-opposed tactics of autoclasm is the longevity, and the strength, of anti-comics stigma. Though it has been directed more at some comics genres than others, this stigma marks the medium as unable to speak for itself or determine its own fate. Through autoclasm, creators picture the disenfranchisement that, to one degree or another, comes with the very act of making comics. Against the mainstream narrative, in which at least some graphic novelists can transcend the stigma of immaturity and vulgarity attached to comics, autoclasm testifies to a struggle with problems of status that binds creators across many genres and production models.

Autoclasm arises out of the lived experience and the conscious attitudes of comics creators, often expressed clearly in their writings and interviews. Take, for example, an interview with five highly respected creators, including Charles Burns and Seth, conducted in 2001. While committed to the medium as a form of expression with boundless potential, all five creators testify to struggles for economic stability (Seth observes that when choosing to pursue comics as a teenager, he "had no idea that [he] was picking a career that [he] would have to back up with another career") and to the problem of cultural indifference toward, or contempt for, comics (Groth, "Six Guys" 70). Burns observes: "I'm always really cautious about trying to explain to people the kind of comics I do. If I say something about doing comics for adults, the first thing they're going to think is, 'Oh, you do porno.' Usually I say I'm an illustrator; that makes it a little easier. . . . [W]hen you try to explain what kind of comics you do, you dig yourself into a deeper hole. . . . 'No, it's not in the newspapers, it's not like *Peanuts* exactly . . . it's something that's not for children'" (61–62). The dilemma Burns describes, in which making comics means either making something for children or making smut, certainly indicates how the idea of the graphic novel has bridged a cultural gap, creating new ways to conceive of (at least some) comics as legitimate for adult readers. Burns takes no comfort from this; the problem of status is still too pressing for the diminishment of anti-comics stigma to offer much consolation.

One might expect a complex awareness of status questions to be stronger among earlier generations of comics artists who spent most or all of their careers with no expectation of even a small degree of cultural legitimacy. In fact, it is when the quasi legitimation offered by the graphic novel emerges that a combination of contentiousness and skepticism becomes more fully articulated. Take, for example, the generational differences visible in the 2005 volume *Eisner/Miller*, a series of lengthy conversations between two prominent creators in which the dominant subject is the medium's status. Will Eisner, a towering figure who began work as a comic book illustrator in the late 1930s, and whose 1978 work A Con-

tract with God was the first comic to be widely recognized as a graphic novel, is even-tempered concerning the abysmal conditions in which many comics creators were forced to spend their careers. His vision of comics' future is decidedly optimistic: "I believe in the future of this medium and think it will be tremendous. More tremendous than it's ever been" (173).[1] Eisner's younger interlocutor, Frank Miller, who became renowned in the late 1970s and early 1980s, resists Eisner's view and speaks of the medium as deeply scarred by long-standing illegitimacy. He believes it is possible to embrace this condition: "I think we are in a young and vital form that has a rather dangerous outlaw aspect to it, and that's one of the things I love about it" (162). Yet his culturally derived memory of comics history is much more resentful than Eisner's personal memory; Miller talks angrily and almost compulsively about the damage the comics code of 1954 inflicted on the medium, though he was not alive when it was first put into effect.[2]

Miller has had expansive creative freedom (incalculably more than Eisner had in his earliest days in the industry) and a measure of cultural prestige; his acclaimed 1986 series *Batman: The Dark Knight Returns* was one of the first widely legitimated graphic novels. Given such achievement and recognition, it is tempting to judge remarks like the following as oddly backward-looking and needlessly defensive: "Why be ashamed of ourselves? . . . In the early eighties, a colleague of mine got a prose novel published. And one of the top people at Marvel Comics turned to me and said, 'As of today, this guy's a giant and we're ants because he's a real writer.' Jesus Christ! His book was remaindered by Berkeley!" (172–173). Miller's active remembrance of such a moment, clearly still suffused with the anger it evoked from the first, is not a perversity born of privilege, and it exemplifies the paradoxical stance of many comics creators who have gained fame in the era of the graphic novel. On the one hand, there is a refusal of low self-esteem, an embrace of creative possibility and a determination to make comics matter (hence Miller's disgust at his fellow comics creator who feels that he is not "a real writer"). On the other hand, there is a strong awareness of the realities of cultural status and of the ways status can influence creative and career possibilities (thus, Miller makes a point of the fact that his former colleague's book was published by a second-rate genre imprint and subsequently failed to sell).

The contrast between Eisner and Miller is, perhaps, too neatly fitted to the argument I will be making; not all creators of Eisner's generation have been so philosophical concerning the poor conditions in which they labored, and not all artists who came to prominence in the era of the graphic novel have been self-styled firebrands, as Miller has. Nevertheless, many of Miller's contemporaries, including those who are now respected in literary and fine arts discourses, share his basic stance. Such skepticism does not preclude awareness of the uses of the graphic novel; the two can sometimes go hand in hand. In a 1995 interview, Art Spiegelman, concerned that the medium's readership will continue to shrink, as it has for decades, proposes that comics ought to "drift over toward 'legitimate' culture," because their access to an audience may well come to depend on "a system that includes university studies, museum shows, the literary 'respectability' that allows them to exist in bookstores. . . . [S]ome kind of pact with the Devil has got to be made for comics to survive" (Groth interview 62).[3] Spiegelman's approach to the question of status is pragmatic; legitimation is seen as a compromise driven by necessity, not as something that might utterly transform the medium's status, much less as an improvement significant enough to change how creators feel about making comics.

A forceful rejection of self-imposed shame, alongside a keen sense of what it means to be viewed as illegitimate and an unwillingness to let this awareness slip away—this complex attitude, far more than acceptance of current conditions or overt optimism, typifies the work of contemporary comics creators. I track this attitude, ambitious yet attuned to the medium's low status, as its tensions manifest, through autoclasm, at the level of the individual comics text. Art Spiegelman's sketchbook doodle gives us a striking instance of an autoclastic icon (figure 0.1). A giant in comics and, since the appearance of *Maus*, a respectable presence in culture at large, Spiegelman draws himself as a diminutive, threatened figure overwhelmed by his situation. He crouches on a tightrope, arms akimbo, head sunk anxiously into his shoulders and body off-balance, one leg poised above the line on which he is situated. The caption reads: "In late middle-age Spiegelman still tries to learn how to walk the line . . ." The most acclaimed and widely respected comics maker in the era of the graphic novel, Spiegelman renders himself with no fixed place, an instant away from a nasty fall.

What exactly is the "line" on which Spiegelman situates himself, and which has just broken loose? It is a link, apparently unsustainable, between two visions of comics and two kinds of culture. The still-attached anchor point behind Spiegelman is the name of underground comix artist Robert Crumb, composed of genitalia and libidinously erect characters. Crumb stands both for underground comix scenes of the 1960s and

0.1. Art Spiegelman, 2007 sketchbook drawing from Be a Nose!, 2009.

1970s in which Spiegelman was also involved and, more broadly, for the *MAD* magazine tradition of lowbrow humor that has been a creative wellspring for many postwar comics artists. The now-detached point ahead of Spiegelman is Saul Steinberg, a cartoonist whose classical balance and delicate, literary wit evoke connections to the fine arts and to fine writing. Spiegelman has often testified to an interest in making art that has both low and high cultural attributes, but this doodle suggests that the gap between the dirty vulgarity of Crumb and the respectable, and exceptional, legitimacy of Steinberg cannot be bridged. Given his artistic proclivities, his roots, and his record of achievement, Spiegelman would be the single creator most qualified to close the gap, but he figures himself as failing. The little height he has attained does not seem sustainable as a kind of cultural legitimacy, and the name of Steinberg stands alone, detached from the irredeemable tradition represented by Crumb.

But as with all the works I will be considering, the cultural struggles represented in this image are even more dynamic than a first glance might reveal. Perhaps the line has not broken loose but is unrolling, in defiance of gravity, as Spiegelman inches forward. In this reading, the name of Crumb, with its erectile solidity, is the reliable point from which Spiegelman can operate. Steinberg then becomes the most unstable element in this cultural equation. The precarious stacking of the letters of his name, together with the discarded G (by which Spiegelman also evokes questions of ethnic assimilation), suggests that the goal ahead is not a secure end point for the creator's journey. Perhaps Spiegelman hesitates, his foot suspended above the line, because he questions whether the respectability toward which he is moving is any improvement on the tradition that lies behind him.

Neither of these interpretations—failed aspiration, skepticism toward respectability—is optimistic, yet the two cannot be reconciled. Spiegelman suspends his life's work between two incommensurable possibilities: either the vulgar, antisocial practices native to his comics lineage cannot be joined to more sustainable goals or the vulgarity of this lineage is precisely what gives it artistic power and cultural significance (if not respectability). This is not a drawing about merely personal artistic uncertainty; Spiegelman defines himself in relation to larger cultural assumptions that keep low and high art separate. Like Spiegelman's line, the image as a whole breaks under the strain of what it expresses, namely, the culturally perilous position of the comics creator, caught between ambition for legitimacy and wariness of it.[4] In each case of autoclasm examined in these pages, we will see this pattern of creative energy arranged against itself, brilliantly picturing the fraught condition of the medium.

By placing the problem of illegitimacy directly in the path of the act of reading, I forgo the usual scholarly practice of sidestepping this problem. In the context of comics studies, illegitimacy is something like a very large elephant in a very small room: impossible to ignore altogether, but difficult to examine with care. Critics do acknowledge the medium's low status, but they often proceed to move around and past it. Thus Scott McCloud, creator of the most widely read theoretical account of comics in the United States, offers this defense of his project: "Sure, I realized that comic books were usually crude, poorly-drawn, semiliterate, cheap, disposable kiddie fare—but—they don't have to be!" (3.4–5). For sheer adroitness, one could do no better than this opening sentence from one of the earliest academic works on comics: "This book presupposes that comic books as cultural productions merit serious critical analysis" (Witek, *Comic Books* 3). Such critical moves are understandable, and the impulse behind them—the desire to talk about something other than status, and to proceed on some basis other than sheer defensiveness—has been crucial to the flourishing of comics scholarship, both in the academy and in comics culture more generally. Narrow focus on the medium's low status would obviously result in a claustrophobic field, and as recent decades have seen the partial mitigation of the worst damage done to comics, a backhanded mention of the medium's cultural condition has often sufficed. However, direct attention to how illegitimacy appears on the comics page is now overdue.

Thus I undertake this study of contemporary US comics from, as it were, the elephant's point of view, and with the comics page itself as the primary focus. In contemporary culture, swayed by the myth that all art forms and media have become equal, we are somewhat out of practice in thinking about cultural status, especially as it affects media. We accept, as indeed we should, the idea that gender, race, religion, class and sexuality can decisively influence writers or artists, shaping thematic or topical concerns as well as form and style. The question of *medium* as one of status, and therefore of creative possibility, is far less familiar to us. We have not grappled with the fact that comics makers can be influenced at every level of the creative process by difficulties that are intrinsic to the cultural position of comics. Later chapters will open up specific works as dealing with problems of legitimacy at many textual strata, from the way Frank Miller confronts the history surrounding the 1954 comics code in *Batman: The Dark Knight Returns* to the way Charles Burns shades his figures in *Black Hole*.

This way of reading makes four assumptions. First, creators can be profoundly influenced by questions of status, whether their work deliberately reflects on them or not (though deliberate reflection is very common). Second, even creators with a foothold in the literary mainstream confront essential problems of audience and public perception that surround comics as a whole in the United States; such problems influence what is expressed on the comics page even when there is no limitation on subject matter, no prescribed narrative direction and no stifling house style. Third, creators' status struggles, in all their fullness and complexity, constitute one of the richest ways creative energy is expressed; attention to this topic will reward careful reading.

My fourth, and perhaps most challenging, assumption is that questions of medium—and related matters, such as reading practice and literacy—constitute a separate horizon of concern, which can overlap other horizons without being identical to them. This assumption entails certain risks. A study that compares various comics creators on the basis of their experience *as* creators might end up erasing, or at least taking too little account of, the ways they differ on the basis of gender, ethnicity, sexuality, religion and class, as well as how they are differently positioned regarding production, distribution and audience. Alison Bechdel and Frank Miller would not describe their own experiences as comics artists, or their relationship to the question of the status of their work, in identical terms. I nevertheless find it appropriate for them to inhabit the same book about the problem of the medium's illegitimacy. Given that this problem, as it manifests on the comics page, is not yet an established concern among scholars, I think it right to focus on common narrative tendencies, ways of understanding cultural categories, and formal tactics that connect the work of disparate creators, no matter how widely varying their identities, aims or circumstances. These commonalities are rooted in the distinctive cultural situation of US comics, and the links between that situation and the comics themselves are my central concerns.

The ways of reading offered here can be applied to many more comics creators than the four major case studies considered in later chapters. Three of the figures I consider are white, and three are male; this is not a representative sampling of the creators and readers, present and future, with a stake in the fate of comics. If my choice of examples risks reinforcing the stereotype of the typical citizen of comics culture as a white male (defensive concerning questions of his cultural status, no less), I here point out that one of the best ways to keep a form of culture marginalized is to claim that it is privileged already. The idea of comics as a white male concern, and of the oppositional attitude of the comics creator or reader as a sort of rearguard maneuver in the name of patriarchal privilege, works less to increase our awareness of the importance of race, gender or class in the study of media than it does to obscure, once again, the importance of cultural legitimacy, in matters of medium and literacy, as a real concern for comics readers and creators across many lines of difference. In emphasizing these stakes, my study may possibly risk a kind of counterconflation in which comics become a figure for social inequities of all kinds; this problem will come into focus most clearly in the last two chapters.

The historical scope of this study is that of contemporary comics, by which I mean comics produced since the late 1970s; in other words, I am concerned with the period typically understood as the era of the graphic novel. In order to frame the comics of this period, I begin with a sketch of the status problems comics have faced since their emergence more than a century ago. The first chapter focuses primarily on what has been said about comics, both in culture at large and in academic accounts of the medium. As part of this discussion, I will complicate and critique the term "graphic novel"—which offers little descriptive accuracy or critical guidance, but has a great deal to tell us about the problem of illegitimacy—and connect it to what I call the *Bildungsroman* discourse that governs the mainstream narrative of comics history. In the second chapter, the focus will shift to what the problem of illegitimacy looks like from the perspective of comics creators themselves, and how this problem manifests on the comics page. I show that behind the *Bildungsroman* discourse centered on the graphic novel is an embattled state of affairs, one in which even the most widely respected comics creators confront the medium's illegitimacy through autoclastic icons. The remaining chapters consist of four case studies, each considering a creator whose career began in the late 1970s or early 1980s and took shape during the era of the graphic novel.

The four creators I discuss have a fundamental stake in questions of status, which influence both their thematic and their aesthetic choices. I see the way these creators incorporate and rework the problem of the medium's status as a source of great strength; without succumbing either to a self-defeating sense of worthlessness or to a discourse of upward mobility, they have made the damage done to comics radically visible in the medium itself. The case studies are arranged so as to begin with a tighter focus on comics culture and on the memories of the suppression of comics that the medium still carries within it, and then to widen the scope, asking how the condition of comics might resonate with other kinds of suppression and marginalization.

My analysis of Frank Miller's *The Dark Knight Returns* shows how comics remember and rework the mid-century moment of the code and its aftermath. In my discussion of Alison Bechdel's *Fun Home*, I examine some of the broader attitudes that tend to arise from the illicit nature of comics creation and reading, particularly a view of pleasure as a disruptive, antisocial force. Turning to Charles Burns's *Black Hole*, I consider how the illegitimacy of comics creates an affinity for other forms of abjection as well as a powerful vision of the exclusionary tendencies of modern social forms. Looking finally at Gilbert Hernandez's Palomar stories in *Love and Rockets*, Volume 1, I demonstrate how the violence done to comics gives rise to a powerful vocabulary for addressing many kinds of suffering, from physical abuse to political oppression. The goal of this sequencing of case studies is not to judge the relative merit or importance of the topics raised by a given creator (much less to evaluate the creator's importance), but simply to consider the kinds of work the illegitimacy of comics does at different conceptual levels.

In my conclusion, I pay tribute to an abiding wariness—sometimes sarcastic, occasionally hostile—toward established cultural forms and values that is strongly rooted in comics. There is sometimes a tendency to assume that the business of comics criticism is made possible by refining and disciplining one's youthful attitudes and attachments. The comics scholar, like the medium itself, seems obligated to grow up in order to gain respectable standing. My conclusion will oppose such a notion and advocate a more paradoxical stance that refuses to take the rhetoric of development that surrounds comics at face value. In these opening gestures I have taken my epigraph from one of the many offspring of MAD, and in my conclusion I will consider the significance of MAD itself, which for more than a century has been the greatest monument to suspicion of legitimate culture in all its forms.

While this study treats comics creators as active agents responding to their low status with creative force, it also explores how the medium as such has lived with its suppressed condition. I yield to what W. J. T. Mitchell calls an "incorrigible tendency to vitalistic and animistic ways of speaking when we talk about images" (*What Do Pictures Want?* 2). Speaking of comics as a living medium, I discuss how a comic can express, respond to, or make visible the problem of illegitimacy, as if the text were sentient, and self-reflexively aware of its status. While hoping, like most comics scholars, that the status of the medium will change, I focus on what is visible if we abide with the long-standing condition of comics and ask what the medium expresses *as* suppressed and illegitimate. In dealing exclusively with the most recent chapter of the history of comics, and with a subset of work produced by respected creators, this study should be seen as an opening inquiry that will hopefully be followed by others. What is disclosed here indicates that the inner life of "low" media can be much more complex than we tend to imagine, and that a medium can speak of its illegitimacy with eloquence.

In the case of the comics I consider, the medium responds to its status with energetically paradoxical thematics and aesthetic strategies, both acknowledging and exploiting its status to powerful effect. To speak responsibly of these characteristics of contemporary comics demands a countertranslation, resisting an urge to recast the object of study in established terms. Thus I have found it useful either to construct new concepts or to rework established categories in accordance with conditions observable in the medium itself. It has been necessary to employ such general concepts as legitimacy, status and power, but I have attempted to do so with an eye to the valences most relevant to the status of comics. One specific concept related to questions of legitimacy, the differend as articulated by Jean-François Lyotard, has proved useful in constructing the idea of autoclasm.

Other concepts arising from deconstruction and from theories of the postmodern have proved less applicable, as has the category of trauma. In earlier work I suggested that comics can be read as a traumatized medium, but I have come to believe that even a purely metaphorical application of the concept of trauma distorts more than it reveals about the condition of comics.[5] I have found some categories associated with trauma, particularly witnessing and repetition, to be applicable, but their function is notably different in the context of comics. In assessing the way comics respond to their status in fine detail, I will be insisting on distinctions not always observed in comics culture, or indeed in culture at large. But attention to the particular forms that illegitimacy takes, and to the precise ways in which creators respond to it, helps us understand the medium's past and present, offering new ways of reading that might help to shape a different future.

Haunting the background of any attempt to discuss the problem of comics' illegitimacy, I suspect, is a stereotype of the comics nerd—a pathetic figure, both driven and inept, and one whom the arrival of the graphic novel has done little to demystify—creeping up from the basement into the light of day to defend the medium before a contemptuous public. Basements, it should be noted, are terrible storage environments for one's comics, and the basement-dwelling reader new to comics studies should immediately invest in a dehumidifier, along with a ready supply of Mylar bags. Having thus rounded the stereotype, I want to insist that any prefatory awkwardness on display in these opening gestures is not intrinsic to comics. It may be tinged by the voice of the author (who is probably not best qualified to judge), but it certainly has to do with the medium's cultural position in the United States. Comics studies must overexplain itself for the same reason comics readers in general have long been on the defensive: because the medium is so marginalized, and so visibly marked as illegitimate. The effects of this illegitimacy on comics creators—most importantly, its profound influence on the work they produce—must now come into focus.

[   ]

In the context of the United States, to propose a new way to read comics is to upset the ubiquitous truism that everyone already knows how to read comics. This truism is certainly linked to the status of the medium, specifically to a decades-old belief that comics reading is, at best, a stepping-stone to the reading of print, so that mastery of the latter necessarily encompasses the former. As teachers who begin to assign comics quickly discover, some beginners find reading the medium's pictorial and design elements more challenging than scanning printed words. Most adults, including many academics, read comics rarely or never, which obviously affects how they take up a book on the subject.

Comics scholars are thus required to divide their critical energy. New work must enrich the existing conversation while providing points of access for those unfamiliar with comics and, for this latter audience, also managing an expectation of facility. Discussion of this problem is accompanied by a certain awkwardness—in the academy, it is bad form to suggest that any person in one's audience might not know how to read something—but it has to be confronted if comics studies is to widen its audience while deepening existing lines of inquiry. There is no ideal way to balance the preliminary and the innovative, but in the remainder of this introduction I account for the choices that structure the argument that follows, together with basic matters of terminology and scope.

Comics studies has passed the point at which each new work must start by defining the medium; existing theory is more than sufficient to allow other kinds of entrance into the field. However, there is considerably less powerful and durable theory devoted to comics than there is, for instance, to the novel as a genre. Scholars of the latter have a vast array of conceptual tools at their disposal. Significant new theoretical contributions arrive infrequently, and existing concepts can be accurately evoked in abbreviated fashion. In comics studies, the tools are fewer, and their uses more unpredictable. Some terms, most notably from the work of Scott McCloud, have passed into common usage, but we can expect new paradigms to expand and alter our understanding often in the years to come. My own sense of how comics might best be theorized has changed more than once in response to work published during the past five years, particularly in such critical venues as *Studies in Comics* and *ImageTexT*. Given this state of affairs, I have chosen to explore the specifics of comics theory selectively, sometimes drawing on an established vocabulary derived from McCloud, sometimes making use of more recently translated work by Thierry Groensteen, and sometimes referring to other new theoretical contributions. My goal has been to present a significant cross-section of the current state of comics theory while offering some purchase for readers new to the field.

The question of audience also has shaped the arrangement of this book's chapters. My key terms are presented not in one chapter, as would typically be the case, but spread over two. Because the first chapter surveys and critiques the existing discourse that has structured a great deal of thinking about comics in the United States, those already conversant with the state of comics studies may find the material in this chapter familiar (but not, I hope, entirely superfluous). An account of the *Bildungsroman* discourse that shapes mainstream views of comics is a necessary background for the alternate critical vision that follows. No thorough and up-to-date account of this discourse exists, so I have taken pains to sum up the current cultural and institutional positions of comics before setting out in a new direction in the second chapter, where I trace the narrative, thematic and aesthetic strategies used by some comics creators to respond to their conditions. This approach might seem to provide two first chapters rather than one; alternately, some readers may feel that the bulk of the argument actually arrives in the second chapter.

One terminological choice should be mentioned: my use of "medium" to denote comics. In current scholarship, this term is often applied to any instance of sequential art (a term coined by Eisner and popularized by McCloud) regardless of its material instantiation, even as most works discussed as examples of comics are in fact books printed on paper.[6] This is certainly the case for the comics I consider, all of which I have read and cited as printed objects. This tacit conflation of form and format requires justification. The number of comics appearing digitally, either exclusively or simultaneously with their print publication, is on the rise, reminding us that the medium, as a sequential form, exists in a variety of "media" in the narrower sense. Moreover, newer or newly translated theories, derived from semiotics or from linguistics, are converging on the idea of comics as a conceptual form or language that resides in the mind, regardless of material format.[7] These theories hold considerable promise, and should they carry the day, any bias toward a particular physical instantiation of comics may come to seem provincial.

However, I doubt this will happen, and I have found attention to comic books as a specific physical medium quite compatible with newer concepts of comics as a language. As my discussion of Frank Miller's *Batman: The Dark Knight Returns* will make clear, there are often good reasons to let the idea of comics as a (physical, paper) medium and the idea of comics as the object of a specific literacy overlap; used together, they help to show exactly how comics are read while also distinguishing comic books from texts composed of printed words. For the generation of creators I am considering, most comics have been printed on paper, and this fact bears not only on the form and content of their work, but also on the history that has shaped it. A material, paper-based concept of literacy has dominated our understanding of comics in the United States, and the printed object known as the comic book has been crucial to the illegitimate status of comics, an issue I wish to keep constantly in view (though admittedly, referring to comics as an object of literacy, or a language, is also likely to evoke such questions of status). All three terms— "language," "literacy," "medium"—make appearances in this study, but I find the third particularly suited to my focus on the comics page as the place from which the problem of illegitimacy is best visible. This book, like most contributions to comics studies, is written in the hope that the status of comics will improve. I welcome a time when a term like "the language of comics" is widely accepted; the medium (both the term and the things it names) can only stand to benefit from such a change.

"Medium" as a category also raises questions of format and publication history. Most of the works considered here (Alison Bechdel's *Fun Home* is the notable exception) were published in serial form before being collected as graphic novels. As already indicated, this latter term is freighted with a host of problems, which the first chapter will explore in detail. However, later chapters still discuss the material objects to which the term refers. All citations, with exceptions that will be clearly indicated, are taken from collected editions. Issues raised by serial format will be addressed when they bear on the line of thinking this book attempts to develop, but otherwise, specifics of publication history are relegated to footnotes or to the Works Cited. As some scholarship on the nineteenth-century novel teaches us, when the issue of serial publication is left unspoken, it becomes invisible; hence, for what little it may be worth, I make this opening gesture. In-text citations of comics give both page and, when appropriate, panel number(s), separated by a period. I am happy to credit this method, which I find both functional and elegant, to my former student who invented it: Jacob Karle. I note also that one of the collected editions I discuss, Burns's *Black Hole*, does not have printed page numbers. For this text I have elected to establish pagination, given in a footnote when it is first cited.

I take it as given that not every critical study of comics must concern itself with canon formation. I did not choose the subjects of my four case studies because I believe them to be the most essential or important creators currently working in the United States. At some point in her or his career, each has certainly been among the strongest, but they are chosen as representative creators of valuable work; they do not constitute a canon. One important criterion guiding my selections has been diversity of style and subject matter; another has been the absence of personal or professional connection. Wishing to underscore the fact that the patterns I am tracing do not arise from a particular coterie, I have chosen creators whose careers have rarely or never crossed paths; none of them has any strong affiliation, personal or professional, with any of the others. The argument this book puts forward is intended to be applicable to other case studies, including both widely discussed and highly respected figures such as Lynda Barry and Chris Ware as well as lesser known, underappreciated creators such as Eve Gilbert and Kim Deitch. But in the confines of this study, I have found it beneficial to proceed narrowly and thoroughly, avoiding the practice of lateral reading, whereby the work of one creator is interpreted through associative linkages to others rather than by close attention to the dynamics of a particular text.

Since the illegitimacy of comics is a central concern in this study, the reader might note that its focus on the United States is deliberately narrow. As some histories have established (and as many citizens of comics culture know), the suppression of comics in the United States has parallels with the medium's history in Canada and, even more obviously, in the United Kingdom. Additionally, there has been a great deal of transatlantic creative traffic since the late 1970s and early 1980s, as British writers and illustrators have found appreciative US audiences. The most famous instance, *Watchmen*, written by Alan Moore and illustrated by Dave Gibbons, is in fact a touchstone in my survey of the contemporary status of comics in the first chapter, and there will be other brief mentions of British and Canadian creators at various points in this study. I believe much of the argument advanced here will prove useful for a discussion of comics in a broadly North American context, as well as in a transatlantic one. I have restricted my central examples, and most of my historiographic gestures, to the United States in order to ground my discussion in more specific and extensively documented conditions.

A final matter of scope is the choice to focus primarily on the relationship between comics and literature. Given that problems of status are my chief concern, some readers might ask why there is not an equal focus on the relationship between comics and art. While definitions of the medium have varied, more than a few have emphasized that it is a hybrid entity, composed of both words and images, and thus susceptible both to acts of reading, associated with the printed word, and to acts of gazing or looking, associated with the fine arts—or, to add an additional complication, with cinema. I am wary of an emphasis on hybridity, which too readily presumes the separation of image and word as a norm (hardly a self-evident proposition, and one that is entangled in questions of status), but it is certainly true that comics have been considered illegitimate from the point of view of the art museum as well as the literary canon. Further, in three of the four cases I consider, I give at least some attention to the fine arts. Any concern that bears on the question of the medium's illegitimacy is of relevance to this study, and as it has taken shape, I have been tempted to add "and Art" to the end of its title. During the latter stages of this book's composition, the first major study of the relationship between comics and the fine arts appeared. I have found Bart Beaty's *Comics Versus Art* an invaluable counterpoint to my own way of reading. Beaty's accounts of contact between comics and the fine arts in the postwar era leave no doubt that this aspect of the medium's struggle for legitimation has been unduly neglected. However, as my survey of the suppression of comics in the first chapter will make clear, I find literary categories, especially as organized by the notion of the *Bildungsroman*, to be most central to the problem of illegitimacy. Public, legislative and institutional pressure on comics has been concerned not with regulating the presence of comics in the museum, but with governing what roles the medium plays in the hands of readers. I believe, as well, that the future of comics is tied in part to its pedagogical functions, and in ways that are likely to keep it more closely aligned with notions of language and critical expression than with concepts derived from the fine arts.

W. J. T. Mitchell has remarked that there are many kinds of discourse—and of thought—to which comics might contribute, but from which they have thus far been excluded: "What would it mean to do philosophy, to theorize in comics, not just about them?" ("Comics as Media" 263). My second chapter will touch on this question and point briefly to the ways in which comics have thus far rarely been employed to theorize comics themselves (to say nothing of their relative lack of presence in the realm of philosophy).[8] Yet any critic who hopes to contribute to the legitimation of comics must imagine, in however utopian a fashion, a point at which comics criticism could take comics form as a matter of course (at which point, one supposes, film criticism might usually take the form of the video essay, and so forth). Meanwhile, in this limited present, this book is the work of a critic who cannot draw and is reduced to words as his sole means of expression. The gambit of print-based contemporary comics criticism, I suggest, is to leverage this one medium to the benefit of a more democratically intermedial future.

ONE

Coming of Age

THE PROBLEM OF THE *BILDUNGSROMAN*

Almost from the moment we begin to describe a literary genre, we become lawmakers. When creating guidelines to identify a genre's characteristics, we must decide which elements to include or exclude, and what starts as discriminating curiosity can become the enforcement of critical legislation.[1] Tangled though such difficulties are in genre studies, the problem of regulation is even more complex in the study of media. "The emergence of the media concept in the later nineteenth century," observes John Guillory, "was a response to the proliferation of new technical media . . . that could not be assimilated to the older system of the arts" (321). The fact that "new technical media," including cinema, radio, television and comics, were at odds with an "older system" of aesthetic expression did not merely prompt scholarly curiosity. During the first half of the twentieth century, artistic and intellectual interest in mass media was driven by anxieties about their dangers, not least their "false resemblance to art," so abhorrent to the values of modernism (Guillory 347). By the early years of the postwar era, it was possible to declare some newer media dangerous in general, regardless of specific cases.

We might hasten to assure ourselves that today, the study of media is free of regulatory tendencies. The sheer variety of contemporary media, and of myriad linkages among them, discourages the idea of the scholar as legislator; being a scholar of a medium is now, we would hope, fully compatible with being its advocate. But the process of legitimating media has not become transparent, and the shift from Adorno and Horkheimer to Henry Jenkins (if one had to sum it up in a phrase) has not dissipated all the regulatory energies at work when we theorize media. Although they persist, in mainstream journalism as well as in the academy, such energies have become more difficult to notice than they were in the middle of the twentieth century.

In this chapter, I trace a dynamic of subtle, and quite powerful, regulation that affects the condition of comics. There was nothing subtle about attacks on the medium when it initially appeared; from their earliest years until the first decade of the postwar era, comics were broadly condemned in mainstream culture and were subject to threats of legislative regulation and censorship. Since this initial period, discussion of comics has been suffused with figures of development, such as maturation, growing up, or coming of age, which now regulate the status of the medium and normalize its ongoing marginalization. I will track the emergence of these developmental concepts and analyze their operation in education, in mainstream journalism, and, to a lesser degree, in academic scholarship devoted to comics and within comics culture itself.

Linking the medium's long-standing illegitimacy to the images of development that surround comics, I will offer a fresh understanding of the story that mainstream culture tells itself about comics today. Once we understand how serious the problem of status is for comics, it will be clearer why their history is understood in terms of maturation, growing up, or coming of age. Such notions might seem to promise freedom from cultural stigma, and the regulatory, often harmful force they exert usually goes unremarked. I will read the developmental discourse surrounding comics against the grain, acknowledging it as a path to better status for specific works but insisting that it perpetuates the illegitimacy of comics as a whole. I want especially to question the supposedly organic quality that is attached to images of growth and development. There has been nothing organic, in however metaphorical a sense, about the medium's struggles, and in the context of comics history, images of natural development are best interpreted as signs of violence. Against the background of these difficult realities, we will be able to see more clearly in later chapters how comics creators might be compelled to dwell on problems of status and to resist normative ideas of coming of age.

We can begin with the problem of illegitimacy in its simplest form. In the first half of the twentieth century, the low status of comics was fixed in mainstream culture without substantial debate. Historians have not yet determined all the processes whereby anti-comics discourse established itself, but it is clear that much early commentary on the medium consisted of outright condemnations that seemed to obviate the need for critical understanding. Even before concerns about mass media reached their height among postwar intellectuals, comics were frequently considered a brutal assault on society and on literacy; "at best," observes Charles Hatfield, they could be designated "a neutral or value-less carrier of themes and ideas better expressed in traditional books" (*Alternative* 34). The 2004 anthology *Arguing Comics*, a collection of writings on the medium from the turn of the century up to the early 1960s, demonstrates that among thoughtful critics, there has been some diversity of opinion concerning the value of comics. However, the volume's editors note: "If . . . we had focused on the enormous volume of writings and speeches of politicians, behavioral scientists, and public moralists, then the final project would be dull indeed . . . " (Heer and Worcester, Introduction viii). Most attacks on comics were dull, even monotonous, in part because they attempted no careful engagement with their subject matter. From the first appearance of newspaper comic strips at the turn of the twentieth century to the massive outpouring of comic books between the 1930s and the early 1950s, harsh critical judgment was the norm, and there were few real attempts at definition or description.

Typical of this state of affairs was Sterling North's editorial "A National Disgrace," a vitriolic attack on comic books published in the spring of 1940 and extensively reprinted thereafter. This short piece struck a note of "fury rare in [North's] journalism and virtually absent in his gentle, elegiac fiction"; for North, as for many others, unreflective outrage felt like a natural response to comics (Hajdu 42). North made a basic distinction between "action 'comics,'" by which he meant comic books, and "'funnies' in the newspapers"; he then proceeded to excoriate the former as "sadistic drivel." What defined comic books, for North, was their opposite—namely, literature; he declared that as regards child readers, "the antidote to the 'comic' magazine poison can be found in any library or good bookstore" (21). North himself was an author of children's literature and thus a party to the case he was claiming to judge, but he obviously proceeded on the assumption that his vocation enhanced rather than diminished his authority. Like most critics, North assumed that comics were to be assigned the cultural place deemed right for them by representatives of culture associated with what Guillory calls the "older system of the arts" (321). If their judgments were not particularly measured in content or in tone, it was presumed that this said more about comic books than about the biases of their detractors.

North's confident declaration that comic books, sold at newsstands, were "poison," and that literature from bookstores and libraries was the "antidote," indicates some institutional and material aspects of the problems comics faced. Unlike television or film, comics did not have the advantage of a new format of presentation—a new medium in the narrowest sense of the term—in which to manifest their particular characteristics; comic strips appeared in an established space of print. This space had, over the course of the nineteenth century, made room for pictorial matter, but the parameters of this sharing were not such as to welcome comics. Even before strips became widespread in newspapers, there was already significant concern that the "austere, print-dense environment" of "high-toned intellectual magazines of early twentieth century America" was being undermined by the increasing number and importance of illustrations in many periodicals (Heer and Worcester, "Early" 1). The earliest attacks on comics could thus follow a ready-made template of grievances concerning the growth of pictures in print.

Such attacks increased in number and intensity with the spread of the comic book in the 1930s. The newspaper strip, a pictorial supplement to what was properly a print publication, was disturbing enough; the freestanding stapled comic magazine, with its flimsy yet unmistakable overlap with the category of the book, was more outrageous yet. The outrage was probably compounded by the fact that comics were cheap. If books they were, they were also books even children could afford to buy with their pocket money and without direct parental regulation. Thus North reminded his adult readers of the importance of the library and the "good bookstore," and remarked on the damage comic books in particular could do to young readers: "Badly drawn, badly written and badly printed—a strain on young eyes and young nervous systems—the effect of these pulp-paper nightmares is that of a violent stimulant" (21). The content of comic books was largely unregulated, unlike that of syndicated strips. Comic books were sometimes far more violent, and the books themselves more poorly printed, than their counterparts in newspapers. But in attacks on comics, it seemed necessary to emphasize differences of material quality and content, less to spare newspaper strips from blame than to underscore how unacceptable it was for comic books to claim legitimacy as worthwhile reading matter by annexing their own space in the field of print.

North and others seemed compelled to associate their belief that comic books were culturally illegitimate with their growing anxiety about the welfare of children growing up in a new age of mass media. Psychologist and leading anti-comics crusader Fredric Wertham claimed that while everyone read newspaper strips, comic books were more exclusively the provenance of the young. His attacks on comic books in the late 1940s and early 1950s emphasized their tendency to implant violence in the minds of children, to damage their capacity for print literacy, and to bar the way to fruitful engagement with serious literature.[2] Not all intellectuals were ready to go as far as Wertham was, even when anti-comics sentiments grew increasingly vociferous in the first half of the 1950s. Leslie Fiedler, in "The Middle Against Both Ends," his 1955 essay on comics and their detractors, took pains to distance himself from Wertham's belief that comics encouraged juvenile delinquency. Nevertheless, on the subject of the cultural illegitimacy of comics, Fiedler and Wertham were in accord.

Fiedler proclaimed comic books, in particular, as "the first art for *post*-literates"; the background logic of this claim was that the more fully comics established their own territory within the realm of print, the more they announced themselves as false copies of real literature that required real reading (18). Though he expressed particular contempt for Wertham, Fiedler would have had no basis for disagreement with Wertham's assertion that "good teachers know they have to get rid of comic books to make their children read real books" (Fiedler 16, 20; Wertham, "The Comics . . ." 28). Both Fiedler and Wertham opposed Classics Illustrated, the long-running series of comics adaptations of print literary classics. For Fiedler, such comics epitomized middlebrow mediocrity; for Wertham, they represented noble cultural achievement turned to the dead end of violence, "blocking one of the child's avenues to the finer things in life" (Fiedler 19; Wertham, *Seduction* 311).

Thus, the cultural priorities even of a self-described contrarian on the subject of comics could easily dovetail with moral panic over children's welfare. And because, regardless of Fiedler's own leanings, objections to mass media and concern for children's development were firmly linked in this way, the fate of comics would inevitably be tied to the question of the medium's maturity. By the early 1950s, comic books had become a primary target for concerns about juvenile delinquency in particular and about the condition of postwar youth in general.[3] Fiedler insisted that there was no intrinsic connection between comics as a medium and children's literacy, pointedly asking, "Why must [comic books] be disguised as children's literature though read by men and women of all ages?" (17). But the "post-literate" status of comic books unleashed a circuit of regulatory energies that have associated the medium with childhood ever since. There was no sound logic in the idea that comics contained "adult" content while the medium was nevertheless so worthless as to be read only by children. But from the standpoint of cultural legislators such as North and Wertham, such a proposition made sense.

It designated the medium as delinquent in a fashion that seemed both to preserve the value of traditional literary culture and to defend the innocence of children. The designation of comic books as children's reading made it seem both necessary and reasonable to control their content more harshly than was deemed necessary for other media.

This regulatory strategy brought about profound changes for comics. In the face of increasing public and legislative pressure, not least a harsh public shaming of comics before the US Senate Subcommittee on Juvenile Delinquency in the spring of 1954, comics publishers tightened their own existing standards in what was effectively an act of self-censorship, creating a new Comics Code Authority. As it addressed concerns over the potential harmfulness of comics for children, the new code issued by this regulatory body necessarily rendered a judgment of the medium's legitimacy that discouraged adult readers. The detailed rules of the code positioned comics as best fitted for children's reading, quite narrowly defined. Although such rules were not absolute creative barriers, in their immediate context they were highly destructive. Many titles featuring what might, in other contexts, be called adult subject matter were eliminated by the code and by contemporaneous legal measures, helping to end hundreds of creators' careers, decimate whole genres of comics, and accelerate the decline of comics readership, which had reached a historical peak in the late 1940s and early 1950s.[4] Yet the tensions inherent in the link between cultural status and childhood kept this regulatory strategy from working exactly as intended, and the aftermath of the code offered little consolation to Wertham. Children continued to read comics, if in smaller numbers, and the medium was marked as children's reading even more strongly than before.[5] The strategies used by anti-comics crusaders ultimately did far more to stigmatize comics as juvenile reading matter, shrinking adult readership and further lowering the medium's cultural status, than they did to raise public commitment to the welfare of children.

While the association of comics with childhood abetted the damage done in the 1950s, this association can be seen in retrospect as having the potential to renegotiate the medium's status, at least to some degree. The opening sentence of the 1954 code evoked ideas of growth and development quite cannily: "The comic book medium, having come of age on the American cultural scene, must measure up to its responsibilities" (Gabilliet 313).[6] As a gesture toward a critical account of comics, this was perfunctory at best. The code managed to cover the distance between optimistic description (a "medium" now reaching maturity) and binding prescription (the obligation to meet certain "responsibilities") in the space of a sentence. The code did not purport to theorize what it regulated; its declaration that comics had grown up was, in a sense, merely a segue to an assumption of new responsibilities and creative restrictions.

Yet the developmental phrase "come of age" did constitute a claim to a degree of legitimacy, since it implied that while the medium fell short of its moral and social obligations (a failing the code was ostensibly proceeding to rectify), it nonetheless had responsibilities in the first place because it was mature enough to be called to account. This implication was, perhaps, little more than a rhetorical flourish; the code came into existence not because comic books had been recognized as mature and fully developed, but because the comics industry was being attacked on all fronts, prompting many publishers to believe censorship was imminent. However, even as it announced a capitulation to legislative pressure, this evocation of the idea of coming of age was an attempt to forestall the medium's total destruction. Postwar concerns about mass media in general, and the efforts of anti-comics crusaders in particular, had made it increasingly difficult to conceive of comics even as a low-grade substitute for print literacy. While sacrificing most of the medium's opportunities for adult readership, the code opened by claiming the "responsibilities" attendant upon serving an audience of children, and thus insisted that comics had a place in culture, however lowly.

This "coming of age" was, at best, a weak effort to deflect the full force of anti-comics crusades, but it foreshadowed the ways that images and concepts of development would continue to surround the medium. Educational discourse on comics has been emblematic of this trend. Beginning in the 1970s, increasing numbers of teachers and librarians have granted comics a role as a stepping-stone in the development of print literacy.[7] This idea had a modest number of adherents during the 1940s, though in that decade the research focused primarily on the reading practices of elementary school students.[8] That line of inquiry had effectively ended by the early 1950s, when the notion of comics as the enemy of literacy held sway; from the 1970s onward, comics have been seen as helpful not just for early readers, but increasingly, in secondary education as well. As with the code's opening gesture, a shift away from unequivocal condemnations of comics has been made possible, in part, by the developmentally inflected terms in which such condemnations have been phrased. Labeled a substitute for real reading, one that could fool only a child, comics could subsequently be valued as offering something that at least resembled reading (perhaps unlike other visual media, such as television or video games).

We would be mistaken, however, to see too much good news for comics in this change. At present, a few genuinely progressive accounts of comics have begun to frame the medium not simply as a stepping-stone to print, but as an integral part of multimodal literacy.[9] Yet this approach is the exception, and there is still a widespread tendency to think of comics reading as a means to some other end. Comics are usually not welcomed as intrinsically important, and are permitted because they can function as aids to print reading, literary appreciation and other traditional educational goals.[10] In other words, comics are allowed, in the short term, precisely so that they may be dispensed with later. In my comics classes, students tell stories of being scolded for choosing comics from the "easy" pile of available books in the classroom because their reading "level" had already progressed beyond the point at which perusing them could be judged appropriate. Young comics readers are now usually seen as potential readers of real books, but until the transition to print literacy is achieved, they are also potential delinquents, developmentally speaking. Thus, more than sixty years after some teachers first appropriated what Fiedler would have termed the post-literacy of comics as a pedagogical tool, the role of comics in education often remains fully reversible. For a significant number of educators today, the medium is a stepping-stone only because it is also a stumbling block, indicating the double-edged nature of the developmental concepts through which comics are usually understood.[11]

Progressive arguments for the importance of comics as multimodal literacy, still numerically rare in the context of primary and secondary education, overlap with what we find in the introduction to the volume *Teaching the Graphic Novel*, which is concerned with comics pedagogy in universities. There, we learn that "graphic novels fit students' sensibilities at a deep cognitive level" because in comics, "the experience of reading text is combined with the experience, omnipresent today on the electronic screen, of viewing," and that "the reading experience of a graphic novel is one with which we are very comfortable in this age of technological speed and visual sophistication" (Tabachnick 3–5). Such claims closely resemble new discussions of comics in secondary education claiming that "traditional, alphabetic literacy and literacies such as information, visual and media literacy can be well served by classroom engagement with the graphic novel," because it is "a medium that combines the visual and verbal as do films, TV and even pop-up ads" (Schwarz 59).

Both these arguments are rightly motivated by a larger awareness of the diverse media ecology in which high school and university students are situated, and the way this awareness is expressed has developmental overtones quite different from those of the more typical rhetoric I am analyzing. There is some sense that the image itself, once seen as the primitive invader of mature, civilized print discourse, has now come of age, thus elevating comics to a new level of importance. But such arguments are uncommon in discussions of comics for adult readers; journalists and academics alike have insisted on the maturity of certain long-form examples of the medium much more often than they have focused on the growing importance of pictorial images in culture and literacy. As Katalin Orbán astutely observes, vanguard voices that have predicted the ascendance of comics as a new, fully viable form of literacy "have underestimated the time lag between technological advancement and a more conservative transfer of cultural prestige trailing behind it" (171).

A tendency toward a "conservative transfer of cultural prestige" is precisely the way in which the introduction to *Teaching the Graphic Novel* diverges from progressive scholarship in secondary education: "The high literary and visual quality of many graphic novels provides the most compelling reason for the study of this new genre" (Tabachnick 3). For such a claim, the value of high cultural achievement trumps the question of media literacy; this more traditional arrangement of cultural priorities, strongly focused on the graphic novel, has had a decisive influence on cultural perceptions of comics over the past thirty years. Turning directly to this larger trend, I want to explore in detail a concept that, from the late 1970s to the present, has been a shaping force in mainstream perceptions of comics, and that has had considerable influence on comics culture and comics studies as well. It does not, at first glance, appear to be a regulatory concept, since it declares that the status of the medium has been improving, but it limits the status of comics precisely through the kind and degree of maturity it grants.

"Status" is a kaleidoscopic term with a range of meanings, including social position on the basis of merit, rank on the basis of custom and tradition, current standing on the basis of influence, legal standing on the basis of citizenship or conduct, and access to economic or political rights and privileges, either because of age or on some other, contractual basis. These meanings overlap in some cases and differ in others, and suggest an array of possibilities for thinking about changes in the legitimacy of comics. For instance, the medium's increasingly transmedial cultural influence, especially on mainstream film and television, gives us a much different set of coordinates than does the trend of gradual, uneven improvements in creators' rights.[12]

In contemporary discussions of comics, however, the meaning of "status" is fairly narrow and is strongly determined by what I call the *Bildungsroman* discourse. This discourse claims that comics have changed, over the past few decades, in the following ways: from a medium intended only for children to one sometimes fit for adults; from crudely and functionally produced commodities, often the product of multiple and interchangeable creators, to aesthetically complex work created by self-directed writer-illustrators; from adventure-romance serials to closure-oriented narratives modeled after the novel—and thus, so goes the logic of this narrative, from a despised medium with little to no credibility as an art form, a literature or a mode of literacy to a respectable kind of reading with an earned measure of cultural legitimacy.[13]

Of the three kinds of changes just enumerated—audience, production and form—by far the most commonly emphasized, in mainstream views of comics, is the first. Accounts of exactly how comics production has changed, or why narrative closure matters, are far less common than general announcements to the effect that some comics are now appropriate for adults. The central feature of the *Bildungsroman* discourse is the graphic novel, which "has become comics' passport to recognition as a form of literature" (Hatfield, *Alternative Comics* ix). The term has a range of applications, but whether it refers to collected editions of previously published work or stand-alone volumes appearing for the first time, it usually names long-form comics judged appropriate for and worthy of adult consumption. Neither the fact that many graphic novels are actually aimed at younger readers nor the fact that staple-bound serial comics are routinely repackaged in square-bound format has done much to complicate the usage of this term, and regardless of its accuracy, its obvious function is to confer a measure of legitimacy on the comics so named.[14]

Successfully put into circulation in the late 1970s, the term "graphic novel" gained widespread currency within a decade, and as Roger Sabin relates in his history of comics for adult readers in the United Kingdom and the United States, the "coming of age" narrative associated with it was well established by the early 1990s (176–177). The *Bildungsroman* discourse has remained in effect since Sabin's study was published in 1993, and documenting even a fraction of the newspaper and magazine articles declaring that comics have grown up would be a daunting task. The repetition of this narrative over a period that now spans about thirty years speaks to the entrenched nature of the medium's illegitimacy. In a strict sense, the *Bildungsroman* discourse has never been fully accepted, since the idea of comic books for adults is apparently still a surprise to some mainstream readers, or at least to a number of mainstream journalists.[15] Nevertheless, this discourse has adequately demonstrated the force, if not the accuracy, of its central ideas.

The vast majority of journalistic accounts of comics declare, or at least strongly imply, that the medium has "come of age" through an organic process of maturation—that the image of growing up is less figural than factual, in other words—and most teachers and scholars of comics know from experience how persuasive such a claim can be. Usually, even a person deeply surprised that adults might legitimately read or study comics can be won over by the idea of a new kind of comic that has matured, through organic growth, beyond the presumed limitations of the traditional comic book. Thus, in the particular way it grants legitimacy to the graphic novel, the *Bildungsroman* discourse successfully elides the most painful features of comics history, which has been governed not by natural processes of maturation, but by dynamics of cultural, economic and institutional power.

Sabin points out that there have been many comics for adults published throughout the medium's history, but that the idea that such comics are a recent development has served the needs of two groups: media outlets newly interested in reporting on comics, and comics publishers interested in increasing their sales (92–95). A journalistic impulse to discuss grown-up comics has colluded with a marketing impulse, on the part of comics publishers, to advertise comics as literature. In both cases, there has been a desire to explain why—or at least announce that—comics can now be presented to adult audiences. For comics publishers, there was also an imperative, particularly in the late 1980s, to cover up the fact that the products being offered to adult readers were emerging from conditions that in no way resembled those of contemporary literary production. Creators' rights were virtually nonexistent when the graphic novel was first gaining currency, and while the injustice of this fact was a matter of increasing contention in the comics industry, a factory mentality prevailed.[16] Thus, while the *Bildungsroman* discourse generally implies that the graphic novel is congruent with the rise of auteur models of production, it has done little to clarify the actual relationship between process and product—an oversight the comics industry has had little interest in correcting.

Contrasted with the open hostility toward comics that characterized the moment of the 1954 code, the *Bildungsroman* discourse must be deemed an improvement. Yet, in the way it is usually deployed, it not only obscures the difficult struggles that have made the idea of the graphic novel necessary in the first place, but also does very limited legitimating work. Consider the case of *Watchmen*, written by Alan Moore and illustrated by Dave Gibbons. On *Time's* 2005 list of the one hundred best novels published since 1923, Lev Grossman praises *Watchmen* as a high artistic achievement, declaring it "a watershed in the evolution of a young medium," a description whose key terms have no appreciable relationship to historical fact (n. pag.). Grossman identifies *Watchmen* as a graphic novel and then defines the latter as "a book-length comic book with ambitions above its station." This anachronistic phrasing may be intended facetiously, but Grossman does little to challenge the low "station" of comics, since his description implies that the best way to discuss a great comic is to speak of it in other, more respectable terms. Note the tightly packed references to music, film and novels: "Told with ruthless psychological realism, in fugal, overlapping plotlines and gorgeous cinematic panels rich with repeating motifs, *Watchmen* is a heart-pounding, heartbreaking read and a watershed in the evolution of a young medium" (n. pag.). *Watchmen* is the only comic on *Time's* list, and the phrase "evolution of a young medium," typically "coming of age" in its overtones, glosses this tokenism as appropriate to the early stages of a natural process of development.[17]

Implied here, for the *Time* reader, is that the literary promise of the graphic novel is new and untested, and best understood against the background of the natural "station" of comics in general. Thus, there is a contradiction: a sense of the graphic novel's legitimation, achieved through natural growth, is at odds with a widespread sense of comics as naturally inferior and immature. The contradiction goes unresolved, and the legitimacy the graphic novel possesses is conflicted and unstable. Thus the term, as it is typically used, does little to challenge the grounding assumptions of mid-century anti-comics crusaders. The latter group saw the phrase "comic book" as a contradiction in terms, and "graphic novel" does not so much overturn this view as accomplish a modest rebalancing of emphasis. The comic—pictorial and immature, therefore illegitimate—book is recast as the graphic—pictorial but legitimate, because lengthy and literary—novel. As with educational discourse on comics, which links the helpfulness of comics reading to the medium's delinquent status, the legitimation offered by typical journalistic formulations is reversible. An organically mature graphic novel is still, naturally, a comic book.

Mainstream journalism's developmental, quasi-legitimating approach to comics is, in its own way, just as grindingly dull as the anticomics journalism of the early twentieth century, and it might not seem to demand close reading. Yet we should observe carefully what the idea of the graphic novel does, and does not do, in the very form of its iteration. I take as an example Charles McGrath's "Not Funnies," which appeared in the *New York Times Magazine* in 2004. The article begins with a gesture of distinction, separating comics worth reading from others that, McGrath implies, should not command serious attention:

> Comics are . . . enjoying a renaissance and a newfound respectability right now. In fact, the fastest-growing section of your local bookstore these days is apt to be the one devoted to comics and so-called graphic novels. It is the overcrowded space way in the back . . . and . . . this section is likely to be a mess . . . [consisting of newspaper comics anthologies] . . . loads of manga . . . [superhero comics], still churned out in installments by the busy factories at Marvel and DC . . . [and] newer sci-fi and fantasy series. . . . You can ignore all this stuff. . . .
> What you're looking for is shelved upside down and sideways sometimes—comic books of another sort, substantial single volumes (as opposed to the slender series installments), often in hard cover, with titles that sound just like the titles of "real" books. . . . These are the graphic novels—the equivalent of "literary" novels in the mainstream publishing world—and they are beginning to be taken seriously by the critical establishment. (25–26)

McGrath designates graphic novels as the kind of comics the reader is (or ought to be) "looking for," unlike others that, he assures the reader, "you can ignore." Such a confident directive sweeps aside the majority of comics on offer even as McGrath momentarily stumbles over the terms he is using to make this gesture, referring to "so-called graphic novels" (though he quickly drops the qualifier "so-called"), and using scare quotes to blur the line separating comics from "'real' books" (though he does not explain why the word "real"—or the word "literary"—might be problematic in the context of a discussion of comics). For a moment it seems that McGrath believes two irreconcilable things: that comics as a whole might not actually be inferior to print literature as traditionally defined, and that graphic novels really are different from most other comics, which are unworthy of adult readership. This apparent indecisiveness certainly indicates that the legitimacy of comics as such, not of a few comics designated as graphic novels, is far from guaranteed, and it also demonstrates the tenuous status of the graphic novel itself.

As McGrath's account unfolds, it more and more readily presumes that distinctions between comic books and real books are worth enforcing. A graphic novel by a significant creator, or, as McGrath terms it, a "comic book with a brain" (30), may fit into literary discourse "upside down and sideways," but it nevertheless belongs in the bookstore, and deserves to be the focus of an article published in the *New York Times Magazine*, in ways that comic books in general do not. Throughout his account, McGrath inadvertently troubles the distinctions on which he insists. He praises Alan Moore as the graphic novelist with "the purest and most inventive literary imagination," a claim he makes no attempt to reconcile with the fact that most of Moore's work has first appeared in what he would call "slender series installments," sometimes in the imprints of mainstream comics publishers, and has often featured superheroes (26). Indeed, almost all of the creators McGrath holds up as respectable graphic novelists published their work serially, later repackaging it in bound volumes, just as mainstream corporate comics producers tend to do. But such inconsistencies only bring into focus McGrath's bedrock assumption that the adult-worthy, literary long-form comic is a rare and valuable thing, and that its numerous and brainless relations are beneath notice. McGrath ultimately assumes that comics are not, and generally should not be, legitimate. Graphic novels are exceptions to this rule, but they do not challenge the rule itself.

This is why McGrath's description of the comics section in the back of the bookstore is so different from the vision most readers probably have of the section located closer to the entrance and labeled "Fiction" and "Literature." There, one can find many books that are not "literary" in the sense in which McGrath uses the term, but few readers would claim it is wrong to place trendy commercial fiction next to more culturally durable works. While McGrath claims that graphic novels should have their place, he assumes they are currently sharing space with other comics that do not belong in the bookstore at all. Some respectable creators, McGrath notes, might feel differently: "The comic-book form until recently has been unable to shed a certain aura of pulpiness, cheesiness and semi-literacy," and "that is what a lot of cartoon artists most love about their genre" (26). The immature qualities creators love, Mc-Grath then explains, are not things their readers must take seriously; they should, at most, cultivate a measured appreciation for them. Mc-Grath concludes by asserting that "no matter how far the graphic novel verges toward realism, its basic idiom is always a little, well, cartoonish," and that "this is a medium probably not well suited to lyricism or strong emotion" (56). In short, McGrath sees the graphic novel as the portion of an essentially juvenile medium close enough to literary "realism" to merit adult attention, though its lack of intrinsic seriousness, not least at the level of "its basic idiom" (the cartoon), is something the fair-minded adult reader need not ignore.

Like most other mainstream journalism on comics, "Not Funnies" registers the clash of two very different goals. The first is to safeguard the value of traditional literary production over and against that of comic books. The second is to identify exceptional comics deemed good enough to be valued in traditional literary terms. McGrath believes that taking such work seriously means at least some status advancement for the medium, since it is "enjoying a renaissance and newfound cultural respectability" thanks to the existence of graphic novels (24). Yet there is nothing in McGrath's discussion to support this belief, since it would seem that recognition of a few important comics creators and graphic novels can be fully compatible with—indeed, through a kind of tokenism, can abet—a dismissive view of comics in general. Given what this kind of journalistic writing about comics actually says, the graphic novel is fully compatible with an assumption that comics should be considered illegitimate, excepting specific creators or works designated otherwise by specific kinds of discourse in other media (and above all by the discourses of print).

This very limited legitimation seems almost endemic to the term "graphic novel," and even scholarly attempts to define it can propagate the problem. In the introduction to *Teaching the Graphic Novel*, the subject at hand is first described as "an extended comic book that treats non-fictional as well as fictional plots and themes with the depth and subtlety that we have come to expect of traditional novels and nonfictional texts" (Tabachnick 2). By specifying an "extended" work, presumably longer than the average stapled comic book, this definition implicitly compares the latter's physical flimsiness with its lack of literary weight. What this definition actually seems designed to exclude is not the short story, which is certainly capable of "depth and subtlety" (in fact, it has been the stock-in-trade of many powerful comics creators, including several who are praised in *Teaching the Graphic Novel*), but the sprawling superhero serial with its endless variations on a fixed set of narrative options.[18] Yet the question of narrative closure, which would make this opposition a great deal more precise, is not raised; the cultural prestige associated with the stand-alone book (together with an assumption that material and artistic substantiality naturally go together) seems to matter more than the specific formal characteristics of the novel—or of other culturally respected genres, such as the autobiography.

Admittedly, such definitions as this can still attempt a nuanced view of the question of prestige: "Because of their basis in the popular comics tradition, most graphic novels and their practitioners offer a style of art and life free of elitism, to which students can relate, regardless of their own social backgrounds" (Tabachnick 6). Here the issue of legitimacy is treated in complex fashion, at least insofar as we might ask why the "popular comics tradition" has given rise to art and culture that is "free of elitism" (the reason is its lack of legitimacy). But this observation praises the cultural multivalence of the graphic novel without looking at the conditions that have given rise to it. While the graphic novel is presented as an elite comic, superior to the "popular comics tradition," its connection to the latter is then advertised as something that ought to broaden its appeal; in short, the graphic novel is offered as an advantageous cultural hybrid that offers literary quality without class-based exclusiveness. This definition displaces its own contradictory cultural investments onto the object it claims to define and thus highlights, without resolving, the high-low cultural opposition that produced the category of the graphic novel in the first place.

As it is usually deployed, the graphic novel conceals or downplays its inconsistencies and contradictions by naturalizing them. This is to be expected from a concept associated with the *Bildungsroman*, since the ideas clustered around this literary form—growth, maturation, socialization, social cohesion and legitimation—are often deployed hegemonically, and used to regulate changes in status. Joseph Slaughter demonstrates the central role that concepts related to the *Bildungsroman* have played in the development of human rights as a global discourse. Tracking a close connection between forms of law and forms of literature, he shows how the idea of human personality development, as both legal and literary narrative, has allowed for the progressive acquisition of human rights (or at least the idea of their acquisition) while determining which kinds of persons, operating within the guidelines of which kinds of development narratives, can be allowed such rights. Slaughter stresses "the *Bildungsroman's* ambivalent capacity to disseminate and naturalize not only norms of human rights but also the paradoxical practices, prejudices, and exclusions codified in the law" (5). In other words, wherever the *Bildungsroman* spreads the good news of human rights, it likewise spreads the various inconsistencies and unequal distributions of those rights as they are legally instantiated and enforced.

Adapting Slaughter's point to consider the less pressing question of the status of media, we can see that the discourse surrounding comics is simply hegemonic regulation of artistic expression and literacy. The persistent tendency to define the graphic novel as a new kind of comic is a means to allow comics into the realm of cultural legitimacy on a limited basis without necessarily altering the status of the medium as such. Since the actual difference between comic books and graphic novels is simply a matter of terminology, it should not be surprising that the developmental concepts applied to comics are so contradictory. In the hegemony that currently regulates the status of media, the idea that comics are juvenile and the idea that adults can sometimes read them without shame do not exist as separate ideas. In fact, they are routinely fused in a single, quite natural-sounding utterance: Comics aren't just for kids anymore.

Yet the *Bildungsroman* discourse has altered, however slightly, the hegemonic status of print literacy. New visual media have been challenging the dominance of print for over a century, but comics literacy presents a threat much different from that of film or television. The comic book is less an alien mode of expression unrelated to print than a quasi book that, from a traditional point of view, pretends to be an object of literacy. Leslie Fiedler, in the same essay that described comics as "the first art for *post*-literates," also noted: "What seems to offend us most is . . . the fact that the medium, the very notion and shape of a book, is being parodied by the comics" (18). More than half a century later, a few progressive voices in educational scholarship are arguing that to read comics is, in fact, to exercise a type of literacy. At the same time, an emerging line of research in cognitive science claims that when we read comics, we are absorbing a grammatically structured language that responds to linguistic modes of analysis.[19] While comics will continue to wield less—and fewer kinds of—institutional power than print, their status as a mode of literacy may well improve (whether this improvement is followed by an increase in readership is another matter).

The *Bildungsroman* discourse mediates between these emergent realities and a ruling idea of literacy that has thus far kept comics in a marginalized and illegitimate condition. The graphic novel serves this function so long as it marks noted achievements in comics as exceptions to a general state of illegitimacy. It remains to be seen whether this kind of cultural and literary tokenism might lead to a more definitive change in status for the medium. As the canon of graphic novels becomes ever more large and diverse, it is possible to imagine a moment, perhaps quite distant in time, when comics as such might be absorbed into, rather than kept distinct from, the term "graphic novel," and when comics reading might become part of a larger, less hierarchical sense of literacy.

Meanwhile, the *Bildungsroman* discourse also seems to suit a cultural moment when the worst scars from the era of the code—gradually reduced in power and now eliminated—have begun to fade. Distribution and readership are diversifying, censorship is rarely a concern, creators' rights are less abysmal, and some kinds of cultural capital are credited to comics on a limited basis. Readers less familiar with comics approach the graphic novel with a desire for new reading experiences, but not an extensive knowledge of comics history. For such readers, the easiest way to understand their altered reading choices is to attribute them to a change in the quality of (some) comics, and to see that change as organic, not as the result of a shift of the power dynamics that regulate literacy and culture. The graphic novel thus offers new or returning readers the enabling sense that they are entering the world of comics at the beginning of a period of legitimacy rather than at another chapter, perhaps not the last, in an ongoing period of difficulty. In my experience, no matter how thoroughly a course on comics delves into historical matters related to cultural status, some students who are not lifelong readers of the medium continue to believe that comics "grew up" between the time they stopped reading them as children and the present. Thus, the *Bildungsroman* discourse enables at least a limited improvement of the historical conditions it does not acknowledge as existing in the first place.

And such conditions do seem less severe, thanks in part to a vast increase in the number of graphic novels being published and their wide availability to a diverse audience. However small or nebulous it was as a category when the term was first circulated, the graphic novel is now a creative goal for many younger comics artists who, were they working thirty years earlier, would probably not have conceived the possibility of making a lengthy bound comic available for sale in bookstores, or in the area of an online retail outlet labeled "Books." A move from short- to long-form comics is not an unusual career trajectory for younger comics artists, and it is an accepted reality for their readers, who have become accustomed to years of waiting between publications by creators engaged in long-form work. In the studios of corporate publishers turning out serials hundreds of issues into their publication run, creators think in terms of arcs that will be collected in square-bound volumes. What might at one time have been a purely instrumental use of the term "graphic novel" to add legitimacy to any reprinted collection of serial issues is now, quite often, an accurate description of closure-oriented narrative designs within long-running story lines. Such adjustments to publication models encourage new readership while also being compatible, if only contingently, with increased recognition of writers and illustrators. Contemporary creators are not merely allowed, but actually expected, to put their stamp on the narrative arcs they create. Further, graphic novels have found a place in libraries of every sort, and if they are often situated in the Young Adult section, they are nevertheless materially available to any reader. In short, the graphic novel is arguably a positive influence on several aspects of comics production and distribution.[20]

The changes just enumerated cannot be attributed to a single cause. It is certainly ironic that one of the most important factors has also been one of the least concrete, namely, the self-legitimating aura that accompanies concepts of maturity and organic growth. This aura is also a primary reason that ideas very similar to those propagated by the *Bildungsroman* discourse have manifested in critical discussion of comics, and in comics culture itself; here we turn back to the harmful effects of discourses of maturation. Perhaps the most notable is an aggressive form of criticism that treats attacks on mediocre work as the best way to advance the medium as a whole. This strategy has sometimes operated in the pages of *The Comics Journal*, which, years before the emergence of comics studies as an identifiable field in the academy, was by far the most influential organ of serious comics criticism.

The *Journal* has made space for a wide variety of perspectives and critical approaches; over the decades of its existence, the viewpoints presented in its pages, and now in its online content, have only grown more diverse. Yet there has been an editorial logic, persistent if not dominant, that can be expressed thus: in the post-code era, comics are unfairly despised and ignored; many comics publishers and creators justify the medium's low status by producing contemptible work; therefore, the best way to support the medium as a whole is to prize only the best comics being produced; hence, harsh condemnations of lesser comics as immature, undeveloped and childish are good for the medium; furthermore, the reading of mediocre work is actually a bad thing altogether, and those who overvalue imperfect examples of the medium should be attacked with as much hostility as the works themselves.

Lest this be judged an unfair caricature, consider an editorial summary addressed to comics readers and creators in the *Journal*'s twenty-fifth anniversary issue:

> If . . . comics creators and audience members . . . [can] present to us a work that is beautiful, moving, profound, invigorating and serves to show us all . . . what comics could become, we will herald you and your work and your appreciation of it as . . . earth-shattering genius. . . . But until that day, we reserve the right to mock and deride you endlessly, constantly noting your failures and inadequacies, reminding you always of those who attempted and failed before you and why they did not succeed because, apparently, that is the only way you will ever learn. So: you suck. Get over it. (A. E. Moore 7)

Precisely out of a desire to promote the medium, the *Journal* has, on occasion, encouraged the assumption that comics are worth taking seriously only when they are exceptionally good. The *Journal* has also done a great deal to encourage medium-specific evaluations of comics—at least as regards form and aesthetics—that do not rely on rubrics appropriate to other media, and its list of "The 100 Best Comics of the Century" was an admirably diverse assortment of work obviously not governed by attachment to the graphic novel as a format.[21] But the *Journal*'s consciously medium-specific set of guidelines for identifying valuable work has not managed to address the overall problem of illegitimacy that the medium confronts. When a novel is judged to be poor, it is ruled a bad example of a kind of writing that is legitimate as a whole. When a comic is judged to be "mature," it is still often seen as an exception to a general state of illegitimacy—and this is the case regardless of what criteria are applied to make the judgment. The editorial statement above, unfortunately, resembles not only mainstream journalistic accounts at their most judgmental, but also what many opponents of mass culture said about comics more than half a century ago.[22] The cover of the *Journal*'s twenty-fifth anniversary issue featured this slogan: "Resisting Arrested Development Since the Ford Administration" (Reynolds, Aragonés, Barr and DeLapp). The way in which the *Journal* has pursued this project has occasionally overlapped damaging ideas about comics that date back much further.

Attachment to literary notions of adulthood and maturity can manifest as a kind of reflex even in the writing of critics who consciously resist the *Bildungsroman* discourse. For instance, as Roger Sabin critiques mainstream notions of "adult comics," his use of the term sometimes shifts from description to prescription; that is, he momentarily seems to assume that comics that are "adult" are also better than other comics, or ought to be, and that being "adult" is the same as possessing aesthetic, moral or political value. Discussing the numerous "revisions of the superhero genre" that followed the success of *The Dark Knight Returns* and *Watchmen* in 1986 and 1987, he comments: "Certainly some titles were imaginative and had something to say; most, however, were dire plagiarists that rightly drew criticism for being obtusely self-referencing and only spuriously 'adult'" (98). When Sabin assumes that inferior superhero comics are "only spuriously 'adult,'" in contrast to others that merit the term because they are "imaginative" and have "something to say," he seems to assume that literature for children is derivative, that superhero comics are childish by nature (despite the fact that adults read them), and that only exceptional examples of the genre have achieved maturity thus far.

Unoriginal and solipsistic narratives appear frequently in every genre and medium, and it would seem strange to argue that a novel, television show or film is not "adult" simply because it is derivative and generic (indeed, depending on what children's literature one has been reading, or what children's television shows one has been watching, the term "derivative" might seem much more appropriate for contemporary culture aimed at adults). To assume that a bad comic is childish, or vice versa, is to reinscribe some features of the very discourse Sabin elsewhere attempts to uproot. While he avoids the false history of mainstream journalism, he occasionally seems to adopt the vision of comics it perpetuates, a vision in which comics are unworthy of recognition until they grow up.

Such slippages run parallel to the influence the *Bildungsroman* discourse exerts on critical understanding of production history. In the early decades of the comic book, creators were treated as interchangeable parts in a publishing machine, and many of them had contempt for the works they made. The comic books of this era are typically very different from those produced with greater degrees of creative freedom, and pre-code genre comics are unlikely to generate the variety or volume of critical interest that has gathered around the most acclaimed graphic novels. Yet we can easily presume intrinsic connections between expanded creators' rights and cultural legitimacy, though even a brief glance at production outside the United States shows us that such connections are contingent. In Japan, the comics for adults that first emerged, and were then rapidly legitimated, in the postwar era were not always produced in conditions of creative freedom; in fact, some comics were made by teams of artists forced to imitate the style of a lead illustrator.[23]

The assumption that corporate control necessarily runs parallel to immature work, and that both factors are tied to the medium's illegitimacy, is therefore untenable, difficult as this is to admit for anyone who wishes to defend creators' rights. Insofar as binaries such as early/late and restricted/free become aligned with the youth/age distinction at the center of the *Bildungsroman* discourse, our sense of how contemporary comics differ from those of previous eras can be exaggerated. In the case studies featured in later chapters, I seek to appreciate the complex achievements of contemporary creators without allowing figures of development to stand as rubrics for those achievements, or to project the more suppressed condition of earlier comics as being more childish. Given the pervasive force of the *Bildungsroman* discourse, I find it likely that this study contains slippages I have not detected.

The pervasive influence of notions of maturity and development points to a key aspect of the medium's legitimation that historians have not fully addressed. Jean-Paul Gabilliet and Paul Lopes, whose accounts of the medium's struggles with status have been the most authoritative to date, describe legitimation as something that begins within the medium, and the culture devoted to it, and then spreads into wider cultural fields.[24] At first glance, this model is simple common sense. Dedicated producers and consumers of any medium are those who first take it seriously, and subsequent legitimation can be seen as following from what initially happens among devotees. But as it is typically understood, this model can ignore the degree to which "internal" legitimation of a medium actually means applying external standards that have been used to devalue it. The intermittent editorial leaning of *The Comics Journal* most vividly illustrates such an internalized understanding of comics as worthless until validated in specific instances, but a parallel problem undoubtedly haunts the advocacy efforts of teachers and scholars, for whom the growth of comics studies has been inseparable from the *Bildungs-roman* discourse. Comics scholarship and teaching has been driven by the passion of scholars determined to make a place for comics in the academy—and it has been dominated by the graphic novel.

It is tempting to claim that material factors alone are at work, and it is true that the existence of a wide array of graphic novels certainly influences the kinds of comics that are typically read in university classrooms, both when they are assigned together with print literature and when comics are the sole object of study. My own comics syllabi, and those of most others with whose pedagogy I am familiar, tend to feature many graphic novels, a few bound short-story collections, the occasional anthology of newspaper comics, some fair-use digital copies of shorter works, and a smattering of online comics, but few, if any, stapled single issues of comic books—this despite the fact that such works are still a substantial (if shrinking) part of comics publication in the United States. Single issues pose more problems of access than do graphic novels; the latter usually stay in print more consistently, and most are less affected by the constraints of direct-market comics distribution. Yet such material concerns run parallel to broader problems of status. Students who are suspicious of comics sometimes have difficulty accepting even acclaimed graphic novels as valid ("I wanted to read a real book," a disappointed student confessed to me after discovering that Bechdel's *Fun Home* had been assigned for a discussion seminar). The stapled single issue, often seen by non-comics readers as both contemptibly disposable and shamefully collectable, tends to raise yet more doubts.

I offer these observations not as a defense of a certain way of teaching comics, but simply as a frank evaluation of the options one confronts when doing so. To select materials for a comics course is, among other things, to negotiate the degree of one's complicity with the *Bildungs-roman* discourse. The disproportionate scholarly attention paid to comic books and graphic novels, as opposed to newspaper or web comics, is a related, though more complex, issue, but it deserves mention, not least because the present study, focused on works currently printed as graphic novels, does its part in adding to the disproportion. I proceed on the assumption that it is possible to focus on examples from the canon of graphic novels while still approaching these works in ways that can both expand possibilities for comics reading and critique the *Bildungsroman* discourse with some effectiveness. Whether this gambit is worthwhile will depend on whether the kinds of reading advanced here prove useful for a wide spectrum of comics outside the canon of graphic novels. Meanwhile, I concede that the selection of works for this study is not free of the influence of the *Bildungsroman* discourse.

Even at its most pervasive, this discourse can still be critiqued; teachers can certainly discuss questions of format and legitimacy in the classroom, for instance. But highlighting the way some aspect of the *Bildungsroman* discourse operates does not cancel its operation. Further, what is most accurate, as an account of the fate of comics, is not what is most likely to get a hearing. It is often more effective to resort to the terms of the mainstream press and explain comics studies as the result of natural changes in comics themselves (a young medium reaching maturity, fit for serious study at last!) than it is to tell a century-long story of struggle. Nor is there always a clear dividing line between tactical deployments of the graphic novel and moments when the *Bildungsroman* discourse exerts an unconscious influence. Lopes, in his detailed history of the troubles comics have faced, closes his introduction with this invitation to his readers: "I hope the following social history of the American comic book will not only enlighten you to the themes I have outlined here about artistic rebellion, the political economy of art, cultural status and cultural politics, but also inspire you to pick up a graphic novel or comic book and discover how comics have truly grown up" (xxv). I find it impossible to tell whether this is a calculated use of a figure of maturation or something less self-aware. In either case, there is nothing accidental about the phrase "truly grown up" as an appeal for a broader scholarly audience for comics, and the phrase is, in fact, appealing, however badly it clashes with the narrative spelled out elsewhere in Lopes's account. The persistence with which this kind of phrasing can reassert itself, even at the beginning of an account that shows why it is unworkable, is one of the reasons I pursue a more aggressive strategy for dealing with the *Bildungsroman* discourse. Material and cultural histories must join ways of reading that do not allow the idea of coming of age to be a measure of quality or of ultimate importance.

To readers deeply invested in comics, much of my account of the powers and functions of the *Bildungsroman* discourse (other than the unwieldy term itself) is at least somewhat familiar. I find it important to highlight both the limitations of this discourse and its importance for understanding not only where comics have come from, but also where, as comics readers and scholars, we find ourselves now. From its first significant utterance in the 1954 code, the idea that comics have come of age arrives far too late to undo the damage that gives rise to it. At best, it negotiates the forms of damage, and often inflects and propagates the regulatory forces to which comics have been subject.

Much is obscured when we look at the story of US comics as an organic process of growth toward adult artistic expression or literacy. Although the aura of maturity has been useful as the guarantee of legitimacy for comics studies, it remains vague to the point of uselessness as a critical rubric. But we will never consign the *Bildungsroman* discourse to oblivion by even the most exhaustive account of its inaccuracies and limitations. Its shortcomings make it insufficient as a *standard*, but its centrality testifies to the fact that legitimacy and maturity are unavoidable as *topics*, and are destined to be conjoined for years to come. By seeing clearly how these topics work together, we can shift their orientation and ask new questions about them. And if this is the case when we consider how best to advance comics literacy as teachers and advocates of the medium, it is also true when we turn to the pages of contemporary US comics as critical readers. The burden of the chapters that follow is to illuminate how comics creators have engaged, critiqued, refigured, and otherwise struggled with the problems of status that cluster around comics. To do this demands both that we set aside the *Bildungsroman* discourse and that we keep it in view—precisely in order to recognize the ways in which comics creators have resisted it.

TWO

Autoclastic Icons

PICTURING ILLEGITIMACY

W hat do comics want?

I am rephrasing the question "What do pictures want?"—a striking inquiry formulated by W. J. T. Mitchell.[1] Offered as a new way of theorizing images, Mitchell's question arrived at the end of a series of theoretical investigations stretching over more than a decade. Early in these investigations, Mitchell offered a strong critique of the "fear of imagery that can be found in every major philosopher from Bacon to Kant to Wittgenstein, a fear not just of the 'idols' of pagan primitives, or of the vulgar marketplace, but of the idols which insinuate themselves into language and thought, the false models which mystify both perception and representation" (*Iconology* 113). In opposition to this widespread fear, which he terms "iconophobia," Mitchell has argued that, while retaining a full critical awareness of their power, we should celebrate the lives of images and value our relations with them rather than attempting to master them through critical suspicion or to eliminate them through righteous iconoclasm. He speaks of images as agents working alongside their human makers; in one of his early formulations, the image is "an actor on the historical stage, a presence or character endowed with legendary status, a history that parallels and participates in the stories we tell ourselves" (*Iconology* 9).[2] Our obsession with controlling images, argues Mitchell, should give way to thoughtful communion.

After opening the door to this affirmative approach to images, Mitchell has continued to urge new kinds of attentiveness to them, not least in his suggestion that "pictures might be capable of reflection on themselves, capable of providing a second-order discourse that tells us— or at least shows us—something about pictures" (*Picture Theory* 38). Images can be seen as a kind of theory that we read not in order to subject them to critical control, but so that we can better understand how our relations with them actually work. Having gone thus far along this trail of thought, Mitchell has urged us to embrace the libidinous nature of our relations with images and ask what they desire from us. Hence the radical new question: What do pictures want? As one of Mitchell's major examples (a still image from David Cronenberg's film *Videodrome*) shows, pictures often want the same thing we do, namely, the expression of desire itself: "If we had only this picture to work from, we would have to say that the answer to our question is, pictures want to be kissed. And of course we want to kiss them back" (*What Do Pictures Want?* xvi). Beginning with a critique of the ways in which we are intellectually hostile to images, Mitchell has eventually arrived at a kind of self-aware paganism: "We might even have to entertain what I would call a 'critical idolatry' or 'secular divination' as an antidote to that reflexive critical iconoclasm that governs intellectual discourse today" (*What Do Pictures Want?* 26).

This suggestion may seem like an invitation to an undisciplined, hedonistic approach to images, but in practice, Mitchell's critical iconophilia hews to common theoretical concerns, and particularly to questions of power. The "libidinal fields" that images generate are connected to the power dynamics in which they are enmeshed (*What Do Pictures Want?* xvii). Insofar as traditional approaches to images have subjected them to discursive and political control, Mitchell's project is a rescue attempt, a "subaltern model of the picture" that "opens up the actual dialectics of power and desire in our relations with pictures" (*What Do Pictures Want?* 34). And it turns out, not surprisingly, that part of what images want is what they typically do not get: clearer, less ideologically motivated understanding from their viewers. Surveying various categories of images—the openly appealing propaganda poster, the mass-cultural racial caricature, the self-enclosed modernist painting, the self-reflexive postmodern art work—Mitchell sees a kind of "lack" operating in each case (*What Do Pictures Want?* 33–48). While several of his examples show how images themselves wield power, often to the detriment of their audiences and others, the recurrence of this lack also indicates, for Mitchell, the power and pervasiveness of iconophobic discourse.

Turning to contemporary comics, I want to specify a "subaltern model" of the image in accordance with the "dialectics of power and desire" that have regulated the fate of comics. A medium's self-understanding and its cultural status are always connected, and Mitchell is right to suggest that in many instances, visual media bear the marks of their subaltern position. In the range of examples he considers, differentials of power are crucial to an understanding of iconophobia's effects. But because not all visual media wield the same kind of influence or possess the same degree of legitimacy, images do not always want the same things. What does a visual medium want when it is denied any legitimacy, when the ambitions of its creators are strongly discouraged, and when the inclinations of its readers are considered shameful?

According to the *Bildungsroman* discourse that dominates mainstream cultural understanding of comics, the medium as a whole is juvenile, and only some exceptional cases are mature enough to be considered worthwhile adult reading matter. Anyone subscribing to this discourse might, in a moment of frankness, answer my opening question thus: In its beginnings, and for several decades thereafter, the medium did not want anything, except perhaps to express itself without standards or consequences. Comics remained too long in a state of unmotivated adolescence, desiring neither artistic achievement nor cultural responsibility. Now, at last, the best of them have aspired to improve their station, and they want to be recognized for literary maturity. Many comics, however, have refused to grow up, because they desire nothing more than to wallow in adolescence forever—and so their delinquent status is, even now, well deserved. This hypothetical response suggests how strongly the *Bildungsroman* discourse is aligned with an iconophobic imperative to regulate our desire for images and their desire for us.

Given that such regulatory tendencies put severe limitations on the medium's status, we should expect the "libidinal fields" comics generate to be distinctive and complex. In the comics I examine, vectors of desire are highly unstable; frequently, they clash or collapse rather than generating a libidinal connection with their readers. Such complex images fascinate, but they can no more be sealed with a kiss of pleasurable satisfaction than they can be wedded to the *Bildungsroman* discourse. The damage done to comics over so many decades now disrupts the intimate process of comics reading, upsetting the expectation—even such admirable hopes as might be inspired by Mitchell's approach to images—that comics and their readers can achieve a legitimate exchange of affections.

The examples discussed in this chapter all feature what I call autoclasm, which is central to the medium's troubled economy of desire. As the roots of the term indicate, autoclasm is present when an image effects a kind of self-breaking, as if it is designed to work against itself.[3] Reading an autoclastic icon with care and following its meaning from one level of interpretation to another, we observe a dynamic of autonomously enacted dissolution, as if self-destruction is its ultimate function as a signifier. Often, the structure of autoclasm is binary: strongly contrasting elements are joined to generate incommensurable meanings. This joining is intricate and tangled, articulating the condition of comics through carefully orchestrated interruption, cancelation, self-censorship or discursive implosion. Far from being a surface matter of aesthetics or style, autoclasm is a formal tendency specific to conditions where the act of making comics is not considered legitimate. Autoclastic icons are resonant evidence of status problems, and through such icons, the medium figures and repeats its own sense of its illegitimacy. This repetition is not an inappropriate holdover from a previous era; nor is it a performative manifestation of low cultural self-esteem. It is fully in accord with the fraught position the medium still occupies in the era of the graphic novel.

Autoclasm arises, in part, out of comics creators' resistance to the *Bildungsroman* discourse. Any creator associated with the term "graphic novel" has understood its legitimating function. Will Eisner, who first put the term into wide circulation, has testified that he applied it to his 1978 short story collection *A Contract with God* as a bid for legitimacy (Arnold, "Silver Anniversary" n. pag.). Yet willingness to employ this term has not kept creators from seeing its limitations. Art Spiegelman has acknowledged its usefulness—remarking that "graphics are respectable, novels are respectable, so whammy: double respectability"—but has remained skeptical of the graphic novel, frequently implying that there is a price to be paid for the legitimacy it provides (Sabin 235). He describes a "Faustian arrangement of trying to dance with the academic and the institutionally and culturally acceptable devils so that this work gets to live for another century. Since this work is this hybrid bastard that sort of is literature, sort of is picture-making, any alliances that allows [sic] it to continue seem like decent ones" (Kidd 37). Spiegelman's analysis highlights the problem of illegitimacy—the choice of the term "bastard" is telling—and admits that comics should agree to be adopted (if I may extend his metaphor) by whatever discourses and institutions will allow the medium a future. Yet the prospect of "literary" respectability is viewed warily; Spiegelman sees the business of legitimation by way of the graphic novel not as a welcome ascension to respectable status, but as a complex deal with the devil.[4]

One of the most troubling aspects of this "Faustian arrangement" is that as it has provided graphic novels with a measure of respectability, articulating the problem of illegitimacy has become increasingly difficult. The present status of comics is rooted in mid-century cultural assumptions, but these assumptions are now dispersed through the *Bildungsroman* discourse rather than concentrated in hostile anti-comics movements and industry codes. A general sense of the medium's contemptibility is still prevalent, but in the case of a given reader or critic, it may take the form of a hazy presumption whose consequences are not worked out. Journalists attached to the idea of the graphic novel have taken little notice of creators' wariness toward it, even when this attitude is bluntly expressed. In "Not Funnies," my central example of "coming of age" journalism in the previous chapter, author Charles McGrath interviews Spiegelman on the subject of the graphic novel. It is, Spiegelman claims, the literary equivalent of "the state of Israel—one big boundary dispute in one little corner of the bookshop globe" (29–30). Where McGrath insists on finding manifest literary respectability, Spiegelman sees a territorial claim made for the purpose of legitimation; McGrath takes no notice of this marked difference of perspective. From the point of view of the mainstream, the graphic novel suffices to give some comics a modest place in literary culture, and little more need be said. From the point of view of the creator, status problems are massive realities that the graphic novel has not eliminated, but has made much harder to express.

Since there is no ready vocabulary to express what it means to be considered illegitimate, as a creator, because of one's choice of medium, attempts to describe the low status of comics put considerable strain on existing terms and concepts. When comics creators articulate status concerns, what they say can be controversial, and sometimes blatantly offensive. In choosing the term "bastard," Spiegelman expresses the idea of illegitimacy in rather archaic fashion, but when he uses Israel as a metaphor, he evokes a live political conflict that impinges on his own ethnic identity. Spiegelman has been skeptical, even contemptuous, of Zionism, remarking that "Israel is a sad, failed idea," so the idea of the graphic novel as "the state of Israel" suggests its insufficiency (Hays n. pag). Yet insofar as comics remain a "bastard medium" lacking recognition or sovereignty, it is not clear which side of the "boundary dispute" they are meant to occupy in Spiegelman's metaphor. Perhaps Spiegelman suggests, if unconsciously, that while he is ethnically Jewish, he is, in comics terms, Palestinian.

Provocative as such an implication is, it falls short of this openly outrageous comparison from Frank Miller: "When I first came in [to the comics industry], during the late seventies, there was this constant sense that we were the 'niggers' of entertainment—and I think that persists and hasn't progressed" (*Eisner/Miller* 191). This metaphor clearly invites condemnation, not least because it obscures the fact that racial diversity— both in terms of creatorship and in terms of the range of characters represented on the page—remains a significant problem in mainstream comics; if Miller's comparison is allowed to stand, one would have to ask what language is left to express this problem.[5] This choice of metaphor can, at the same time, be read as a symptom of the problem of articulation. If Miller unconsciously suggests that working in comics is the closest he has come to feeling a loss of white privilege, his overstatement also indicates a struggle most creators have in common (even as its quality and intensity are affected by many factors, including race).

In the face of this struggle for adequate language, how is illegitimacy made visible within the medium? Mitchell claims that a kind of image he calls the "metapicture" can offer a "self-analysis . . . directed not only at the medium, but at the determining conditions of the work—its institutional setting, its historical positionality, its address to beholders" (*Picture Theory* 36). Within the context of comics' status difficulties, the idea of the metapicture should prompt us to be on the lookout for comics that theorize their own illegitimacy. At the same time, the force of this illegitimacy can be expected to influence the way such theorization is expressed. The medium is not usually deemed suitable for producing ideas about itself; authoritative descriptions of comics are almost invariably phrased in print. The most obvious exception is Scott McCloud's *Understanding Comics* (1993)—a work that has had an overwhelmingly positive reception in comics culture and has garnered significant acceptance among academics—but McCloud has had no substantial body of successors. In fact, comics theory in comics form remains rare even among practicing cartoonists, most of whom express their ideas about comics in live interviews or in print.

Notably, on occasions when McCloud is criticized, the form of critique often implies a distrust of comics' ability to express thought in image form. Discussing academic critiques of *Understanding Comics*, Charles Hatfield notes a "tendency to bracket off McCloud's claims because they come from a book without academic cachet—a comic book at that," and predicts that "this tendency will persist, and *Understanding Comics* will be cited, over and over, as the 'seminal' yet 'problematic' *Understanding Comics*, the 'provocative' yet 'flawed' *Understanding Comics*, the indispensable yet dangerously seductive *Understanding Comics*"

2.1. *Chester Brown, first page of two-page strip*, New York Times Magazine, 2004.

("Thoughts" 89). The attitudes Hatfield describes are a stark reminder that comics have been, for the most part, a medium that is not permitted to give a legitimate account of itself.[6]

While comics devoted to understanding the formal or expressive *capacities* of the medium are quite rare, there are many comics that picture what Mitchell calls "the determining conditions of the work," which is to say, the medium's discredited *status*. Such representations are typically autoclastic, because this formal strategy can make glaringly visible the difficulty the comics creator confronts. I return once more to the 2004 issue of the *New York Times Magazine* in which Charles McGrath's

"Not Funnies" appeared. Accompanying the article is a two-page comic written and drawn by Chester Brown, and it provides a take on the question of the graphic novel that is very different from McGrath's (figures 2.1 and 2.2).

The first page of the comic, featured on the cover, shows a conversation between a journalist and a graphic novelist. "Aren't graphic novels just comic books? Comic books with more pages and better paper but

2.2. *Chester Brown, second page of two-page strip,* New York Times Magazine, 2004.

comic books nonetheless," the journalist asks. His interlocutor responds by defending graphic novels on the basis of their serious, well-developed narrative and thematic content, observing that increased length means a larger "scope for telling stories of greater complexity and depth." The graphic novelist then claims that "creators who are interested in more mature themes are more likely to—" but gets no further in his defense; the journalist interrupts him, saying they will "have to continue this discussion inside the magazine." On the second page of the comic, which appears opposite the first page of McGrath's article, the graphic novelist is surprised—and quickly becomes indignant—upon finding that the journalist has been replaced by a duck. In the fourth and fifth panels, the graphic novelist declares, "Graphic novels are a respected art form now! I don't have to put up with this sort of juvenile nonsense." He then departs, leaving the duck to observe, in the final panel, that he is "overly sensitive." This comic orchestrates, and is wholly animated by, conflicting approaches to the question of legitimacy.

Brown raises this question in unmistakable fashion. Note the interviewer's opening move: "Aren't graphic novels just comic books?" Brown then begins to answer in the vein of "Not Funnies"—clearly, the graphic novelist is about to say that creators with "mature" ambitions are more likely to make graphic novels—but then he brings this answer to a sudden halt. Unlike the character he creates (and unlike McGrath), Brown does not believe the graphic novel is a superior form of comics. A 1990 interview indicates that he sees it simply as a format that presents specific practical considerations regarding publication possibilities and deadlines. It does not, in his view, possess different creative horizons, and the graphic novelist is thus not to be trusted when defending long-form comics as a special case ("Sacred to Scatological" 89–90). Yet the way his voice is silenced, far from reducing the comic to a simple critique of the graphic novel, is dizzyingly complex. On one interpretive level, the journalist's opening question, the rude interruption and the appearance of the duck are all ways for the literary establishment to mock comics. At this level, Brown strips away the veneer of the *Bildungsroman* discourse and indicates the seriousness of the problem of illegitimacy. Yet it is ultimately Brown, not the journalist, who introduces the talking duck in order to make this point, and thus the creator invites exactly the kind of condemnation he purports to challenge. The comic seems designed to induce a dilemma for readers: How can we take Brown's critique of the *Bildungsroman* discourse seriously when he is, after all, being so childish?

We could try to resolve this problem by arguing that when Brown interrupts high-flown talk of literary comics and uses the duck to drive away the graphic novelist, he performs an elegant, perverse involution that shows there is something immature about obsession with maturity, and something sophisticated about deliberate recourse to the seemingly juvenile. At this level, the graphic novelist is suspect, because he shows a cultural insecurity poorly veiled by his claim that "graphic novels are a respected art form now." Perhaps, then, it is the duck that speaks for comics, and for Brown. Such a reading is appealing, but we must revert to our earlier interpretation and acknowledge the degree to which the creator is invested in the very concerns he claims to reject. After all, the sole theme of Brown's comic is the question of status that the graphic novelist is mocked for taking to heart. The graphic novelist may in fact be "overly sensitive," but only a comics creator deeply sensitive to the kind of subtle delegitimation effected by articles like "Not Funnies" would make this comic. Brown seems simultaneously to engage the problem of legitimacy as central, by critiquing the *Bildungsroman* discourse, and to disavow this critique as unproductive status-seeking. At the center of this short-circuited arrangement of meanings is the ambiguous duck, who is at once an agent of literary culture, used against comics with ambitions for respectability, and an agent of comics culture, attacking comics with snobbish literary pretentions.

Brown does not actually blame himself for caring about the marginalization of comics; nor does he indicate that all responses to it are equally futile. He simply suggests that the graphic novelist is wrong to believe that long-form comics, called by a culturally respectable name, can be the answer to questions of status. Yet the same forces that motivate the graphic novelist's mistake influence Brown, who seems compelled not to defend the medium but simply to picture its status. Through deliberate mockery of the graphic novel (and thus of the premises of the article that accompanies his comic), Brown resists the path to legitimation promised by the *Bildungsroman* discourse. He does so with good reason, since that path ends in a cul-de-sac of tokenism from which there is no easy escape for the medium as a whole. Yet clearly, this refusal is not motivated by a sense that there is some other way to make the medium respectable. Brown's creative strategy is less an aspirational move for higher status than a way to keep faith with the problem of illegitimacy, and a determination to make this problem consistently visible. And keeping it visible can best be accomplished if the medium keeps repeating its understanding of the ways in which it is seen as illegitimate, without offering a false resolution to the problem. The fact that comics lack cultural authority is, it would seem, the thing Brown believes they have the most authority to express, but this expression is, paradoxically, most powerful when it is arranged in autoclastic fashion.

In the case of Brown's comic, it might seem that autoclasm is inspired by the chance to respond to "coming of age" journalistic discourse like McGrath's, but very similar dynamics operate when there is no such immediate motivation. I turn to a one-page comic by Michael Kupperman entitled "Are Comics Serious Literature?" that first appeared in 2005 in the first issue of his series *Tales Designed to Thrizzle* (figure 2.3). It features two cowboys, one claiming that comics are serious literature, the other claiming that they are not. "Let's settle this question!" the first cowboy exclaims as he punches his interlocutor. A dialogue-free fistfight ensues, full of hackneyed visual drama and poorly chosen sound effects; the knockout blow, delivered by the first cowboy, is accompanied by an especially unfitting "CLOP!" (a sound better used, the reader might speculate, to accompany the movement of some off-panel horse). The final panel shows the first cowboy confidently proclaiming, "Now who else says comics aren't serious literature?" as his opponent lies unconscious behind him. This comic very pointedly names its topic and gives it a sense of urgency. No reader can be in any doubt that the medium's legitimacy is the issue at hand, and that there is a conflict over this issue that can be won or lost. Yet the comic deliberately undercuts its chances at triumphing in this conflict by offering evidence against the medium; in place of an argument, it presents a fistfight.

The pro-comics cowboy raises the debate, throws the first punch, and wins, but at every moment he is a ridiculous figure. On its own terms, his final question is rhetorical, and it is clearly meant to be followed by awed silence. On any other terms, the likely answer to the question is "Everyone," including, it seems, Kupperman himself, who betrays the enterprise of defending the medium not just by his choice of content, but through his execution. Note the irregular grid, which seems designed to draw the eye to the curiously shaped fourth panel, positioned in the middle of the second tier. Its asymmetrical form suggests a stubborn attempt to force it into position, like a wrongly fitted puzzle piece, so that it is both awkward in itself and disruptive to the panels around it. This panel is, not accidentally, a moment of suspense; the pro-comics cowboy appears to be losing the fight. Far from helping his protagonist, Kupperman seems determined to support the opponent's position by committing a number of compositional sins. The edges of

ARE COMICS SERIOUS LITERATURE?

2.3. *Michael Kupperman, one-page strip from* Tales Designed to Thrizzle *issue 1,*
2005.

buildings that intrude into the corners of four panels are painfully awkward, as is the offhand rendering, at once blocky and loose, of the two
figures. Kupperman thus works to make a bad comic in glaring ways,
confronting the critic with a paradox: immature and aesthetically dubious work is offered as the measure of the creator's skill and intelligence—
and of the medium's worth.

In a 2009 interview, Kupperman indicates both that he sometimes
intends to make bad comics and that his interest in them is derived
from the medium's history: "In early comics, you see this amazing awkwardness and bizarre reasoning in the storyline, and it's because comics
hadn't really been invented yet. There was no format for them to follow.
They were just making it up. . . . I try to incorporate that kind of awkwardness in my comics quite frequently. . . . I will try to make the artwork look bad, occasionally" (n. pag.). This artistic strategy has nothing
to do with kitsch or primitivism; "Are Comics Serious Literature?" is neither an exercise in nostalgia nor an embrace of naïve art unfettered by
convention. Rather, form and style raise questions of status; Kupperman
makes his work "look bad" in order to express how the medium itself is
perceived.

Kupperman refuses to say why comics ought to be granted legitimacy, but he does demonstrate the hollowness of any simple declaration
that "comics are serious literature." Instead of a progress narrative claiming the medium has naturally grown up, Kupperman displays a conflict
that does not proceed in any credible sequence, instead unfolding in a
fashion at once generic (the protagonist seems to be losing at first, then
makes an implausible comeback and triumphs) and incoherent (the flow
of the action tracks poorly in the fifth, sixth and seventh panels, the moment when the momentum of the fight is reversed). The fourth panel focuses our attention on the fact that, regardless of the stakes of the conflict, force alone settles it. Whoever wins the fight will claim that his
position is correct, quite apart from any actual points of debate. Kupperman thus suggests the arbitrary nature of the violence to which comics
have been subject.

When yet another mainstream news article declares that comics are
not just for kids anymore, it never questions the background assumption that for some unspecified length of time, comics *have* been just for
kids. This premise is taken as given, and, by default, as appropriate (one
finds no articles entitled "Comics Not Unfairly Stigmatized Anymore").
In other words, both the declaration of a modification in the status of
graphic novels and the backhanded sanctioning of the medium's over-

all illegitimacy are rhetorical maneuvers backed by supposition; the *Bildungsroman* discourse provides them the illusion of coherence. Kupperman expresses what is obscured by this discourse: the illegitimacy of comics and the recent mitigation of this illegitimacy (the triumphant pro-comics cowboy) are contingent effects of force, not conditions regulated by sound argument. Kupperman's imitation of the "bad" style of early comics reinforces this point by suggesting that, despite the illusion of change, the status of comics has not progressed, and this status has determined the medium's fate. The question of what comics really are, or might be, is overwritten—given Kupperman's bad art, perhaps we might say overdrawn—by the problem of how they are still perceived.

In the world of "Are Comics Serious Literature?" perhaps every debate is resolved through fisticuffs. But if we read allegorically, we can see the pro-comics cowboy as a fan who thinks well of the medium and embraces its possibilities, and his opponent as someone who despises the medium, or at least believes its value is limited. Outside the ten panels of the comic itself, readers agreeing with the first cowboy are likely to see "Are Comics Serious Literature?" as sophisticated and clever; those on the other side of the question will not. As this comic arranges matters, the more readily and crudely the pro-comics cowboy turns to violence in order to defeat his opponent, the more difficult it will be for any of his real-world supporters to speak on his behalf (what, the skeptic might ask, is so valuable about a badly drawn fistfight?). The comic could certainly proceed otherwise; for instance, its protagonist could make an actual argument. Instead, Kupperman turns to a language of pictorially expressed violence long associated with especially contemptible genres of comics, a language that, in this context, might well please insiders with its clever crudeness, but will certainly perplex or irritate outsiders. Yet, as Kupperman arranges matters, internal legitimation inevitably leads to a confrontation at the boundary separating comics from "serious literature." In the last panel, having won the fight against his opponent, the pro-comics cowboy is positioned in the extreme foreground and looks forward to another conflict and outward to the reader's world, where his reception will be uneven, to put it mildly. Autoclasm here takes the form of an impossible dare, which Kupperman seems to acknowledge as too risky to work even as he refuses, like his protagonist, to back down from it.

Both Brown and Kupperman engage the question of the medium's legitimacy without answering it. Instead, they simply picture the dynamics of power that make the question itself so troubling. Likewise, these creators critique legitimating discourses in order to show how they per-

petuate the very conditions they claim to alleviate. Through such critique, creators express not a dislike of the category of the graphic novel,
or of literature as such, but a deep awareness of the way cultural cat-
egorization exerts power. Brown disrupts a conversation about the legitimacy of comics in order to reveal in full the nature of anti-comics
stigma. Kupperman desublimates the violence of critical discourse on
comics, figuring high-toned talk of comics as "serious literature" as the
prelude to a brawl rather than as an invitation to responsible public discourse that could alter the medium's status. We are meant to understand
that this is not a fight the comics creator, through some natural belliger-
ence, is interested in starting; it simply cannot be avoided. Yet—outside
the world of the pro-comics cowboy—the fight cannot easily be won, because the medium is not permitted to express its capacities in a way that
can be recognized on its own terms. Thus, autoclasm articulates the medium's conditions and, at the same time, illustrates the ways that this articulation is limited by those very conditions.

The ability to dwell with this paradox, to embody it in visual form, is
one of the chief achievements of contemporary US comics creators. To
see this achievement clearly, we must grasp how it arises from the conditions in which creators find themselves and how it constitutes a significant creative response to those conditions, a complex act of making them
visible and of bearing witness to them. If this witnessing is deliberately
limited or self-canceling, this is not because of a legacy of pessimism
or low expectations (though, given the challenges many comics creators
have faced, such expectations would be thoroughly justified); nor is it
a matter of accumulating some kind of subcultural cachet. The comics discussed here do not capitulate to the marginalized position of the
medium any more than they strike a deliberately stylized pose against it.
They simply keep a watchful eye on the stigmatizing discourse that has
never ceased to fix its gaze on them. This is not a matter of taking up a
wounded posture; it is a focusing of creative energies in the face of real
barriers to legitimacy.

As comics enter the bookstore, the library and the classroom in
greater numbers, some of the more material barriers to legitimacy have
been at least partly overcome. As Brown and Kupperman suggest, however, the essential problem of comics as illegitimate expression has remained. Because comics are not granted the power to speak of themselves with authority, they are subject to a differend. As Jean-François
Lyotard articulates this term, it names both a discursive inadequacy that
makes fair adjudication of a conflict impossible and the injustice result-

ing from this inadequacy. A differend, in the sense of an inadequacy, is possible whenever two conflicting parties express their concerns across a discursive gap, and injustice occurs whenever the claims of one party cannot be fairly expressed because "the 'regulation' of the conflict . . . is done in the idiom of one of the parties while the wrong suffered by the other is not signified in that idiom" (9). Whenever comics are discussed as "serious literature" (or not), or as being not just for kids anymore (or as still mostly for kids), a differend is operating—not simply because such utterances are made in verbal or print discourse, but because their phrasing obscures and perpetuates the very conditions that make it impossible for comics to be seen justly, either as a medium or as an object of literacy.

This is not a case of a minor distortion, correctable by rearrangement of available phrases; here we confront the inadequacy of an entire phrase regimen, as Lyotard would term it, that cannot grant comics authoritative expression of their own capacities and conditions—and thus cannot fundamentally alter their status as a medium and a mode of literacy.[7] Unfortunately, this problem is also present in Lyotard's own sense of what counts as a phrase regimen, which is limited to what can be expressed in language: "To give the differend its due is to institute new addressees, new addressors, new significations, and new referents in order for the wrong to find an expression and for the plaintiff to cease being a victim. This requires new rules for the formation and linking of phrases. No one doubts that language is capable of admitting these new phrase families or new genres of discourse. Every wrong ought to be able to be put into phrases" (13). The problem confronting us in the case of comics is that language, as Lyotard clearly means it to be understood, must incorporate not "new phrase families or new genres of discourse," but a new conception of what counts as language (either in the general sense of communication or in a more specific, linguistic sense).[8] At present, comics are still marked either as a site of illegitimacy that no rephrasing can eradicate or, at best, as a medium that can be rephrased (usually in the terms of the *Bildungsroman* discourse) and then granted a measure of legitimacy. The limitation in Lyotard's formulation is correctable, but it highlights the intractability of the differend that governs the relationship between comics and literature. Autoclasm is best understood as a tactic for making this differend visible, and readable, in the medium itself.

Autoclasm allows us not only to read the power relations in which the medium is caught up in culture at large, but also to glimpse the inner struggles of the comics creator, who is aware of the problem of status at the very moment creation occurs. I do not profess to have seen what goes on in the minds and bodies of comics artists when they are writing and drawing, but I do claim that creative impulses, no less than ambitions for cultural recognition, can be affected by the differend to which comics have been subject. There are occasional hints to this effect in creators' writings and interviews. Take this anecdote from Neil Gaiman:

> I remember once at a party running into the editor of the literary page of a major newspaper. . . . [H]e was asking me what I did, and I said, "I write comics." And I could see him turn off—it was like, This is somebody beneath my nose. . . . [A]nd then I said, "I also do this thing called 'Sandman,'" and he went, "Wait, hang on, you're Neil Gaiman!" He said, "My God, man, you don't write comics, you write *graphic novels*." And I suddenly felt like someone who had been informed that she wasn't a hooker, that in fact she was a lady of the evening. (Erikson n. pag., italics original)

Like the two comics examined above, this story is a critique of the *Bildungsroman* discourse. The editor seems to confer a new status on Gaiman's work, but the pronouncement "you write *graphic novels*" actually sustains the conditions it purports to set aside. In the simile Gaiman uses to describe his reaction to this remark, he also touches on the creative impulse. While the comparison to sex work is clearly an overstatement, it suggests how, when comics themselves are considered shameful, the comics maker is a figure of illicit desire. The editor is, it would seem, a fan of *Sandman*, so he softens his disapproval of Gaiman's work to justify himself. Behind this polite concession, Gaiman suggests, is a dirty act of displacement; in comics reading, as in the sex industry, the consumer can find a way to project shameful feelings onto the other party. Gaiman is not suggesting that sex workers must be motivated by their desires; he speaks of stereotypes rather than realities. His point is simply that being a comics creator means being told, perhaps in veiled terms, that one's most essential impulses are blameworthy.

The effects this stigma can have on the dynamics of creation are vividly expressed in the comics of Dori Seda, whose work frequently connects comics making to transgressive desire. Especially powerful is the elegantly titled "Fuck Story" (1986), which Seda begins by confronting readers with their own desire for pornographic comics while simultaneously admitting her own anxieties as an artist. A confidently posed Seda in lingerie declares, "I know why you bought this comic book with the lurid cover!! You wanted a . . . FUCK STORY!" A second image of Seda below the title shows her hunched over a blank sheet of paper, telling herself, "OK. . . . I think I can do this . . ." (86.1). As the story unfolds, illicit desire and artistic uncertainty become increasingly entangled, and both become increasingly implicated in a crisis of legitimacy that bears most directly on the status of the creator.

By the standards of pornographic narrative, things begin innocuously: a man and woman meet in a laundromat and, after exchanging clichéd suggestive dialogue, go to the woman's apartment for sex. Another man and woman arrive, turning the encounter into a foursome, and after a while, one of the men looks out a window and spots Seda herself in a nearby apartment. When he suggests they invite her to join the group, one of the women says, "She's this weird cartoonist. . . . [W]e invited her over to fuck once, and that was enough! She just doesn't fuck nice!" (88.3). The woman then explains exactly how Seda "doesn't fuck nice": she brings her dog into the sex act. As the woman is narrating how this happened, one of the men suddenly shouts "STOP IT!" (89.1). He is not, it turns out, addressing the storyteller, but Seda herself, who is suddenly revealed at her drawing table, looking at the foursome, who have, it seems, emerged from the paper on which they were drawn and now stand above it, doll-sized, confronting their creator. The man continues: "We were having a lot of fun, and you ruined it with your bullshit about fucking dogs! Look! . . . Maybe you fuck your dog, but nobody else fucks their dog, and nobody wants to read about it!" (89.3). The group then walks off the drawing table, leaving Seda with blank paper (90.1, figure 2.4). Beginning with an appeal to the reader's desire and an admission of creative struggle, Seda then orchestrates a scenario of rejection and failure.

Such a story succeeds (if that is the right verb to apply) precisely insofar as it achieves autoclasm, disrupting established reader-creator relations and turning its "libidinal fields," to return to Mitchell's formulation, against themselves (*What Do Pictures Want?* xvii). Seda manages this by employing a distinction between kinds of transgression. Beginning with an acceptable script for dirty comics, which is likely to find an audience, she then introduces bestiality, which many readers will reject. Within the comic itself, Seda the artist appeals to the principle of innovation: "I was just trying to make the plot a little more interesting . . ."

2.4. *Dori Seda, detail from page 90 panel 1 of "Fuck Story," 1986, collected in* Dori Stories, *1999.*

Her human creations, however, cling to propriety, displaying a "Not in my neighborhood" attitude: "We're leaving!! There's lots of better places to fuck than here! We don't want any dog-fuckers around *us!*" (90.1). Examining this panel, the reader may experience a kind of social and ethical vertigo. On the one hand, some substantial objections can be made to bestiality, and perhaps even to pictorial representations of it. On the other hand, in the context of a "fuck story," the puritanical tone of the outraged, fist-shaking man is rather odd for someone who has just been in a foursome and is interested in adding a fifth participant. Seda is not, we can assume, confused as to why bestiality is more controversial than group sex, but she does suggest that sexual mores are often visceral prejudices based on fetishes rather than ethical principles. The outraged man is not concerned with animal rights; he is angry because Seda has taken her fantasy beyond the limits of his own preferences. His claim that "nobody wants to read" about sex with Dori's dog is less an affirmation of community standards than a kind of self-righteous consumerism. What really concerns Seda, I suggest, is how widespread cultural prejudices can affect the individual creative impulse. The indelible image of Seda's creations walking off the page as they reject her storyline expresses precisely this problem.

This image is not to be confused with other tropes of creative difficulty associated with more legitimate arts or media. The modern tradition of creative frustration—abandonment by one's muse, writer's block, and so forth—references scenarios in which the artist is denied access to utterance not because of a problem of medium or reception, but because the creative impulse is absent or frustrated. Seda's comic pictures a wholly different situation in which the creative impulse is thwarted because the medium in which it finds expression is subject to prejudice. Bestiality is the sign of comics' illegitimacy; Seda arranges her narrative so that her troubles begin the moment the creator becomes visible in her work and is labeled a "weird cartoonist." Not all the concerns raised by such a scenario are unique. In "How My Family Encouraged Me to Become an Artist!" Seda worries about how her family's perception of her as a failure will affect creative possibilities for the next generation. The final panel of the comic shows one of Seda's nieces attempting to draw as her father shouts, "Don't do that! You're gonna wind up like your Aunt Dori! (137.6)" A parallel experience might easily befall a poet, novelist or filmmaker. But in "Fuck Story," when Seda's figures first stigmatize her and then depart from their medium, leaving the creator's drawing paper blank, something very specific to comics is happening: figures that initially express a libidinous creative impulse are redeployed to depict the problem of illegitimate expression. The artist is halted not by a lack of inspiration, but by social stigma so strong it seems to sever the creator from her work.

The medium-specific nature, and thus the unavoidability, of such creative difficulties distinguish autoclasm from other discursive practices that it might, at first glance, seem to resemble. For instance, autoclasm differs from the act of placing a term under erasure. Admittedly, there is deliberate thwarting of expression in both cases. But autoclasm functions to make the overall illegitimacy of the medium visible; it is not, like erasure, focused on a single concept or term. This latter practice usually occurs in discourses that have garnered extensive legitimacy, such as literature as a culturally sanctioned kind of writing, or philosophy as an academic discourse. Overall discursive legitimacy is what makes the localized gesture of erasure meaningful. The usual goal of erasure is to challenge an element of a discourse (or, in more ambitious cases, an entire system of thought or signification) from within; the speaker is, from the outset, part of the legitimate conditions the new utterance seeks to challenge. Erasure is at once a divestiture, an admission of complicity, and an exploration of the limits of possibility for new thinking— all of which are feasible only when one is already on the right side of the boundary line of legitimation.[9] And one can remain complicit, often deliberately, in the use of a given term even after placing it under erasure, insofar as it remains part of a legitimated whole.

The comics creator is outside the boundaries of legitimation, and autoclasm expresses the creator's lack of expressive authority. Thus, autoclasm also differs from strains of postmodernism that engage self-critically with questions of legitimation. What we see in "Are Comics Serious Literature?" or "Fuck Story" is not "complicitous critique" as described by Linda Hutcheon in *The Politics of Postmodernism*, whereby a work of art acknowledges its implication in the ideological conditions it seeks to challenge (13). It is certainly possible to read Seda's comic in terms of, say, its self-reflexive complicity with the reader's gaze, but autoclasm takes such concerns in a direction very different from what Hutcheon's approach to postmodernism would lead us to expect. As the conclusion to "Fuck Story" shows, the illegitimacy of the medium, if it is strong and pervasive enough, strikes at the heart of the creative act, and it does so in a way that can overlap other issues, such as sexual exploitation on the basis of gender, while also remaining quite different from them. Based on the evidence of this comic, Seda is concerned less with her own implication in a sexualized economy of the gaze than she is with problems of cultural status specific to her medium. Some readers may judge Seda's priorities misplaced; nevertheless, "Fuck Story" pictures a stigma specific to creatorship and distinct from gender.

Autoclasm is motivated by a desire for legitimacy; that is, low status is assumed to be a bad thing. This point may be self-evident, but I underscore it because theories of postmodernism have too readily collapsed the category of legitimacy into that of ideology. In her discussion of complicitous critique, Hutcheon observes: "As producers or receivers of postmodern art, we are implicated in the legitimization of our culture. Postmodern art openly investigates the critical possibilities open to art, without denying that its critique is inevitably in the name of its own contradictory ideology." In this passage, cultural legitimation and ideological complicity are treated as equivalent (15); it is unwise, however, to assume that legitimation, in the broader sense of being seen, read or heard without interference from a differend, is necessarily the same thing as complicity. It is possible for a work in an illegitimate medium to be fully complicit with some ideology or other in terms of its content (mid-century comic books could and did express racism and sexism). Conversely, a work of art can be strongly counterhegemonic in various ways and yet still be given a hearing, and thus a measure of legitimacy, because of its institutional placement or the respectability of its genre.

Theories of postmodern culture have not paid attention to such differentials, leaving us unprepared to grasp how and why autoclasm can express status concerns without necessarily touching on problems of complicity. The postmodern era is imagined as a great cultural leveling that distributes legitimacy evenly across all cultural forms and media. In Andreas Huyssen's durable formulation, "the great divide that separated high modernism from mass culture and that was codified in the various classical accounts of modernism no longer seems relevant to postmodern artistic or critical sensibilities" (196–197). Since the status of cultural forms is no longer deemed a matter for concern, it is understandable that legitimacy of utterance is conceived of in a rather one-dimensional fashion that makes little distinction between the culturally acceptable and the ideologically complicit.

Given this shortcoming, it is possible that the depthlessness sometimes ascribed to postmodern cultural artifacts is, on occasion, an illusion projected by theorists whose lack of attunement to status questions results in a rather flattened perspective. Certain cultural forms, particularly highly legitimated media such as literature and film, do lend themselves to a democratic mixing of high and low cultural energies formerly kept separate; observe the way Thomas Pynchon combines mass culture genre tropes with modernist exploration of interior consciousness in *Gravity's Rainbow*, or the way Quentin Tarantino fuses propaganda film, grindhouse pulp and arthouse cinema in *Inglourious Basterds*. Comics creators, by contrast, do not naturally grant themselves the freedom possessed by postmodern novelists or filmmakers to evoke various "high" and "low" cultural discourses and then freely rearrange them, whether through pastiche or some other method. Much more often, differing aesthetics or discourses are presented on the comics page so as to emphasize their irreconcilability. This tendency toward binary thinking should not trouble comics critics. The oppositions that a creator establishes can in fact rest on oversimplification; creators sometimes treat literary texts or other cultural artifacts containing both "high" and "low" cultural strata as if they belonged only to one realm or the other. While acknowledging these oversimplifications as the misperceptions they are, I am skeptical of the tendency in literary and cultural studies to assume that binary thinking is perforce a transgression that must be corrected before it is well understood.

In fact, a suspicion of cultural binaries can sometimes be an expression of cultural privilege. If comics creators seem to perceive culture as divided into legitimate and illegitimate phenomena, this reflects not a stunted mindset attendant on the choice to make comics, but a shaping of perception intrinsic to the cultural position in which creators find themselves as a result of that choice. (Likewise, the freedom with which Pynchon and Tarantino use disparate kinds of cultural raw material is made possible by the legitimate status of their chosen media.) Note how Kupperman begins by raising a debate about comics as "serious literature" and then immediately recasts it as a fistfight between two cowboys; the shift from intellectual discourse to stereotypical physical action is designed to maximize the contrast between literary culture and pulp, and thus between a desirable condition of legitimacy and the stigma blocking the creator's access to that condition. For Kupperman, as for many comics creators, the question of whether a particular kind of cultural expression is legitimate or not becomes central in a way that it is unlikely to become for a novelist, whose vocation is granted legitimacy in advance. The importance of the question, and not some innate immaturity or simplistic thinking, drives the binary assumptions that often ground autoclastic iconography.

This deployment of binaries, and the conditions that produce it, also distinguish contemporary comics from modernist aesthetic production. David Ball argues that today's most ambitious creators draw upon "the most recognizable characteristics of modernist literature" to produce what he terms *"comics against themselves*: an ambivalent, yet determined resistance to the generic conventions and mass media associations of conventional comics artistry within the emergent field of graphic literature" (106). In a reading of a short series of comics by Chris Ware, Ball points to several characteristics I would term autoclastic, observing that "in Ware's work, for every exploration of a high-minded, literary theme, Ware's narratives ensure that those meditations are relentlessly undone" (116). This formulation, like the concepts I have presented in this chapter, suggests both that comics creators are strongly engaged with the question of legitimacy and that this engagement manifests through strategies of self-opposition. Expanding his reading beyond Ware's comics, Ball claims that "this unwriting, this working at odds with itself . . . is the hallmark . . . of an entire generation of graphic novelists who aspire to the status of literature. It is a rhetoric of failure, one of conspicuous difficulty and willed ambivalence learned from literary modernism, and extending both its intellectual anxieties and intellectual rewards" (120). Here I differ from Ball on a number of points. Some respected contemporary creators—Ware and Spiegelman most of all—do have a conscious relationship to the modernist tradition. However, to suggest that contemporary creators "learned from literary modernism" what they needed to produce work that is "at odds with itself" is to underestimate the direct influence of status problems, with which today's creators are intimately familiar, and out of which they have developed formal tactics of self-opposition.

Such tactics express creative ambition and wariness toward categories of false legitimation, and this is quite different from what we see in the modernists. The latter, as Ball rightly points out, had a tendentious relationship to mass culture because its influence was so pervasive; precisely because of their cultural ambitions, artists working in highly legitimated media felt they had no choice but to engage with their mass cultural surroundings (105–106). For the contemporary comics creator, the mass cultural status of comics is a first principle of creation, a grounding fact so unavoidable that, while frustration concerning it is likely, "willed ambivalence" is not. Ball's claim concerning "resistance to the generic conventions and mass media associations of conventional comics artistry," together with the notion of "conspicuous difficulty," makes some sense in the context of a discussion of Ware, who is concerned with the deleterious effects of commodity culture and makes comics that are not easy to consume. But to apply this idea more broadly is to perceive a divided loyalty where none exists, and to ignore the medium-specific cultural commitments on display in contemporary comics. When Ball claims that "what makes recent graphic narratives so thoroughly and persistently modernist is their continued desire to disassociate themselves from the mass media forms in which they were first produced," he suggests that ambitious comics creators express their aspirations by putting distance between their work and other, lesser comics (106). What I see in autoclasm is a commitment to working on the problem of illegitimacy in comics-specific terms and an expression of unwavering loyalty to the medium as such. Though contemporary creators openly represent the problems attendant upon being associated with mass culture, they do not usually attempt to "dissociate themselves" from their less respected forbears.

The patterns I am describing do resemble postmodern cultural production in one respect: like the latter, contemporary comics exhibit a distrust of progress narratives. The focus of such distrust in comics is, however, specific to the medium. There is less concern with the burden of complicity and more attention to the actual effectiveness, or lack thereof, of a particular avenue of advancement. The *Bildungsroman* discourse is treated with skepticism not because it implicates the creator in cultural hegemony, but because it fails to provide the legitimation it might seem to offer. Desire for genuine improvement of status for the medium as a whole, rather than for a certain kind of comic or for an individual work, is a guiding impulse for many creators.

This is not to say that they are uninterested in more conventional creative and vocational dilemmas, such as the economic security offered by corporate comics publication and its attendant creative constraints, or, as previously discussed, the pragmatic benefits of calling one's comic a "graphic novel" despite the misperceptions that accompany the term. Yet a concern with the status of comics as such is visible above such local concerns. Recalling Spiegelman's discussion of legitimation games as a Faustian bargain, what should strike us is that, whatever cost-benefit calculations are implied, the essential goal is that comics should be able to "live for another century" (Kidd 37). That is, the very existence of the medium as a living form of communication is at stake. Autoclasm is a powerful witness to the persistent dilemma that confronts the comics creator, the reader, and the medium as a whole in relation to its illegitimate past, its quasi-legitimate present, and its uncertain future.

I have sought to foreground the persistent, comprehensive effects of illegitimacy on comics. The medium has been shaped by the fact that creative energy must perpetually be devoted to the problem of status. When I first began to note the repetitive and self-opposed fashion in which this energy is expressed, I put forward the idea that comics are a traumatized medium.[10] As Raymond Williams observes, the "materiality of works of art is . . . the irreplaceable materialization of kinds of experience" (162). I found it possible to imagine the problem of illegitimacy "materializing" traumatically in comics as the medium absorbed decade after decade of suppression and marginalization that impinged not just on this or that creator, but on comics making as a collective endeavor. However, it has become clear to me that even aside from the ethical risks of this idea—which carries Mitchell's animistic view of media quite far—autoclasm does not manifest the same dynamics as discourses of traumatic witnessing. Comics may be denied legitimate status, but they can still testify eloquently, if paradoxically, to this fact, and in a manner quite different from the paradoxes of inexpressibility associated with trauma.

In her study of graphic memoirs by women, Hillary Chute argues that "graphic narrative, invested in the ethics of testimony, assumes . . . *the risk of representation.* The complex visualizing it undertakes suggests that we need to rethink the dominant tropes of unspeakability, invisibility, and inaudibility that have tended to characterize trauma theory" (*Graphic Women* 3, italics original). Chute suggests that the medium's will to visibility, if I may phrase it thus, should prompt us to consider that inexpressibility is not quite the hallmark of trauma that many theorists have assumed. Thus, the explicitness of autoclasm might not rule out the idea that the medium is—if this stretching of the term is permissible—traumatized. Yet in the way comics express their illegitimacy, acts of witnessing and repetition work differently than they do in contexts shaped by traumatic experience. In comics, repetitive articulation of status problems occurs because these problems are still present; autoclasm is a conscious act of creative agency that makes sense of current conditions, rather than a compulsion rooted in past events. Among comics creators, there is often a deep awareness of the medium's troubled history, but this does not mean the present is grasped as posttraumatic.

The distinction I am making between comics-specific conditions and traumatic phenomena is not always observed by comics creators, who sometimes interweave their sense of the medium's difficulties with reflections on some form of trauma. In two of the four case studies that occupy the remaining chapters of this book (Miller and Hernandez), the problem of articulating trauma and the problem of expressing the status of comics become, in highly concentrated instances, versions of one another. The fact that some comics creators seem to represent the medium's history and condition in traumatic terms raises the question of how readers might responsibly weigh the authority of autoclastic icons. Are they to be trusted as accurate witnesses to the contemporary condition of comics? To phrase the question less suspiciously, could there be a moment at which creators continue to repeat their sense of how the medium is suppressed while culture as a whole moves forward to a new view of comics? Some might claim this shift has already occurred, but I trust that the body of evidence presented in the previous chapter demonstrates that the problem of illegitimacy is fully ongoing. It is nevertheless worth asking whether contemporary comics creators are interested in tracking contemporary conditions to see if the status of comics might be changing, and if so, to what degree.

A tentative answer is suggested by the difference between the first two examples I have discussed. In the case of Kupperman's "Are Comics Serious Literature?" we see a strong sense that, while the question of status can be asked in new ways, the real conditions of the medium have not improved since the earliest days of comic books and seem fixed beyond alteration. In Brown's comic, by contrast, there is a more nuanced interest in how comics are faring in the era of the graphic novel. The picture Brown provides of contemporary conditions is not significantly different from Kupperman's, but Brown's comic prompts the reader to a more precise consideration of them. How justified is the graphic novelist in walking away from the talking duck? How justified is the duck in judging the graphic novelist "overly sensitive"? Such questions suggest a readiness to detect and respond to changes in the medium's status—though, given the tenor of contemporary journalism on comics, no major changes are in the offing. Observing the difference between Brown's approach and Kupperman's, we see a shift of emphasis rather than substantial disagreement. The task of articulating the continuity of the struggles that comics have faced is slightly in tension, but not at odds, with a curiosity about possible improvements of status.

Nor are these two activities mutually exclusive, as indicated by the work of comics writer Joe Hill, from which I take two final examples of autoclasm. The first is from the concluding pages of "Freddy Wertham Goes to Hell," an early story written by Hill and illustrated by Seth Fisher and Langdon Foss that appeared in the horror anthology series *Grave Tales*. The story is an attack on the "Freddy" of the title, the most famous mid-century anti-comics crusader, and it opens with Wertham's murder at the hands of young thugs who seem to be under the influence of comic books (n. pag.). In the afterlife, Wertham is shown the untimely deaths of creators whose careers were ruined by the 1954 hearings on comics before the US Senate Subcommittee on Juvenile Delinquency, for which Wertham was a key witness. Hill makes clear that Wertham should be considered responsible for these deaths, and in an image both hellish and humorous, Wertham is crushed in a press so that his body can be turned into pages for printing comics, specifically, the same issue of *Grave Tales* in which "Freddy Wertham Goes to Hell" appears. This issue is shown for sale in a comics shop, and the two thugs, who are looking for new comics to read, are horrified when they detect traces of the issue's raw material (an imprint of Wertham's face) on the cover. Autoclasm here is produced by the sense that Wertham's punishment is both an act of poetic justice for his attacks on comics and a sort of gruesome overkill that even Wertham-hating comics readers may find excessive. The story's message seems to be that the business of producing and consuming comics is fundamentally informed by, perhaps even based on, the violence done to the medium. In other words, comics are made out of the damage the medium has suffered and continues to endure. In "Freddy Wertham Goes to Hell," the worst moment of comics history may be past, but its cultural effects are fully present.

This overtly defensive picture of the medium's status can be contrasted with a subtler approach in the horror series *Locke & Key*, written by Hill and illustrated by Gabriel Rodriguez. The story follows multiple generations of the Locke family and their friends as they seek to master demonic energies that can be forged into magical keys. Both the keys themselves and their relationship to their creators seem to be metaphors for comics. The keys have powers that recall various popular comics genres (some keys grant superpowers, such as strength or flight) or evoke the medium's formal capacities (an "Anywhere Key" allows the user to turn any door on earth into a point of access for any other—a vivid image of the way comics can join disparate locales through juxtaposition).

Most importantly, the keys have a curious and historically variable relationship to memory. In the main action, which takes place in the present, only children and young adults know about the keys; some time in their late teens, people forget them and become unable to perceive their operation. The youngest Lockes seek to uncover and correct the evils committed by their elders (who do not remember what they have experienced with the keys), while facing the risk that they will forget their own efforts and pass on their successes and failures to others. This is an obvious metaphor for the way comics reading is associated with childhood, so that adult comics reading is considered illegitimate. Hill imagines that at a previous point in history, adults could still remember the keys, and this era is explicitly associated with classic newspaper comics (particularly the work of Winsor McCay, one of the most respected early strip creators). As Hill arranges things, the era when adults could fully recall their own youthful powers and transgressions is also the era when contempt for comics had not yet become the norm.[11] While portraying the present era of comics as characterized by perpetually forgotten violence, Hill also looks back to a previous, less fraught moment in the medium's history, and forward to the possibility that cultural memory might improve, even if the status of the medium does not.

I turn to a single page that shows how Hill figures the contemporary situation of comics (figure 2.5). The first page of the second issue of *Locke & Key* shows a one-page comic ostensibly drawn by Bode, the youngest of the current generation of Locke children; the comic is held by his mother, whose thumb, drawn in Rodriguez's usual style, is visible on the lower left. For new readers of the series, the comic Bode has drawn summarizes the plot thus far: the murder of his father, the family's subsequent move to the magical locale of Keyhouse, and Bode's discovery of the first of many keys. From the perspective of Bode's mother, only the first three panels are factually accurate; since she cannot perceive the operation of the keys, even when it occurs before her eyes, the idea that Bode has a key that can separate his spirit from his body is pure fantasy. What is certainly real to her is the teacher's note complaining that "some of the kids saw this comic and were upset." The teacher uses the word "comic," not "drawing" or "picture," and Hill's script for this image specifies: "We can't see what Bode drew next, because stuck over the final panel of his comic is a yellow sticky note" (Script 202). This note is motivated by a desire to protect "some of the kids" without hurting Bode. It interrupts our reading nevertheless, and the final panel of Bode's comic is never shown. It is meant to remain unread, covered two layers deep by the teacher's act of soft censorship—a sort of offhand suppression, indicating how illegitimacy affects the medium now—and the parent's failure of perception.

Both the covered panel of Bode's work and the page as a whole connect adult perception to the dismissal and forgetting of comics. The page critiques the *Bildungsroman* discourse, according to which adult readers naturally outgrow comics reading (perhaps excepting some graphic novels). Hill suggests that such an idea "ghosts," and is thus haunted by, childhood experiences with comics like Bode's. Hill invites this interpretation without guaranteeing that full memory or complete reading practice can be recovered, though, as in other instances of autoclasm, the damage done to reading and memory can be made profoundly visible. Here we see a typically self-opposed strategy for manifesting the despised state of the medium. Bode's crude, visually unimpressive comic has been permanently censored, but this fact itself remains readable for those willing to see it. And insofar as this page invites a new kind of reading that avoids the mistakes of Bode's mother and teacher, it presents

2.5. *Joe Hill and Gabriel Rodriguez, page 1 of* Locke & Key: Welcome to Lovecraft *issue 2, 2008.*

an opportunity to gauge the current status of comics, asking whether they must, necessarily, continue to be misperceived as juvenile, dangerous and contemptible. Hill is not being overtly optimistic, but unlike "Freddy Wertham Goes to Hell," this page from *Locke & Key* allows for a (very cautious) anticipation of better things for comics.

At the time he was writing *Locke & Key*, Hill offered the following remarks on the subject of comics' status:

> I hate it when comics creators get bitching and moaning about how their art form doesn't get the respect it deserves, isn't honored the way theater or painting or mainstream literature is honored, and all that blah-de-blah-de-fucking-blah. Oh go cry a river somewhere over your twenty-year-old copies of *Maus* and leave me alone. Then there are these card-carrying members of Fanboy Nation who want to establish a "read-comics-in-public" day, to make funny books seem more socially normative. Fuck that. I don't want comics to be respectable. . . . I want the act of reading comics to feel dirty and unhealthy and transgressive. (Introduction n. pag.)

The offhand mention of Art Spiegelman's *Maus* is not intended as a criticism; Hill proceeds to extol the complexity and richness of ambitious long-form comics before discussing the kind of violent, antisocial works he prefers to read. His point is that the mere existence of certain decorated and enduring works must suffice to console those who want comics to be respectable; decades have passed since *Maus*'s publication, and legitimate status is still denied to the medium as a whole. Aspirations to legitimacy on the part of "Fanboy Nation" are pointless, and pro-comics fanaticism is condemned as deadening normativity.

Hill is mistaken when he suggests that a naïve desire for literary standing is widespread in comics culture; few creators or readers view respectability as an end in itself—Spiegelman perhaps least of all. Still, something more is at work in Hill's sentiments than a penchant for subcultural infighting, or an immature resistance to improved status. Like the other creators discussed in this study, Hill wishes to make the illegitimacy of comics unavoidably visible, and to display the marginalization to which the medium has been subjected—something that has become more of a challenge in the era of the graphic novel. It is in this sense that he wants comics reading to feel "dirty and unhealthy and transgressive." However, such a goal is not incompatible with the hope that the medium may someday exist on a different footing. The pessimistic aggression of "Freddy Wertham Goes to Hell" and the more nuanced consideration of status concerns in *Locke & Key* are two points on the same spectrum of struggle.

Within contemporary comics, we can see the emphasis shift back and forth between stark witness and cautious anticipation, between a "closed" autoclasm that confronts us with enduring problems of status and a more "open" variety that invites us to assess the potential for improvement. As Hill's work demonstrates, a creator can engage both modes. Thus we see in broader perspective the challenge that contemporary comics creators face. There is a commitment to portraying current conditions in all their difficulty and historical specificity in order to achieve accurate self-representation in medium-specific terms. There is also a desire to remain open to the possibility of real improvements of status. There is a practical tension here, but no actual contradiction. Even at their most hostile and pessimistic, autoclastic icons can be charged with dazzling creative energy, and even at their most open and anticipatory, they retain a strong wariness. To read across this range of possibilities is to acknowledge the full significance of the medium's difficulties in the present, and—precisely through keeping faith with these difficulties—to anticipate possible changes that might exceed the restrictive terms laid down by narratives of "coming of age."

THREE

Pop Art Comics

FRANK MILLER

I have argued that the *Bildungsroman* discourse is at best a mixed blessing for comics, and at worst an actual detriment. For new comics readers, it is an appealing narrative that explains why now is a good time to pick up a graphic novel, but it obscures why many adult readers in the United States still need special persuasion in order to do so. The abiding problems that this narrative covers up are certainly visible to the writers and artists who make comics, as are the ways that the *Bildungsroman* discourse perpetuates those problems while seeming to obviate them. Awareness of the medium's illegitimacy, and resistance to the hegemonic notion of "coming of age," have pushed contemporary comics toward a variety of formal and thematic paradoxes.

Frank Miller's creative strategies have been so paradoxical that, at times, they seem to stem from two unrelated perspectives. While desiring a broader readership for his work and improved status for comics as a whole, Miller is best known for his elaboration of violent pulp mythologies, often from the realm of superhero comics or from hard-boiled detective fiction, and his take on them has been provocatively antisocial.[1] Highly aware of the infantilizing tendencies of the Comics Code and determined to make "adults-only" fare, he has nevertheless chosen to produce the kind of action-packed, lascivious stories that, as he well knows, abetted the conviction of public figures of the 1950s that comics are unfit reading for anyone.[2] Miller's most powerful work follows such contradictions to extremes rather than seeking their resolution. *Batman: The Dark Knight Returns* (1986, hereafter *DKR*), which will be my focus, expresses a perverse fascination with the unstable, even untenable nature of the protagonist around which its narrative is structured.[3] Refusing either to remain in a state of innocence or to grow up, Miller's Batman enacts a spectacular self-destruction that makes visible the fraught condition of his medium.

Given the differences between comics and postmodern cultural production discussed in the previous chapter, my term "pop art comics" might seem oxymoronic, and some clarification is needed. I will be analyzing DKR not as an example of pop art—certainly not as the Batman television serial of the 1960s is considered pop—but as a work that achieved in comics what the work of artists like Andy Warhol and Roy Lichtenstein accomplished in the fine arts: a new power to make cultural and institutional status visible within the medium itself. The status of comics, as Miller pictures it in DKR, is radically different from that of painting in the Warhol era; hence, my comparison is somewhat ironic. As I will discuss briefly at the end of this chapter, while pop art can be seen in retrospect as clarifying, and also reinforcing, the legitimacy of the fine arts by highlighting the art object as commodity, DKR can be read as making comics' lack of status more fully readable by underscoring the way comics have been publicly attacked.

Further, while the message of pop art rapidly became obvious to its various audiences, DKR's way of making status visible has been largely misunderstood or overlooked. Critical and journalistic accounts converged rapidly on a coherent understanding of the new and powerful ways that pop art phrased the question of art as commodity, but DKR has consistently been misconstrued as a more or less straightforward attempt (successful or not) at literary seriousness. What Miller actually does, however, is consciously to appropriate the medium's despised status as his central theme and as an impetus for formal experimentation. Without repeating my earlier analysis of the "coming of age" journalism that first emerged in the late 1980s (and that used DKR, together with Spiegelman's Maus and Moore's Watchmen, as talking points), I will argue that Miller's work is important because it makes status problems central to the act of comics reading and gives us a new way to grasp the limitations of traditional Warholian pop art. This kind of art has long been understood as thematizing, and then breaking down, the barriers between high and low, fine arts and mass culture; what it has actually done is to make it more difficult to phrase the question of illegitimate culture at all. Yet DKR manages to accomplish this task; read carefully in light of questions of status, it shows us what medium-specific treatment of illegitimacy really looks like.

My reading of DKR assumes that the way Miller treats the figure of Batman is a way of talking about the condition of comics. DKR's portrait of Batman as a highly stigmatized and conflicted figure in the world of the narrative reflects the illegitimacy of the medium as a whole. Two clarifications are needed here. First, as an icon circulating through many different media, Batman is not identified exclusively with comics at present; nor was he in the mid-1980s, when *DKR* was published. Cultural studies research on Batman has demonstrated both the ubiquity this figure has attained and the extraordinary variety of meanings that have been attached to him over the decades since he first appeared in the pages of *Detective Comics*, in 1939.[4] While costumed crime fighters have often been associated with childhood and immaturity, and while this certainly has something to do with the status of comics, Batman has served many different public roles in different media, and his cultural authority has waxed and waned over the decades. Thus, one cannot assume in advance that Batman stands for comics; but as we will see, Miller takes great care to build a connection between the two.

Second, as Will Brooker has pointed out, the meanings of Batman are determined partly by the character's current corporate ownership; though he has been appropriated by various audiences over the decades, "Batman and his meanings are still tethered to a multinational institution, rather than floating freely in the public domain" (*Unmasked* 10–11). While problems of corporate control might bear on questions of legitimacy, Miller engages broader questions of status without focusing on matters of intellectual property. *DKR* is concerned not with what DC Comics forces Batman to do, or prevents him from doing, but with how, as an avatar of comics as a whole, Batman is treated in culture at large. Admittedly, this approach was probably made easier by the latitude Miller was granted in his treatment of the character. Having gained fame from his revival of the failing Marvel title *Daredevil*, and then writing and illustrating the acclaimed original miniseries *Ronin* at DC, Miller was offered the narrative universe of Batman and told that he could do as he wished (with the understanding that his story would not be a part of the official continuity of Batman narratives).[5] Miller thus had a large degree of narrative freedom, which he used to establish a link between Batman as a controversial figure of vigilante justice and comics as a despised medium.

Early in *DKR*, this parallel is not fully in view, as Miller approaches Batman from an unusual direction that might seem to have little to do with questions of cultural status. Miller imagines Bruce Wayne as an aging, disillusioned man in his fifties, long retired from fighting crime in Gotham City, his lifelong home. Superheroes are either outlawed or allowed to operate only covertly, under strict regulation, but Bruce is content to be retired for reasons of his own; he is burdened with guilt over the death of Jason Todd, the second person to serve as his sidekick, Robin. Miller shows Bruce confronting the psychological and physical trials of age (a topic Batman comics have, for obvious reasons, usually avoided) and working toward an acceptance of Batman's irrelevance to contemporary life. At times this acceptance takes the form of despair, as Bruce meditates on the emergence of a "purer breed" of criminal who can commit murder without remorse, and even with enjoyment (14.3). Yet Bruce seems to hope that even the worst criminals can be rehabilitated using humane methods, and he publicly supports the release of Harvey Dent, a longtime nemesis, remarking that "we must believe that our private demons can be defeated" (17.8). The modifier "private" suggests the deeper conflict underlying this oscillation from despair to optimism: Bruce continues to struggle with his own desire to assume the role of Batman. At the same time, the condition of Gotham, which Miller portrays as a war zone beset by a hyperviolent gang of criminals called the "Mutants," opens the question of whether Bruce's vigilante alter ego is relevant beyond his own "private" needs.

Out of this melancholy and troubled scenario, Miller turns to the traumatic origin of his protagonist and proceeds to explore in detail its relationship to Batman as a public figure. It is widely accepted that trauma is central to the origin stories of most comics superheroes, and this is certainly the case with Batman. When he is eight years old, Bruce Wayne sees his parents shot and killed by a mugger. He subsequently vows to fight crime in Gotham, and he assumes the identity of Batman in order to do so. Not all superhero mythologies have an equally long and productive life-span in culture, and the longevity of Batman owes a great deal to the dynamic tension between the personal origin of Bruce Wayne's trauma and the larger purpose to which he dedicates himself.[6] For Bruce, the two are inextricable and mutually animating, though their relationship is actually contingent. One can imagine Bruce coming to terms with his parents' death but never giving up on his determination to end crime in Gotham; alternately, he might well accept that he will never change the city for the better, but still be forever traumatized by what he witnessed as a child. These possibilities are, of course, never realized; the origin of Batman remains a powerful narrative motor so long as there is neither personal healing nor adult success and, at the same time, neither personal nor vocational despair. Bruce Wayne will always be haunted by the wrong that shaped his childhood, will always attempt to right this wrong by acting as Batman, will always fail to end crime in Gotham, will always feel both unresolved and undefeated, and will always press on in his attempts. The impossibility of mourning and the impossibility of stabilizing the social order are two very different kinds of impossibility, but when joined in the figure of Batman, their mutual resonance seems endlessly fecund as a narrative device. It is this resonance that Miller proceeds to explore in *DKR*; Bruce Wayne is driven to resume his role as Batman by a sudden clash of personal past and public present.

Miller represents this clash through two series of images that precipitate a psychic break once they intermingle in Bruce's consciousness. One image thread consists of his memories of his parents' murder, and the other is a discontinuous series of television clips. At the opening of the passage in which these two threads appear, Miller provides an initial link between them: a Zorro film is playing on television, and Bruce, who is idly channel surfing, recalls it as the film he saw the night his parents died. This recollection gives way to images of the murder itself, interspersed with more television clips, as Bruce continues to change channels in increasing agitation. The resonances between Zorro and Batman, both costumed heroes, are obvious enough, and yet the present stream of media data and the memories of Bruce's trauma feel quite separate even as they are visually interwoven on the page. The television clips are mostly reports of violent crimes, each truncated and anonymous, while Bruce's memories consist of increasingly detailed images, paced as moment-to-moment transitions.[7] It is obvious that repeated mentions of violent crime exacerbate Bruce's distress at his traumatic recollections. At the same time, there is a clear distinction between the precise texture of suffering suggested by those memories and the sound-bite nature of the reports of suffering in Gotham as a whole. Miller vividly stages, both visually and thematically, the gap that Batman always attempts and fails to close—that between his personal suffering and the collective distress of the community in which he intervenes—and thus the creator codifies, at the level of form, the essentially nondevelopmental structure of the Batman myth.

This passage is typical of the tactics Miller uses in most of his widely read work; he generates thematic, narrative and formal energy by returning to essentials. Miller delineates the central features of Batman's story and brings their contradictions into sharp relief. In the early pages of *DKR*, building up to and including the psychic break, Miller emphasizes how isolated Bruce has become. He derives little companionship from his butler, Alfred, and is no longer in touch with Dick Grayson, the first Robin; he is also alienated from other longtime friends, allies and sometime enemies. His relationship to Gotham as a whole can thus take the foreground, and as soon as he resumes the role of Batman as a result of his psychic break, the paradoxes of that relationship play out in full. Batman lives to serve Gotham, and he genuinely desires a safer social order in which both individual and communal values can flourish. Yet in the service of these goals, he is willing not only to commit crimes, but also to wield authoritarian power, and his sympathy for the innocent is much less evident than his determination to prevent wrongdoing (other than his own). In the face of widespread chaos resulting from a blackout in Gotham, which he cannot manage alone, Batman allies himself with the Mutants and with a vigilante group calling itself the Sons of the Batman; eventually he imposes martial law on ordinary citizens.

The more he protects the social order through illegitimate means, the clearer it becomes that Batman will never recover from his childhood trauma; nor will he compensate for it by changing Gotham. He will, at best, displace his trauma into a complex "adult" form. Though Batman is dedicated to changing his city and making it whole, the more his actions attempt to force this result, the more alienated he becomes from Gotham's citizens, many of whom turn against him. Further, while the looming paternal figure of Batman may induce less criminal behavior and more social cooperation, such changes are portrayed as temporary. At the conclusion of *DKR*, Batman fakes his own death and retreats underground, where he trains the Mutants and the Sons of the Batman (together with Carrie Kelly, a new Robin) as a sort of militia group, "an army," in Bruce's words, "to bring sense to a world plagued by worse than thieves and murderers" (199.4). This society of children, for whom Batman is the guardian and authority, seems designed to fill the otherwise empty chasm between the childhood trauma of Bruce Wayne and the world he has failed to change; it also reveals how impossible his goals actually are in ordinary circumstances.

Miller's take on the central mythology of Batman might seem to be a bid for cultural legitimacy, and this is how *DKR* has been most commonly praised since its publication. When it first appeared, it was widely discussed in the mainstream press as an example of a new, adult kind of comic, and this reception certainly had something to do with Miller's willingness to critique, or at least to dwell on the weaknesses of, both the politics of Batman and the sensibilities of comics readers.[8] The conclusion of *DKR* makes explicit an authoritarian subtext of the Batman narrative; the disorder of life in a democracy is replaced by a fantasy of a martial society under patriarchal discipline. This new society is populated almost entirely by the young, and Batman's followers could be stand-ins for the stereotypically "juvenile" superhero comics fan who is willing to allow his or her psychic life to be ruled by an idealized authoritarian figure. To read the conclusion of *DKR* properly, by these lights, is to judge that the Batman narrative has been an untenable, politically dangerous wish-fulfillment all along; it is also to participate in those aspects of the *Bildungsroman* discourse that associate superhero comics with immaturity.

Alternately, the conclusion might be a complex repetition of a tendency to avoid political critique that Philip Sandifer claims is common among superhero comics. Sandifer argues that "by and large, the traumas that make up superhero stories are not ones that tie into questions of political identity," and that by identifying with superheroes, comics readers experience empowerment through a separation from the social order and from political struggles (179). I will presently take issue with this claim, but it should be admitted that while the conclusion of *DKR* might be a critique of Batman's politics, it might just as easily be a cancelation of the possibility of political engagement altogether, despite Miller's own conviction that comics can and should express political content.[9] Insofar as the attempt to build a new society seems like a fantasy even more destructive than Batman's earlier caped crusading, readers might well be encouraged to prefer business as usual in the world of superhero comics, and accept larger-than-life fictional struggle—which, insofar as Sandifer is correct, is separate from real-world political engagement—as the best available option.

However, both these possible interpretations, the one "mature" and political (*DKR* condemns Batman's crusade as veiled fascism), the other "immature" and apolitical (*DKR* suggests that real social change is the most dangerous fantasy of all and tacitly approves of superhero stories in their ordinary form), fail to encompass the text's treatment of Batman. Miller seems at pains to expose the contradictions inherent in the Batman mythology more fully than any previous creator, and the central burden of *DKR* is simply that *Batman is not legitimate*. Miller makes this point neither to advance an antiauthoritarian political agenda nor to separate comics from politics. He finds Batman's illegitimacy fascinating, and is interested in all of the various discourses that emerge from the central contradictions of the Batman narrative, not just the microcosmic authoritarian society that he marks as its final destination.

In fact, little about *DKR* encourages us to focus on narrative closure, and Miller encodes other, more challenging reading possibilities into its form. Such possibilities are often present in his work; in an interview given after completing the *Sin City* series, Miller observes:

> [A] huge amount of my job is trying to fight that old nemesis time. . . . A film director, for instance . . . can control how long you sit in your seat staring at his image. Whereas a comic book technically can be read in 5–10 minutes—even a rather thick one, you can technically read it in a very short period of time. My job is to find ways to deceive, cheat, and charm your eye so that you stay longer, not by loading it so much with words . . . but by making my drawings just delightful enough, or when I'm really on my game, slightly confusing so that you take an extra few seconds to study them. (Mitchell interview)

The passage that shows Bruce's psychic break contains exactly the kind of "slightly confusing" tactics that slow the eye and encourage critical study. The flashback panels are disordered, seeming to alter the flow of time in order to pass back and forth over the moment of the parents' murder. Important in this respect are panels showing Bruce's mother's necklace, a string of pearls, at the moment it is stretched and broken by the mugger's arm. On the page most central to the passage, the pearls are clearly coming apart in four early panels, yet several panels later, they appear still joined (24.1–2, 5, 7, 18, figure 3.1). On the facing page, they then appear to separate once more (25.9). As Scott McCloud informs us, panel-to-panel transitions most often proceed—in a way that seems somehow natural to the pace of reading—from one moment of action to another.[10] At the moment of Bruce's psychic break, Miller not only slows the progression of images down to a moment-to-moment pace, but also forces us to read differently, concerned not with causal relations (childhood trauma leading to adult crusade), but with a network of images that enables other, synchronic linkages to be made. The images of the string of pearls naturally function as a figure for a series of comics panels, and by breaking the string, Miller indicates that *DKR*'s images are not meant to be neatly threaded together; the links between early trauma and later events will not unfold in one direction.

A similar effect is generated by repetition of a panel showing the murderer's gun being fired, an empty casing visible as it is ejected from the chamber (23.8, 25.4). In his discussion of how comics panels are typically read, Thierry Groensteen notes that "the eye does not apprehend

3.1. *Frank Miller, Lynn Varley and Klaus Janson, page 24 of* The Dark Knight Returns, *1986–1987, collected in 10th Anniversary Edition, 1997.*

the panel frontally . . . in the way that it takes in a painting. It slides . . . along the surface of the plane of the page. It always arrives . . . from another point situated within the plane. . . . . An exit is always indicated, pointing to another series (the following panel), which in turn solicits our attention" (*System of Comics* 47–48). Initially, the image of the gun might seem neatly both to illustrate and to enable this reading process, which "fires" the eye into each new panel as it "ejects" each already-scanned panel into peripheral awareness. However, Miller arranges the visual elements of the panels to thwart this reading; the gun is pointed to the left, seeming to fire into previous panels, while the casing moves to the right. This repeated panel thus images a recursive reading process that pulls the reader against the scanning vector most common to English-language comics literacy. Later in the narrative, it should be noted, readers are confronted with further repetitions of the murder of Bruce's parents, including the panel of the gun being fired, and for these Miller employs the exact same panels—not redrawn, but facsimiles—that were used earlier, in the first iteration of the childhood memory (132.3–4). Such formal tactics are obviously appropriate to a trauma that seizes Bruce's consciousness again and again. But they also cue us in to how Miller wants to encourage his readers to approach *DKR* as a whole. Through this fusion of form and content, he makes *DKR* intrinsically nonlinear and recursive as a necessary effect of its subject matter; its "general arthrology," to use Groensteen's term for large-scale networks of comics images, is structured as an effect and a repetition of trauma.[11] We are meant to read *DKR* in order to encounter and contemplate the complex and fractured networks of meaning that play out before Bruce's trauma undergoes its final, troubling displacement.

Approaching *DKR* in this fashion, we must take seriously the amount of space Miller devotes to discourse about the meaning and value of Batman. Far from overlooking the potential fascism of his protagonist until the conclusion, Miller makes this aspect of Batman unavoidable much earlier. Once Bruce resumes the role of Batman, we see lengthy televised debates concerning his social influence. Miller's portrayal of these debates foreshadows the polarized nature of televised political discourse today; on a show called *Point Vs. Point*, a Batman advocate with the classic Bat-symbol behind her squares off against an opponent backed by a similar symbol overlaid by a red circle with a line through it. The supporter praises the return of Batman as "a symbolic resurgence of the common man's will to resist" and "a rebirth of the American fighting spirit" (41.5–6), while her opponent excoriates Batman as "an aberrant psychotic force," "a danger to every citizen of Gotham," and "a social fascist" who inspires violent behavior and "knows exactly what he's doing" (41.8,9, 42.6).

Neither of these views is fully authorized by *DKR* as a whole. Far from being a populist of any political stripe, Batman acts by his own lights and out of his own motivations, and his authoritarian charisma becomes less an inspiration to the "common man" than the organizing force of a martial regime that polices ordinary citizens at a time of crisis. However, he is not, in the body of the narrative, the calculating "social fascist" his opponents suggest. In fact, he has little real understanding of the consequences of his actions. As this particular televised debate plays out, the Joker, long confined and catatonic, suddenly comes to awareness and to a renewed interest in crime once he realizes his old opponent has returned (41.3–10). The Joker's subsequent killing spree, together with brutal vigilantism committed by the Sons of the Batman—and clearly inspired by Batman's return—suggests that while the anti-Batman contingent might not understand the hero himself, their diagnosis of his social effects may be correct.

What seems true of all the debates over Batman in *DKR*, along with all the actions, destructive or otherwise, taken in response to his presence, is that they express only fragments of what the character means. In his essentially personal struggle, nevertheless aimed at a change in society as a whole, Batman seems to embody fundamental contradictions so massive and complex that, the text suggests, one can be neither for nor against him in the usual sense. Thus, even while insisting that Batman is not legitimate, because he is compromised by the motives and means of his quest, Miller also figures him as "too big" to critique. This phrase is introduced by Batman's ally Jim Gordon, Gotham's police commissioner, at the moment of his retirement. In private conversation with his replacement, Ellen Yindel, who is determined to have Batman arrested for his vigilantism, Gordon tells a story about his memories of World War II:

> [W]e were scared. Rumors were flying, we thought the Japanese had taken California. We didn't even have an army . . . and there was Roosevelt on the radio, strong and sure, taking fear and turning it into fighting spirit. . . . We won the war. . . . A few years back, I was reading a news magazine—a lot of people with a lot of evidence said Roosevelt knew Pearl was going to be attacked—and that he let it hap-

pen. . . . I couldn't stop thinking how horrible that would be . . . and how Pearl was what got us off our duffs in time to stop the Axis. But a lot of men died. But we won the war. It bounced back and forth in my head until I realized I couldn't judge it. It was too big. He was too big. (96.5–6, 9–12)

Yindel observes, "I don't see what this has to do with a vigilante"; Gordon responds, "Maybe you will" (96.12–13). Gordon's point is that morally ambiguous choices—Roosevelt's decision not to provide warning of Pearl Harbor, Batman's vigilantism—are, at moments of crisis, as inevitable for a figurehead vigilante as they are for a world leader.

Yindel eventually reaches the same conclusion: when Batman recruits members of the Mutants, newly escaped from jail, to police Gotham during the blackout, she orders her officers not to interfere, observing that Batman is "too big" (176.3). Even as this phrase suggests that the meaning of Batman cannot be captured, it seems to demand further interpretation and threatens to impose, in a slightly different form, the alternative readings evoked by the text's conclusion. In what exact sense is Batman "too big"? On the one hand, Miller might be portraying him as an authoritarian figure who, by taking upon himself the burden of impossible choices, is above societal judgment; this reading leads us back to Sandifer's sense of superhero comics as setting the reader apart from politics. On the other hand, Batman might be merely symptomatic, an embodiment of deep social, political and moral contradictions, in which case his "bigness" is an effect of Gotham's inability or unwillingness to confront and solve such contradictions. This second reading offers more political possibilities. But what is most telling is Miller's lack of interest in resolving the question of whether Batman is a self-directed, authoritarian patriarch or a mere by-product of societal ills. This apparent indifference has little to do with Miller's own political commitments (though, notably, the latter have shifted a great deal over time).[12] The problem most central to *DKR* is not the social and political import of Batman, were he an actual vigilante in a major US city, but the discursive fallout of Batman as a comics hero in a situation where the medium is illegitimate. Approaching *DKR* in this fashion, we can clarify how and why Batman is, in Miller's view, at least, "too big" to be encompassed by any one political position or moral code.

In scholarship on post-code superhero comics, questions of political content are usually treated as separate from questions of cultural sta-

tus in general or the status of superhero comics in particular. Take Sandifer's indictment of superhero comics, which sees their use of traumatic
origin stories as a way to keep readers free of the burden of politics:

> To take pleasure in the structure of the superhero narrative is funda-
> mentally to take pleasure in our own exile from the machinery of polit-
> ical engagement. The position we, as socially constituted subjects, oc-
> cupy is the position explicitly rejected by the affective consciousness
> of the superhero, who merely possesses a social identity . . . instead of
> embodying one. . . . Since [the] social order is at once an excised back-
> formation and the site of the affective superhero's violent testimony to
> his traumatic consciousness, our position in the structure is a position
> that is always the object instead of the subject of action. . . . [T]he fea-
> sibility of creating the modern day comic fan as an audience stems in
> a large degree from the way in which superhero comics engender plea-
> sure through a fantasy of being protected. (Sandifer 183)

While Sandifer may be right to see the traumatic origins of superheroes
as a potential bar to political engagement, it is tempting to point out
that such ideological effects are scarcely unique; narrative genres rooted
in plausibility (such as the broad tradition of literary realism) have their
own ways to diffuse the import of their characters' social contexts. However, making a parallel between, say, Victorian novels and Marvel superhero comics of the 1960s would once again ignore problems of legitimacy that affected the latter, but not the former. Unfortunately, such
problems are set aside all too often. Discussions of the political dimen-
sions of superhero comics (whether critical of their ideologies or not)
sometimes proceed without any reference whatsoever to cultural status.

Reading such discussions, one is prompted to assume that a fully legitimate, perhaps even culturally dominant, form of expression is under
investigation.[13] Sandifer does take some account of the status of superhero comics, noting the "popular culture rhetoric" that surrounds them
as "power fantasies" with "appeal to teenage boys" (182), but he does not
seriously consider how the status of superhero comics as socially backward and culturally bankrupt might affect their ability to offer readers
"a fantasy of being protected" from politics. The fact that so many superheroes created after the code have traumatic origin stories—not least
Spider-Man, who is Sandifer's key example—suggests that something
more is at stake than withdrawal from political engagement. Samuel R.
Delany argues that to read marginalized "paraliteratures," such as com-

ics, is, in one way or another, to be engaged in politics, even if only in a political struggle over what counts as culture or literacy.[14] The traumas at the center of superhero comics may well be indexes of cultural struggle more than barriers to political engagement.

This is undoubtedly Miller's assumption—largely, if not entirely, conscious—when he simultaneously arranges critiques of Batman and sets him apart from critique. At the center of *DKR's* anti-Batman discourse is Bartholomew Wolper, a criminal psychologist modeled on Frederic Wertham, the best-known anti-comics crusader of the 1950s. Though his was one of many voices raised against comics at mid-century, Wertham most successfully put forward a view of comics as inducements to violence, not least in the testimony he provided in the 1954 hearings held by the US Senate Subcommittee on Juvenile Delinquency, which were the immediate impetus for the code. Miller's views of Wertham have been quite condemnatory, particularly as regards Wertham's most famous anti-comics work, *Seduction of the Innocent* (1954, hereafter *Seduction*). In his introduction to the hardbound collection *Absolute Dark Knight* (which collects *DKR* and a sequel, *The Dark Knight Strikes Again*), Miller claims: "When I first entered my field, That Abominably Crappy Book still cast a long shadow" (Miller's capitals, n. pag.). Wolper's analysis of Batman often echoes, with satirical amplification, claims that Wertham made about comics in *Seduction*.

At first glance, Miller clearly uses *DKR* as an opportunity to expose and mock such claims. Here is Wolper on the effects of Batman: "Every anti-social act can be traced to irresponsible media input. Given this, the presence of such an aberrant, violent force in the media can only lead to anti-social programming. . . . [A] whole new generation, confused and angry . . . will be bent to the matrix of Batman's pathological self-delusion. Batman is, in this context . . . a social disease" (66.1–3). Here is Wertham on the destructive effects of comics: "Crime comics are an agent with harmful potentialities. They bring about a mass conditioning of children, with different effects in the individual case. A child is not a simple unit which exists outside of its living social ties. Comic books themselves may be the virus, or the cause of lack of resistance to the social virus of a harmful environment" (*Seduction* 118). Throughout *Seduction*, Wertham varies the amount of blame that crime comics (which, for him, most certainly included any comic featuring Batman) should bear for violence committed by young readers. In the passage just cited, comics are sometimes the virus of crime itself, and sometimes they are the facilitator of a virus existing in a child's social conditions. Miller's take on Wertham is obviously a hostile exaggeration; Wolper claims that "Batman should be considered personally responsible for every human being murdered" by the Sons of the Batman (113.11). Later in *DKR*, Wolper is murdered by the Joker after attempting to rehabilitate him, and this would seem to put paid to his credibility as an analyst of criminal behavior.

Yet Miller eventually makes it clear that, at least in the world of *DKR*, Wolper is more right than wrong about Batman's social effects. His reappearance does, after all, cause the Joker to return to crime precisely as if he were "bent to the matrix of Batman's pathological self-delusion." Further, the "social disease" of Batman's vigilantism spreads to others, especially to the young, in a fashion that seems like something Wertham himself might have predicted. Even before the Sons of the Batman emerge, Carrie Kelley, who will become the new Robin, is inspired to attempt crime fighting by an encounter with Batman himself. As we see her donning a homemade costume for the first time, a news reporter observes: "Incidents of violence to criminals continue to abound in Gotham. We cannot be sure which are the work of Batman . . . and which he has inspired" (59.6, 8–9). If such a Wertham-like claim is a rather lopsided analysis of larger social problems, of which Batman is only one symptom, it is nevertheless a valid account of the ways that, as Miller arranges his plot, Batman sometimes directly inspires, and at other times is at least implicated in, the forces he seeks to oppose.

But given the historical context Miller introduces into the narrative—given, in fact, the way that what was claimed about comics around the time of the code is both repeated and made literally true of Batman himself on the pages of *DKR*—it should be clear that his implication in the crimes he fights is primarily a statement about the cultural status of comics, not about their possible social effects. At the level of plot, Batman commits acts of vigilantism because of his childhood trauma, but if we take the thematics of legitimacy into account, we can see a very different dynamic of victimization and agency. Stigmatized by accusations that strongly resemble the long-standing stereotypes leveled against comics, Batman also fulfills these stereotypes, making them more vivid than his detractors ever could.

It may be tempting to see Miller as enacting a self-consciously subversive performance of the social crimes of which comics have been accused, but in the immediate context of *DKR*'s publication, such a reading would make little sense. During the early and mid-1980s, comics culture experienced a spike in an ongoing state of anxiety about its cultural position, mostly thanks to critiques of violence in comics from prominent religious conservatives. In a public interview that Miller gave together with Denny O'Neil, his editor during his time working on *Daredevil*, Miller made clear that he thought the entire comics industry could easily be destroyed by social and legislative pressure from such groups as the Moral Majority. Discussing a controversial *Daredevil* story that Marvel hesitated to publish, O'Neil observed that he was afraid "it would get all of the pressure censorship groups in the country down on our heads because they're sort of cruising around looking for targets anyway and comics are in a fairly undefended position if somebody really wants to mount an attack on us. . . . If they came down on the comics industry now they would really destroy it" ("Relevancy in Comics" 52–53, 57). Miller expressed very similar opinions; when an audience member asked, "Is the comics industry gearing up for another '50s?" he responded, "Well, the only thing is, we'd be an after-dinner mint for these guys. We wouldn't have a chance" ("Relevancy" 57). The anxiety expressed in these sentiments, which are from 1981, was still present in 1986; in fact, shortly after publication of *DKR*, Miller, together with Alan Moore, was active in a protest against a possible ratings system that DC Comics was considering in order to placate exactly the kind of pressure Miller and O'Neil had discussed years earlier.[15] Thus, when Miller writes a Wertham-like figure into *DKR* and then proceeds to shape a narrative trajectory that, in many ways, actually fits Wertham's critiques, his goal is not performatively to rehearse widespread anti-comics sentiments. Instead, it is precisely to confront their inescapability—less a complicitous critique, to use Linda Hutcheon's term, than an articulation of ineluctable stigma.[16]

One of the most memorable ways that Miller rehearses this stigma is through a confrontation between Batman and Superman. While Bruce has endured a decade of retirement, Superman has agreed to work in secret as an agent of the US government. The president, clearly modeled on Ronald Reagan, uses Superman in an attempt to tilt the balance of power in the Cold War. This tactic fails when the Soviet Union, in response to Superman's intervention in a conflict in the fictional nation of Corto Maltese, launches a nuclear attack; Superman redirects the missile but is unable to prevent its detonation—hence the blackout that descends on Gotham. Prior to this event, Superman is given a presidential directive to encourage Bruce to retire once more; the public visibility of Batman is, it seems, a threat to governmental legitimacy. After Batman imposes martial law on Gotham during the blackout, a showdown with

Superman is inevitable. At the heart of the conflict is a debate over the role and function of the superhero that strongly resembles a debate about the social role of comics. In the era of Reagan, comics were not asked to perform an ideological function, as they had been in World War II. Even the ostensibly militaristic Cold War–era series *G.I. Joe: A Real American Hero* was complex in its politics, officially nationalistic but often expressing alternate views as well.[17] There was little opportunity for comics to become a tool of US foreign policy, which is, rather harshly, how Miller portrays Superman. Miller's real interest is in the difference between Batman's attitude of open rebellion against legitimate authority and Superman's willingness to serve authority while staying out of public view.

While Superman is fighting for the United States in Corto Maltese, Miller gives him this telling interior monologue: "You were the one they used against us, Bruce. The one who played it rough. When the noise started from the parents' groups and the subcommittee called us in for questioning—you were the one who laughed. . . . 'Sure we're criminals,' you said. 'We've always been criminals. We have to be criminals.' . . . I gave them my obedience and my invisibility. They gave me a license and let us live. . . . But now the storm is growing again—they'll hunt us down again—because of you" (135.1,2–5, 139.4–7). In the 1954 Senate subcommittee hearings, to which Miller is undoubtedly referring, and in the attacks on comics, many written by Wertham, leading up to the hearings, crime comics were in fact a major target, the genre "used against" the medium as a whole (horror comics were a close second). In attempting to push mainstream comics to places they had been afraid to go since the code, Miller was aware that he and other innovators were risking censorship, and as his 1981 comments make clear, he viewed the risks as substantial. Yet *DKR* clearly sides with Batman's acknowledgment that "we have to be criminals," refusing the possibility of legitimacy.

This phrasing is irreducibly ambiguous—Miller could be saying either that superheroes will be seen as criminals no matter what they do or that in order to accomplish their goals, they must inevitably become criminals—and this ambiguity pertains to Miller's vision of comics as well. In conversation with Will Eisner, Miller remarks that innovation in comics is always accompanied by some kind of public outcry; various new achievements "were creative triumphs precisely because they were outrageous and daring, which is what I think comics are made to be. I think there's something outlaw about the medium that's gotta be who we are, and the worst thing we've ever done is sanitize ourselves" (120). The curious phrasing "made to be" and the claim to a transgressive quality "that's gotta be who we are," like Batman's observation that "we have to be criminals," blur the line between what comics themselves naturally might be and what, historically, has been declared about them. The difference between description and prescription collapses under the pressure of anti-comics stigma; here, as in his best work in comics, Miller expresses himself most vividly through self-opposition. Such compact observations/injunctions are precise verbal articulations of the differend that results from comics' cultural position. Juxtaposing Superman's sanitized invisibility and Batman's bold announcement of criminality, Miller clearly phrases the illegitimate condition of his medium.

The outcome of the fight between Batman and Superman is unclear; at a point when he has the upper hand, Batman uses drugs to simulate a heart attack in order to fake his death, and thus appears to lose. This uncertain outcome is common whenever famous superheroes face off; the nature of serial reading, the conflicting demands of comics fandom, and the endless revision of major narrative universes all make it impossible for any major superhero permanently to defeat another. Notably, Miller pushes this trope in an unusual direction (his protagonist appears to accept defeat as part of a deliberate strategy), but the point he makes by pitting Superman against Batman has little to do with the outcome of the fight. The fascination of the encounter lies partly in the fact that the two opponents are so unevenly matched: a vigilante who is aging, increasingly prone to injury, psychologically unstable and entirely human (Bruce Wayne has no actual superpowers) must confront an almost incalculably powerful being from another planet. It is not difficult to see this asymmetry as a vivid illustration of Miller's own view of his medium's position relative to the forces arrayed against it.

As a citizen of comics culture, Miller has not wallowed in a self-reflexive sense of victimization; instead he has been a vocal supporter of nonprofit work to improve the legal position of comics. He has recently been given a seat on the advisory board of the Comic Book Legal Defense Fund, which has defended comics creators, shop owners and readers against legal prosecution since 1986.[18] Yet the strength of comics, for Miller, ultimately lies not in their ability to answer their detractors, but precisely in their power to inhabit and embrace their fragile condition, much as Batman does in the face of Superman's overwhelming strength. This choice is presented as preferable to propping up any social or political status quo (an effort which, as Superman's dubious role in *DKR*'s Cold War suggests, is not likely to succeed anyway).

Batman is able to fight Superman through a combination of directness and cunning, using a number of technologies, and in this respect the protagonist figures Miller's own mixture of bold mythography and self-reflexive formalism. Central to this mixture is a deliberately orchestrated control of page design and of the kinetics of comics reading. Understanding this aspect of DKR requires a brief look at book studies from the perspective of comics, and of (bound or stapled) comic books in particular. I refer not to the familiar discipline known as history of the book but to a newer field that, as Garrett Stewart observes, approaches "the book as an instrument as well as a medium . . . not just a repository of useful cultural data but a mechanical construct for its processing, where page layout cues a certain performance by the reader" (413).[19] This new field has thus far been focused on early centuries of the book's existence—understandably so, since later periods saw "the routinization of books as objects of consciousness" such that printed pages could effectively "inoculate against response to their own physical format" (Stewart 437).

The emergence of the novel coincides historically with this inoculation against format-specific response, such that most writers of fiction have not been able to control the precise pagination of their work and usually do not write with such control in mind.[20] For many, though by no means all, works of fiction, the page as such (as distinct from chapter breaks or breaks within chapters) is simply not a significant unit of expression. Comics, meanwhile, have often been just as able as early modern books to prompt deliberate "response to their physical format." Repagination of a comic can often change its meaning radically, and many creators know exactly what will appear on each page of their work and which pages will be facing one another. This control allows for a great deal of creative attention to which images will be visible together, and what effects can be generated through the displacement of one two-page spread of images by the succeeding spread.

DKR's page designs brilliantly activate the kinetics that are always in play when the comics reader turns a page. This action has its own particular physical dynamics, and it can evoke parallels to other, similar or related, actions. Take, for instance, a sequence in which Batman attempts to confront the leader of the Mutants. On the right side of one two-page spread, Batman is safely situated inside an anti-riot tank, looking out through a camera or periscope at the Mutant leader as he taunts Batman and dares him to fight. The first panel, which occupies about a third of the page, is a bleed showing Batman surrounded by controls and readouts, and the remainder of the page is occupied by eleven smaller panels. Four are close-ups of Batman as he decides to emerge and face his enemy; the other seven feature the Mutant leader, either his face in close-up or other portions of his body. Six of these panels are circular, indicating Batman's first-person view of his enemy through some kind of camera, but the seventh, on the lower right, is rectangular, and its color is significantly brighter than that of the other images. These changes in shape and color are explained once the reader turns the page to discover a full-page bleed showing Batman as he emerges from his tank, fists clenched in readiness for combat. Visible behind him is the hatch he has presumably just opened. This image uncannily makes visible, on the page, the action that has brought the page itself into view.

This fusion of the manual/kinetic (the turning of the page) and the narrative/pictorial (the opening of the hatch) positions the reader as the agent who operates the narrative, bringing Batman into conflict with the forces he seeks to control. In this particular narrative instance, Batman fails and is badly beaten (he later changes tactics and succeeds). But as with the conflict between Batman and Superman, Miller's interest is less in the specifics of plot than in the thematic concerns that surround his protagonist; it is the ongoing struggle against crime and chaos, and the perpetual quest for clarity in a cluttered moral landscape, that Miller expresses when Batman leaps into combat. Throughout *DKR*, Miller alternates between dense, text-heavy panels and large images, often splashes, that usually feature Batman in action. These latter images (eight, including the one just analyzed) are invariably on the left-hand side of the spread in which they feature, a seemingly elementary design decision with powerful effects. Following the usual conventions of English-language print literacy, in which the eye begins to track any two-page spread of text from the left, these splashes seem to be the first thing to appear as readers turn the page—that is, as readers, operating the page as if on a hinge, bring the image into visibility—and, in addition, become available to the reader's eye as they are tactilely in the reader's grasp. Most of these pages feature Batman in some sort of classic pose, often leaping through space, alone or accompanied by Robin. Their composition is usually uncluttered, allowing the eye to focus and then to linger, primarily on Batman. In contrast to these heroic images of the protagonist, the pages featuring public debates about him usually feel cramped and disjointed; the eye must slow down to parse each utterance and its accompanying visual image. The effect of reading these pages is a sense of narrative and thematic velocity first accelerated by the action of the reader's hand, bringing the iconic protagonist into clear view, and then decelerated by a struggle over the meaning of this protagonist.

Miller is thus able to establish maximum contrast, at the level of reading, between Batman as he sees himself—and, perhaps, as he is seen by the reader who identifies with him—and Batman as his social effects or meanings are dispersed throughout the discursive economy of Gotham. Further, Miller establishes this contrast in a way that maximizes its connection to the workings of comics literacy; at basic levels of reader engagement with design and format, we read (not merely read *about*) the multiple meanings of Batman, who appears alternately as driving social force and mere societal symptom, subject of action and object of critique, dominant icon and embattled discursive token. It is this dynamic—activated by the reader, who, in Gordon's phrasing, "bounces back and forth" between two very different approaches to Batman—that makes him "too big" for any final critique. Miller reworks and reproduces the illegitimacy of his medium so that, far from being timid and confined, it is simultaneously massive in its monolithic refusal to conform to any social norm and elusively distributed across discontinuous narrative and thematic trajectories. Miller thus expresses not a maturity that could answer the stigma of illegitimacy, but, as it were, illegitimacy in its mature form—self-aware, ideologically mobile, wary of cooptation, and rich in visual and thematic possibility.

I turn to a thematically central page in *DKR* to examine more fully how Miller produces and orchestrates the illegitimacy of his work and his protagonist. The page in question is a variation on the eight splashes discussed above; itself a left-hand page, it is vertically divided so that one long panel occupies the left side while five smaller panels occupy the right (figure 3.2). In a sense, the page encapsulates the dynamic of the text as a whole, though on one page instead of across a two-page spread: a larger image on the left followed by smaller, more densely packed panels to the right. At this point in the narrative, Batman is attempting to find out who supplies the Mutants with weapons, while Carrie Kelley, shortly to become his official third Robin, is beginning to experiment with vigilantism. At first glance, the page organizes these two plot threads through spatial separation; Batman is on the left, Carrie on the right. It seems we are invited to examine vigilantism in two very different modes—one a deadly serious use of violent force, the other a whimsical, if somewhat misdirected, pranksterism—that can be considered separately. Carrie seems to leap from the panel on the lower right, and

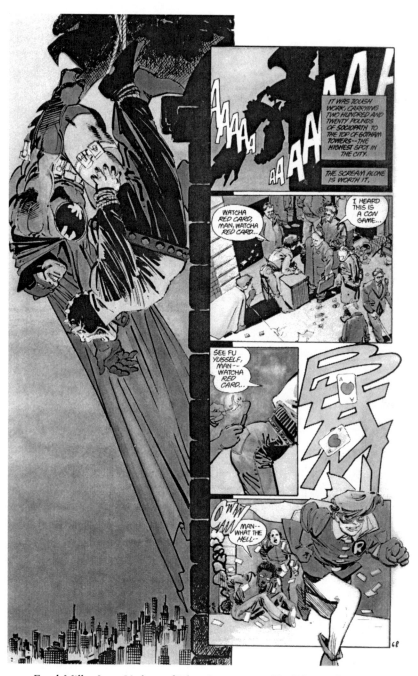

3.2. *Frank Miller, Lynn Varley and Klaus Janson, page 68 of* The Dark Knight Returns, *1986–1987, collected in 10th Anniversary Edition, 1997.*

as a reading vector, this leap suggests her movement off the page and away from Batman. If we read with more care, however, apparent contrast turns into entanglement. Note that the top right panel also features Batman; his interrogation of a Mutant, whom he has hung upside down from the top of Gotham Tower, continues for a moment before the narrative turns to Carrie's rather less sadistic action: using fireworks to disrupt a street con. The stone blocks of Gotham Tower, upon close examination, form a visual rhyme with the stacked panels abutting them on the right, indicating spatial and thematic overlap. Thus, the page is arranged to suggest narrative connections between the two plot threads (Batman's actions seem to flow into Carrie's) along with nonlinear relations between the two that are best represented spatially. Here, as elsewhere in DKR, a dynamic of cause and effect, in which Carrie's vigilantism is inspired by Batman's, is drawn into a multivectored thematic network in which there is another, more complex circulation of energies.

The page renders a vivid image of how, in Miller's view, the energy of vigilantism plays out; it also constitutes a meditation on the perpetual instability of the Batman myth that is animated by this energy. As we examine more closely the relationship of Batman's narrative to Carrie's, uneasy parallels begin to surface. Batman himself is engaged in a sort of prank; "It was tough work," his interior monologue reads, "carrying two hundred and twenty pounds of sociopath to the top of Gotham towers— the highest spot in the city. The scream alone is worth it" (68.2). Presumably, Batman could find other ways to induce fear in the Mutant he interrogates (indeed, he possesses chemical technology for this purpose), but his chosen method is, for lack of a technical term, more fun. Carrie, for her part, certainly seems to enjoy her first attempt at crime fighting, which is inconsequential in itself. But given the dangerous challenges that await her on future pages—and any reader seeing her in the classic Robin costume already anticipates these dangers—something quite serious is beginning for her. The page is thus an image of the adult struggles into which she is rapidly being drawn, despite her youth, at the same time that it pictures the hero of those struggles as something of an overgrown child. Notably, if we invert the page and examine Batman's expression, it bears an unmistakable resemblance to Carrie's grin.

Inverting the page also makes clearer that while drawing Batman in a classic pose, Miller has arranged his figure in visual opposition to the Gotham skyline. This spatial opposition foreshadows the increasing antagonism between Batman and his city as well as his alignment with the very criminal elements he is sworn to defeat. Returning the page to its usual orientation, we might note that a strange confusion of Batman and the Mutant he interrogates is already present in the interior monologue; "two hundred and twenty pounds" is roughly Batman's usual weight. Whether or not this implies that Batman is himself a "sociopath," his eventual alignment with the Mutants and the Sons of the Batman, together with his inspiration and later recruitment of Carrie, give him a trajectory that leads back to youth even as it moves forward into authoritarianism. The relationship between Batman and Carrie, then, is not harmoniously cyclical, but asymmetrically weighted toward youth and immaturity. Batman is what Carrie may soon become; Carrie is what Batman has never ceased to be. Batman's sadistic enjoyment and Carrie's innocent glee are thus connected, but not, despite the design of the page, as mirror images or inversions. They are two ways of expressing a violent, unstable energy that can be provisionally organized as binary—youth/age, innocence/experience, immaturity/maturity—but that then collapses in on itself, reverting to a fundamentally immature aggression. This page is perhaps *DKR*'s most powerful and complex instance of autoclasm.

For readers invested in superhero comics, the most disturbing aspect of the page is probably its treatment of the figure of Robin, who Miller suggests is a deceptive lure. Superhero sidekicks have long been seen as reader surrogates, and Jonathan Rikard Brown has demonstrated how Miller figures Carrie as such in *DKR*. While this form of identification can be seen as a point of entry into the narrative and thematic complexities of superhero comics, on the page in question Miller's focus is less on the value of the sidekick as an avenue of reader access than on the cynicism—in which Miller himself participates—of exchanging one sidekick for another. As already discussed, Carrie is a third Robin, arriving after the retirement of Dick Grayson and the death of Jason Todd. A potential customer/victim in the third panel suggests that the card game Carrie disrupts might be a "con game," and in the fifth panel, in which her firecracker goes off, we see clearly that this suggestion is correct; the con's deck has two identical aces. Just prior to the explosion, the con encourages us to watch the "red card," thus setting up the revelation that follows. There is, however, a further suggestion that Carrie is herself a false "red card" who has been put into the place of her deceased predecessor.

From the moment of her first act of vigilantism, Carrie essentially *is* Robin, but this symbolic moment, in which Miller confirms her identity, simultaneously establishes the illegitimacy of her lineage. Miller's troubled view of the narrative genealogy of Batman's sidekick is not primarily a matter of gender; Miller does not see a female Robin as any more or less viable than a male one. He does, however, unsettle any notion that the Batman narrative is natural and organic; the mantle of Robin can no more pass legitimately from one character to another than the violent heritage of Batman can pass from him to his followers. In his treatment of Robin, as at every other point, Miller disrupts the mechanisms whereby the mythology of Batman is usually stabilized even as he manages to celebrate this mythology in all its instability.

Miller's representation of Batman's illegitimacy makes the status of the medium powerfully present to the eye and intrinsic to the process of reading, as unmistakably visible as it is concretely unavoidable. Miller is determined to portray the circulation of comics' illegitimacy along myriad narrative circuits, examining the way Batman is discussed in Gotham's mass media; the appropriation of his image by others (including the Sons of the Batman, who paint the Bat-Symbol on their faces); the tendentious relationship between his notion of justice and that of Superman, or of the police; and the (potentially quite disturbing) scenario of Batman as the direct instructor of Gotham's youth. In the belated sequel *The Dark Knight Strikes Again* (2001–2002), Miller's tracing of these various modes of circulation is more overtly humorous, even campy, and thus more recognizably "pop"—as the term is colloquially understood—in its treatment of Batman as a malleable and widespread public symbol. But in *DKR*, despite its grim tone, there is already an iconological approach to Batman; the book is a space of analytical, at times almost nonnarrative, *display* of its protagonist in terms of his cultural position. Here I return to my opening claim that *DKR* is a leading example of comics that reflect explicitly on the medium's cultural standing, and thus accomplish in comics form what pop art accomplished in the fine arts: an overt rendering of status in the text itself.

The parallel I am suggesting differs from the usual critical options for understanding the relationship between pop art and comics. From the perspective of its creators, and perhaps especially of Warhol, pop art may well have appeared to be a liberating development that allowed newly equitable relations between high and mass culture. From the comics creator's point of view, pop art's appropriation of mass cultural artifacts, and of comics in particular, has looked much less positive. As Bart Beaty points out, "pop art has helped to open up the reading of popular culture by those [i.e., painters and others in the realm of the fine arts] who had the cultural capital to do so. Now, in the wake of this opportunity, it is common to encounter cartoonists who are resentful of the fact that the opportunities suggested by pop art have not been quickly or fully realized in the field of comics itself" (*Comics Versus Art* 54–55). Miller can certainly be classified as one such "resentful" comics creator; portions of *Sin City* reference the work of Roy Lichtenstein in a way that clearly challenges his appropriation of comics images, sorting with Beaty's observation that, in comics culture, "Lichtenstein . . . is seen not as honoring comics with his paintings but as further devaluating the entire form by reaffirming the long-standing prejudice against cartoonists that has existed in the realm of high art" (*Comics Versus Art* 58).[21] Beaty suggests that "pent-up aggressive feelings toward the world of fine arts" on the part of some creators "can become an all-consuming passion that threatens to poison their work with an easily diagnosed bitterness"; my own view of how creators' "aggressive feelings" manifest in their work is, obviously, more approving (*Comics Versus Art* 52). I would suggest that the best way to value creators' deep awareness of status inequities is to ask what their sense of the medium's illegitimacy might tell us not just about the kind of condescending appropriation typified by Lichtenstein, but also about the broader phenomenon of artistic legitimation—from which comics continue, on the whole, to be excluded.

Confining my scope to pop art, I offer closing thoughts concerning its legitimating power. On its first appearance, pop art seemed to force viewers into an encounter with disreputable products of mass culture in the last spaces they expected to find them: museums and galleries. Within a very few years, however, it became possible to view pop art either as far more culturally respectable than it at first appeared—if only because it propped up the cultural and economic status quo—or as avant-garde work that could be valued precisely for its transgressive and critical qualities.[22] In either case, it was perceived as projecting a power that however much it differed from the Benjaminian aura available to works less implicated in mass production, was nevertheless substantial. That is to say, pop art knew virtually nothing of illegitimacy and, while heralding the advent of the postmodern, did not actually pose a radical challenge to existing concepts of art.

It did, however, reconcile collectors and museum audiences to the fact that works of art were commodities and that the art world was a market for them. Detailing the explicitness with which some gallery owners self-consciously adopted the language of retail advertising in order to market pop art, Sara Doris observes what she calls "a blatancy about art's commodity status unheard of in the art world. Generally, then as now, galleries were extremely secretive about such matters . . . [partly] to sustain the illusion that art was not a business" (126). Thus, regardless of the intentions of its various practitioners, what pop art quickly accomplished was to encourage *and* to normalize awareness that art is in fact a business. It did so by announcing the commodity nature of the art object so obviously as to make it unavoidable.

The degree to which this obviousness quickly seemed unthreatening did not, despite appearances, signal a collapse of all high/low cultural distinctions. The reverse is more nearly true: pop art has come to be a new way of demonstrating the difference between legitimated artistic production and whatever is refused legitimation. The work of Lichtenstein has not dignified the comics creators whose work he appropriated, and the minimal distance (in terms of resemblance) between the former's canvases and panels—drawn by, for instance, Jack Kirby—has proved a remarkably solid barrier in cultural perception. The vanishing difference at the level of appearance, which was what initially announced the arrival of mass culture in the museum, has at length played its role in the maintenance of the very difference it initially seemed to threaten. Despite the steady growth of an art market for comics, there remains a widespread cultural assumption that Kirby is not to be placed in the same category as Lichtenstein.[23] The legitimating aura of fine arts cultural production has, perhaps, proved all the more durable in those instances where its actual, visible difference from its mass cultural raw materials is almost nonexistent. The aura of legitimacy associated with the fine arts can, it turns out, outlive the aura of the traditional art object, and pop art can remain separate from mass cultural forms while— perhaps *by*—appropriating them wholesale.

Pop art thus represents a moment at which the fine arts could express a new kind of self-understanding. At the advent of pop, the art work's legitimation as a commodity, formerly hidden from view (insofar as this was possible), became expressible in the work itself. The degree to which this expression was quickly read, and soon accepted, should be seen as an effect of legitimation. An entirely different state of affairs has obtained for what I have ironically termed "pop art comics." Like other respected long-form works that have followed it, *DKR* has been defined in terms of the *Bildungsroman* discourse, that is, as a newly serious and literary kind of comic book. While its formal and thematic complexities are certainly notable, *DKR* is better seen as giving new form to the low status of comics. The problem of articulating this status is, perhaps, the very reason Miller's strategies have not been noticeable to many critics, despite the fact that the explicitness with which they are executed on the page nearly matches the obviousness of commodity discourse in pop art. An extended meditation on the stigma attached to comics, *DKR* was quickly misperceived as a "serious" work separate from the very lineage of which it was so obviously a part. So long as comics are denied legitimacy, autoclastic icons will likely remain as difficult for some critics to read as they are necessary for many creators to draw.

FOUR

The Scandal of Pleasure

ALISON BECHDEL

From Frank Miller to Alison Bechdel: If we allow our thinking to be guided by their respective cultural positions at present, this is a sudden move; we leave the world of violent pulp to enter the more respectable zone of "literary" comics. Bechdel's career has certainly unfolded along a path very different from that of Miller. Whereas he worked toward creative freedom within mainstream comics, Bechdel pursued a rigorously independent route, publishing her long-running comic strip *Dykes to Watch Out For* in newspapers and magazines for queer audiences; Bechdel has referred to this option as self-syndication.[1] Collections of *Dykes to Watch Out For* sold well, but they did not gain Bechdel even a fraction of the mainstream recognition and respect that greeted the publication of her memoir *Fun Home* in 2006. This work was highly praised in comics culture, winning major awards, and was admitted into the canon of comics deemed respectable among mainstream readers even more rapidly and decisively than *DKR* had been in the 1980s. But while its contrast of closeted father and openly queer daughter bears no easy resemblance to the ideological conflict between Superman and Batman, *Fun Home* is likewise concerned with the perils of legitimation and with the paradoxes that confront the comics creator seeking to realize new ambitions in a medium long excluded from cultural respectability. Bechdel addresses these paradoxes in ways that shape *Fun Home* just as decisively as questions of status shape *DKR*, which suggests a commonality of struggle along a spectrum of US comics production.

In Miller, we have a creator whose generic and medium-specific allegiances are self-evident. Reading Bechdel, we confront the much stranger and more symptomatic case of a cartoonist whose elevation to broad cultural legitimacy has been accompanied by a certain hesitation to point to her work and say "comics." Some critics have been forthright about the specific kind of triumph *Fun Home* represents, observing that it "invests a particular faith in its author's chosen medium" (Lemberg 130), or that it is "a story so thoroughly integrated with its medium that it literally could not exist in any other form" (Edidin 297). Most thorough and persuasive in the pursuit of such claims is Hillary Chute, who argues that *Fun Home* celebrates "the capacities of the comics page" in ways that are inclusive of other forms while evincing the specificity of the medium (*Graphic Women* 207). Quite commonly in discussions of *Fun Home*, however, there are hints to the effect that it is not just a comic, or is somehow *more* than a comic, and that both its formal complexity and the breadth of the raw materials visible on its pages—including photographs, handwritten and typed documents, and, above all, a wealth of references to works of print literature—ought to complicate its classification.[2] Such claims are not perforce elitist in their intentions, but traditional print novels that draw their subject matter from other media, including comics, are not thereby deemed unclassifiable. No one thinks Junot Díaz's Pulitzer-winning *The Brief Wondrous Life of Oscar Wao* cannot be described as a novel because one of its epigraphs is taken from *The Fantastic Four*, or because its pages are littered with myriad references to the various subcultures of what its author calls "the Nerd Age" (22).

It could be argued that because they combine words and pictures, comics are more readily "multimedial" than traditional print. Yet there are certainly other comics whose reference points and raw materials are as diverse as *Fun Home*'s, and whose deployment of such materials is as obtrusive, that are nevertheless understood without qualification to be comics. The perceptions or motives of this or that critic may vary, but the pattern of characterizing *Fun Home* as possessing special generic or formal status sorts with the dynamics of legitimation examined in my account of the *Bildungsroman* discourse. Understanding the hegemonic nature of this discourse, we can see how, in cases where a text that is perceived to inhabit a fully legitimate realm of cultural expression, such as a print novel by an acclaimed writer, reaches "down" to incorporate less respected kinds of culture, there is little pressure to account for this incorporation by a change of terms. It is the move in the opposite direction, the emergence of work in a culturally subordinate medium that displays formidable literary reach, that calls for additional categories. I will work against the tendency to resituate *Fun Home* outside its own medium; at the same time, I will ask what is at stake in this comic's vast accumulation of literary material.

Although the formal and thematic density of *Fun Home* is not as unprecedented as some critics have assumed, its self-consciously literary texture does matter to an attentive reading of the text. Not all the text's references to writers of canonical print literature, and to their works, demonstrate a deep investment on Bechdel's part. Discussing her use of Proust, who is referenced in *Fun Home*'s fourth chapter, Bechdel has remarked: "I never actually read all of Proust; I just skimmed and took bits that I needed" ("An Interview" 1005). But there are other references, most notably Bechdel's use of Joyce's *Ulysses*, that seem more deeply suffused in a reading of the source and serve ample structural and thematic purposes.

I suggest, however, that it is the status of comics, not the import of Bechdel's more sustained engagements with literary modernism, that motivates scholarly claims like the following: "Through the depth and frequency of literary reference, Bechdel is clearly stating the legitimacy of the graphic narrative as inheritor of the modernist tradition" (Freedman 130). As with some instances of the *Bildungsroman* discourse discussed in the first chapter, this claim projects its own conflicted investments onto the text it discusses. While there is an assumption that Bechdel's deployment of literary references must be saying something about the status of comics, and about the kind of comic *Fun Home* is, the question of medium and the problems of legitimacy it raises are instantly deflected by the claim that Bechdel belongs in a literary lineage. This claim is qualified by the observation that Bechdel's "relationship to the modernist tradition is playful and sometimes combative," but this playfulness is not seen to alter Bechdel's project of literary legitimation (Freedman 130). I will argue against this perspective, not because Bechdel is uninterested in legitimation, but because her interest is much more thoroughgoing, complex and self-aware than such critical framing assumes.

Fun Home should, in fact, be seen as a turning point in Bechdel's career as a cartoonist, a point at which she experimented with a genre she had rarely employed (autobiography), a format she had never previously attempted (the long-form comic) and a density of specifically literary allusions far different from her penchant for occasional, and usually whimsical, literary flourishes in earlier work. A variety of creative impulses motivated this experiment, but it was undoubtedly tied to ambition for wider readership. In the mid-1990s, the period leading up to her beginning serious work on *Fun Home*, Bechdel observed: "I am a little disappointed that my cartoons haven't reached more people. Rather than tailor my work to make it more accessible to a broader audience, though, my instinct is to continue with as much lesbian-specificity as I can" ("Across Borders" 169). Although she remained committed to a queer perspective, Bechdel was indeed interested in getting her work into the hands of more readers, and it is thus no accident that *Fun Home* adds an overtly literary sensibility to the "lesbian-specificity" of *Dykes to Watch Out For.* As Hillary Chute observes, "one of the reasons that *Fun Home* may have been so quickly accepted as serious literature is that it is explicitly 'literary'" (*Graphic Women* 185). I agree that the rapid canonization of *Fun Home* suggests that this aspect of the work has almost certainly helped Bechdel to gain a new audience, reminding us once again that however disconnected the *Bildungsroman* discourse might seem to be from the most difficult realities of comics history, this discourse still has real cultural effects. I cite as anecdotal evidence a remark made by a friend of mine who had received *Fun Home* as a gift; though initially quite skeptical, he told me he quickly "forgot it was a comic" and found himself enjoying it "as a book."

Bechdel herself seems fully aware of the cultural dynamics that inform this kind of reading; her thoughts on the reception of *Fun Home* demonstrate a sharp attunement to questions of literary respectability: "[It] makes me happy . . . when people just talk about it as a book, and not as a graphic novel. . . . It has made a couple top-10 graphic-novel lists, but I'm kind of dismissive. I know that's really wrong. I mean, I'm very grateful to be on any top-10 lists, whatever the category, but I can't help feeling like, 'What do you mean? It's a great *book!*'" ("Life Drawing" 40). The fact that Bechdel is "dismissive" of medium-specific acknowledgment does not mean she wishes for *Fun Home* to be viewed as something other than a comic; Bechdel has identified herself as a cartoonist for decades.[3] Rather, she wants whatever is meant by "book" to be expanded, so that it can be applied to print and comics alike without distinction. We should note the precise reason she gives for thinking that being "dismissive" about recognition as a comics artist is "really wrong." It is not that a desire for "literary" recognition shortchanges comics as a separate medium with its own particular capacities—certainly she doesn't seem to suspect herself of any shame about making comics—but rather that being recognized for making great comics is preferable to not being recognized at all. Bechdel acknowledges the low status of comics at present, regardless of her hopes for future respectability.

Further, she immediately connects her wish for unequivocal recognition in culture at large to a desire for her previous work to reach the wider audience she hoped it would have all along: "But this is my great hope, that eventually the *Fun Home* frenzy will translate into more acceptance of the *Dykes to Watch Out For* books ("Life Drawing" 40–41). *Fun Home* was meant not to stand apart from her previous works, but to serve as a gateway to them, and this conscious attention to strategies of legitimation suggests quite a pragmatic attitude toward what it means to be seen as a "literary" cartoonist. One can imagine Bechdel's approach as reversing the pedagogical conception of comics as a stepping-stone to literature. Lessening the shock of difficulty that reluctant comics readers might feel by providing references to James, Woolf and Joyce, *Fun Home* gently guides such readers toward the fact that reading a comic full of such references is still reading a comic.

And yet—as indicated by critical and anecdotal evidence—apparently it somehow is possible to forget *Fun Home* is a comic; its medium-specific lineage does not announce itself to all readers. And to the careless reader of the remarks just cited, it could seem Bechdel is, perhaps unbeknownst to herself, leery of being associated with comics as such. Her choice of the phrase "great book," redolent of canonical privilege, might suggest that, while she officially calls for an end to the cultural distinctions that have marginalized comics, she might unconsciously want to preserve, and to possess for her own work, the status that adheres to print literature over and against comics that are not canonized. Such a suspicious reading of Bechdel's remarks would be a mistake, however, and would underestimate the richness of *Fun Home*'s treatment of the subject of legitimation. Far from avoiding the kinds of questions raised by Bechdel's comments on its reception, *Fun Home* is a lengthy meditation on the special allure of the cultural legitimacy associated with literature.

This is not a matter of literary lineage as typically understood, but a messier question of cultural ambiance. Discussing the influence of her education at Oberlin College, Bechdel has remarked: "I . . . picked up a dilettantish, quasi-intellectual, pseudo-academic kind of avant-garde attitude that proved to be socially useful. I learned a little bit of everything on a Sunday crossword level" (Rubenstein interview 115). This bit of self-deprecating wit demonstrates Bechdel's cultural self-awareness and suggests that a college degree from an elite institution produces, if nothing else, the sense of being cultured. Substantial portions of *Fun Home* can be read as an extended exercise in this kind of wit; Bechdel constantly invites readers to bask in the glow of the literary life. *Fun Home*, I want to suggest, is less a serious exploration of high literary tradition than a droll exercise in feeling well read.

It is here, in the overt quality of the text's meditation on the subtle, and highly suspect, pleasures of a nebulous sense of "literariness," that Bechdel's more comics-specific lineage will come into focus. Reading *Fun Home*, we cannot help but feel bookish from the start, but the value of such a feeling diminishes the more closely we read. In the tradition of *MAD* magazine, which was formative for Bechdel and has a significant presence in the text, *Fun Home* is a self-conscious rehearsal of a siren song it both mimics with uncanny perfection and rejects as a destructive fiction. In addressing these aspects of the text, I will by no means do justice to all the literary traditions, or kinds of reading, that *Fun Home* pictures and encourages. Chief among the projects undone here is, in Ann Cvetkovich's phrasing, "to link the high culture references to the equally dense proliferation of lesbian and feminist texts" (122). To disclose exactly why the critical tendency to reclassify this work interferes with our ability to read its pages with care, I will focus on narrower but crucial strata of *Fun Home*, asking what it says about comics and about the relationship between comics and literature.

The best approach to this issue is through a neglected aspect of Bechdel's work: its sense of humor. To discover what Bechdel does or does not find respectable, we should first ask what she finds funny. In the preface to the eleventh collection of *Dykes to Watch Out For*, Bechdel tells us: "At first, I admit, what attracted me about lesbianism was the sex" (n. pag.). A typical Bechdel joke: deadpan enough to be missed at first glance, suddenly hilarious once it becomes visible, it then resonates with lingering irony. Bechdel quickly learned that lesbianism means more than sexual desire. She tells how, in the early days of her development as a queer subject, she "fell in with a rough crowd—women who were always blockading Wall Street, or going off to Nicaragua to help the Sandanistas with the coffee harvest," and describes how she "stood on the sidelines gaping with awe" at this kind of activism, which was challenging, enjoyable and inspirational all at once (n. pag.). While pleasure in the narrower sense of her own sexual experience initially seemed opposed to (or at least much different from) political commitment, the two quickly came to seem indistinguishable: "If in my excitement I confused the personal with the political, well, that was part of the idea" (n. pag.). The claim that the personal is political is probably not new to anyone reading the preface; indeed, it is the necessary background of the joke that precedes it. The joke itself, however, reminds readers that, while queerness means more than sex, it generally begins, developmentally, as it were, as an itch to get laid.

What resonates after the joke is the clause "I admit," a small confessional extravagance that makes us wonder just why the primacy of pleasure is something that must be disclosed (not assumed), and exactly how youthful desire sorts with mature joining of the personal to the political. It may be nothing more than a pause to let us know that what follows is meant to be funny, but it cannot take place without bringing with it the suggestion that desire and politics are not naturally compatible. We must "admit" the gap between them, and let this gap occupy space in our reading of Bechdel's comics. Throughout the long run of *Dykes to Watch Out For*, the entangled fates of the protagonists serve as a way to explore increasingly broad political horizons. Bechdel uses the lives of her characters to convey the idea that the realm of desire and the realm of ethics and politics are bound to comingle. However, at a less explicit, but perfectly visible, level, Bechdel assumes something else entirely: that desire comes before, goes beyond, and often stands apart from whatever counts as viable political subjectivity or mature and respectable citizenship. If in its confusion this dynamic calls into question exactly what such citizenship is worth, to borrow Bechdel's language: that is part of the idea.

The more distressing any mismatch of politics and pleasure becomes, the more amusing Bechdel seems to find it. Take a *Dykes to Watch Out For* strip in which Lois, one of several characters working at a feminist bookstore called Madwimmin Books, has to deal with a male customer whose interests are clearly prurient rather than progressive. Taking him unawares in the section of the store featuring erotica, Lois cheerfully suggests some publications he might consider, including a magazine featuring "a hot photo spread of three totally tattooed babes with strap-ons doing an armpit-shaving scene." The man flees without purchasing anything, and when her coworkers congratulate her on his rapid exit, Lois remarks that she is "losing [her] touch." She goes on to explain: "Last week I flustered a guy so bad he spent sixty bucks before he left" (*Essential Dykes* 99.7–11). Most obviously, this punch line suggests that if Madwimmin workers must put up with the presence of the heteronormative gaze, they can at least make a profit from it. Yet, upon second reading, it becomes unclear whether it is her failure to sell lesbian porn to straight men or her recent, perhaps accidental, success in doing so that prompts Lois to say she is losing her touch. Which is the preferable outcome: keeping straight culture from the pleasure of appropriating lesbian sexuality by enjoying images of it, or failing to get paid for such appropriation?

Bechdel's complex gag is set up by an earlier debate between Lois and lead protagonist Mo; they discuss a lesbian friend of theirs who is in a relationship with a man. Mo comments: "It bugs me that she can come in here and soak up lesbian culture, then go home to her safe, societally approved boyfriend." Lois's view is more accepting: "There's room for everybody! I say the more people soaking up lesbian culture, the better!" (99.4).⁴ The ensuing encounter with the straight male customer reminds us that in this case, cultural specificity and integrity may be matters of buying and selling, but Bechdel's real concern is the clash of political values on the one hand and pleasure on the other.

The fact that the clash seems funnier the more violent it becomes, and that, as *Dykes to Watch Out For* unfolds, political and cultural boundaries must be readjusted to account for the unorthodox paths desire takes, suggests that pleasure—at least in the form of humor—always wins. However, in Bechdel's work, the triumph of pleasure is never the same thing as its legitimation. Even if, as we will see in *Fun Home*, pleasure might seem to be its own reward and its own justification, invariably it must enter a political and social economy that works to value it on other terms. Such revaluation cannot wholly succeed, and pleasure remains an unruly and disruptive phenomenon, neither adding force to any existing system of values—even those Bechdel supports—nor offering a coherent set of its own. Hence my use of the term "scandal." *Fun Home* brings to light a Bechdel family secret: the sexual encounters Alison's father Bruce had with underage boys, and his closeted sexuality, which were mostly kept concealed from his community even after his death—indeed, were concealed from the world at large until the publication of *Fun Home*. While Bechdel defends neither his affairs nor his decision to keep his queerness hidden, *Fun Home*'s critique of Bruce targets his obsession with legitimacy much more than his ethical or political shortcomings.

This approach to Bruce extends to a larger critique not only of heteronormative culture, but also of prescriptive notions of literary and cultural respectability. Bechdel attacks the very ambitions that motivate her literary allusiveness, and the pleasure she takes in doing so is both something she must figure on the page and something that undercuts the legitimacy of all attempts at literary figuration. One of the ways Bechdel invalidates the literary, however, is to celebrate it, not on the basis of its

cultural authority (much less because of any political value it might possess), but on the basis of its pleasurability. In other words, she simultaneously undercuts and takes pleasure in literary—that is, culturally respectable—ambition; mocking and indulging her middlebrow bookishness,
she uses her work to stage the dilemma she confronts in the very act
of "literary" cartooning. As with *DKR*, one of *Fun Home*'s central concerns is the ongoing crisis of legitimation specific to comics; Bechdel
brilliantly displays this crisis and leaves it unresolved.

As this project manifests in *Fun Home*, Bechdel constructs cultural
binaries that, as discussed in the second chapter, often appear in the
work of contemporary comics creators. Admittedly, these binaries distort some of the cultural artifacts Bechdel brings into *Fun Home*. For
instance, her portrayal of her experience with studying *Ulysses* in college is designed to maximize a contrast between the intellectual ambiance of her classroom, where her professor takes a deadening inter-
textual approach to one of the most canonical works of print literature,
and Bechdel's growing investment in and exploration of her sexuality,
which are tied to the act of cartooning. Bechdel recalls herself wondering, "Once you grasped that *Ulysses* was based on *The Odyssey*, was it really necessary to enumerate every last point of correspondence?" (206.4).
Bechdel portrays herself falling behind in her Joyce seminar as she reads
more and more lesbian literature, viewing "literary criticism" as "a suspect activity," and eventually drawing pictures on the pages of her copy
of Joyce's opus rather than carefully reading the text (206.3, 209.2). At this
point in *Fun Home*, Bechdel seems to view *Ulysses* primarily in terms of
its postwar status as a lapidary monument of the high-modernist cultural
establishment. When she eventually argues that *Ulysses* is a testament to
"erotic truth," she offers an ostensibly subversive reading that is—given
the richly erotic power of the novel in question—so justifiable as to be
merely apparent (229.4).

The point of the binaries that Bechdel sets up is not to enforce an
absolute distinction between high and low culture (Bechdel portrays the
works of Collette, for instance, as both culturally respectable and "good
for a wank" [207.5]), but to remain aware of the ways in which power
organizes culture, and to highlight the troubled status of the medium
in which she works. This status remains distinct from that of the mas-
terpieces of print modernism, no matter how many times Bechdel cites
them or uses them as structural elements of her narrative. When comics themselves are figured on the pages of *Fun Home*, they appear in contrast to "literature" proper. And as we will see, Bechdel orchestrates this

contrast with great care, demanding readerly attention that, while perhaps not as exhaustive as that required by her Joyce professor, has thus far not been granted in critical studies of *Fun Home*.

I turn to the highly deliberate placement of mid-century horror comics in a scene that Bechdel constructs using letters her father wrote to her mother during their courtship in the late 1950s. This scene occurs in the third chapter, "The Old Catastrophe," and it is one of the most elaborately fictionalized moments in the text; Bechdel offers a scenario in which Bruce might have written the letters that is obviously pure speculation. Interspersing images of the letters (rendered by hand, as are all physical documents that appear in *Fun Home*) with interpretations of their meaning, Bechdel portrays Bruce as a closeted gay man who learns, through certain kinds of reading and writing, how to appear to be a straight lover. Key to Bruce's education is F. Scott Fitzgerald, whose works he reads while he is in the army. As Bruce writes love letters to his future wife, he reads both Fitzgerald's fiction and Arthur Mizener's 1951 biography.

While serving partly as a point of comparison for his own psyche—Bruce says that he, like Fitzgerald, suffers from "emotional bankruptcy"—Fitzgerald is mainly a stylistic model and thematic inspiration (62.3). Around the time Bruce was engaged in this course of reading, his letters, "which had not been particularly demonstrative up to this point, began to grow lush with Fitzgeraldesque sentiment" (63.2). As textual proof, Bechdel offers a letter that reads: "Do you know I love you. That made me feel so good I'll say it again. I love you I love you I love you, you crazy wonderful girl. This would be our night to sit and drink and look at one another" (63.2). The fact that testifying to his love for his future bride can make Bruce "feel so good" that he repeats himself shows that his efforts to adopt a straight identity involve pleasure of a kind, but the pleasure seems largely to be in success at performance. The sentence "This would be our night to sit and drink and look at one another" is rather a chaste fantasy of intimacy, and its conditional phrasing suggests that Bruce prefers his nicely expressed image to any actuality (he expresses no desire to depart the scene of writing for a direct encounter).

The context Bechdel creates for this self-education in heteronormativity is highly specific; she portrays Bruce sitting on his bunk, surrounded by other soldiers, one of whom is behaving flirtatiously toward him. Examining a picture in Bruce's book, the man asks if Fitzgerald is Bruce's "boyfriend," and remarks, "He's even prettier'n you"; Bruce's quietly pleased expression suggests erotic possibility (63.1). While this subtle exchange takes place in the foreground, a more straightforward economy of reading pleasure takes place behind (figure 4.1): A soldier is reading an issue of *The Haunt of Fear*, one of the three horror titles from comics publisher EC (the other two were *The Vault of Horror* and the well-known *Tales from the Crypt*). Bechdel's choice of this title is not accidental: while all three series trafficked in disturbing stories and grotesque imagery (to be discussed further in relation to Charles Burns in chapter 5), *The Haunt of Fear* has become, for comics culture, the most emblematic. The story "Foul Play" from issue 19 was a central exhibit in the 1954 Senate subcommittee hearings concerning the influence of comics on juvenile delinquency.[5]

This connection is nowhere mentioned in *Fun Home*; the comics-reading soldier might initially appear to be nothing more than an amusing bit of period color. Yet Bechdel researched the period scenes of *Fun Home* intensively and would have known that *The Haunt of Fear* and other EC horror titles had been eliminated by the 1954 code, before Bruce joined the military. The anachronistic insertion of a horror title that had, in effect, been censored out of existence by 1955 is crucial to this scene of reading and writing, which is also a scene of legitimation. While the soldier reading comics does so, presumably, because he wants to read comics, Bruce reads in order to gain access to social and cultural acceptance. Bechdel thus establishes a contrast between two acts of reading that is also, in effect, a contrast between illegitimate and legitimate forms of culture and ways of being.

The skeptical reader may wonder if this interpretation hangs too much weight on a bit of scene dressing. Perhaps Bechdel is actually on the side of the literary, and references *The Haunt of Fear* to mark a contrast between the era of the comics code and the moment of *Fun Home*, which has quickly become one of the most culturally respectable English-language comics.[6] Just as her deployment of literary allusion has had an intrinsic appeal for her new readership, Bechdel was scarcely unaware of the depth of her creative ambitions in making *Fun Home*, and has openly admitted as much. Asked if she has been surprised by the level of critical acclaim it has received, she responds: "Somewhere deep down I knew that it was a good book . . . like it *should* get attention" ("Life Drawing" 36). But however much *Fun Home* might seem not only to invite, but also to anticipate, its positive mainstream reception, Bechdel's portrait of literary and cultural legitimacy is deeply critical and self-reflexive. Readers who, at this point in the narrative, forget

DAD WAS PASSIONATE ABOUT MANY WRITERS, BUT HE HAD A PARTICULAR REVERENCE FOR FITZGERALD.

MY MOTHER HAD SENT HIM A BIOGRAPHY OF FITZGERALD BEFORE THEY MARRIED, WHEN DAD WAS IN THE ARMY.

HE'D BEEN DRAFTED AFTER DROPPING OUT OF HIS GRADUATE ENGLISH PROGRAM, OVERWHELMED WITH THE WORKLOAD.

REFERENCES TO THE BIOGRAPHY CREPT INTO HIS LETTERS TO HER.

THE TALES OF SCOTT AND ZELDA'S DRUNKEN, OUTRAGEOUS BEHAVIOR CAPTIVATED HIM.

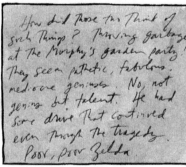

4.1. *Alison Bechdel, page 62 of* Fun Home, *2006.*

they are reading a comic are not paying attention to a glaring compositional cue. In the midst of Bruce's literary elaboration of a straight subjectivity, Bechdel plays a visual prank on her father by seeming to put *The Haunt of Fear* in his hands. This gag occurs just after the soldier who is flirting with Bruce asks if, behind his copy of Fitzgerald's biography, he is actually reading *Playboy* (62.1). In a precisely composed panel, Bechdel seems to place *The Haunt of Fear* in Bruce's line of sight. The head and body of the soldier who is actually holding the comic are not visible, but his arms—while too small to be Bruce's (which are also visible in the frame)—are positioned as if they could be; it is as if the arms of a young comics reader were momentarily extruded from Bruce's body (62.5, figure 4.1, last panel).

This bit of visual slapstick is a joke on readers who may have been momentarily lulled into conceiving of their own reading of *Fun Home* as essentially "literary," since they are doing what the soldier reading *The Haunt of Fear* is doing, not what Bruce is doing. The scene not only suggests a vision of comics reading for pleasure as being more valid than literary reading for the sake of legitimation, but also asserts the specific status of the object that rests in the reader's hands, and the cultural implications that come with reading a comic book, called by whatever name. To read *Fun Home* for the literary references, this scene suggests, is not unlike concealing a copy of *Playboy* behind more respectable reading material (or claiming that one reads it "for the articles").

At this carefully orchestrated moment, the intricacy and daring of Bechdel's project becomes fully visible. We are confronted not just with creative self-opposition, insofar as Bechdel attacks the very cultural respectability that *Fun Home* might seem to court, but with the multivalence of the book's politics. As discussed in chapter 1, the 1950s were, to put it mildly, a bad time for comics, and this scene offers a glimpse of the history that lies behind the need some critics feel, more than half a century later, to call *Fun Home* something other than a comic book. Given the stakes of *Fun Home's* political project, this observation might seem frivolous. Surely, in a scene where queer desire must be concealed in order to survive an environment of institutionalized homophobia, the point is that the 1950s were a bad time to be gay, in the military as elsewhere. And while it might seem easy to align comics and queerness in this scene, the way Bechdel figures comics does not suggest such an alignment. The soldier holding *The Haunt of Fear* is doing so openly; his choice of reading matter is much less respectable than Bruce's in culture at large, but it is not portrayed as something that need be hidden. A few panels later, this comics reader is engaged in playful wrestling with a fellow soldier that looks like a don't-ask-don't-tell scenario of barely concealed desire, yet this does not indicate that Bruce's decision to stay closeted is merely personal (65.1).

In fact, the scene makes clear why the problem of legitimacy associated with comics is a separate horizon of social and political concern that overlaps others, but also differs. As a queer artist publicly discussing her family history, Bechdel possesses a kind of legitimacy that Bruce Bechdel never knew. However, as a cartoonist whose work should have come to widespread public attention long before the publication of *Fun Home*, and whose reception was limited by her choice of medium as well as her focus on queer life, Bechdel faces her own distinct struggle, with which a literary mind such as Bruce Bechdel's would probably not have sympathized. And if this struggle sits uneasily adjacent, yet distinct from, the book's queer politics, this, too, is part of the idea. In *Fun Home*, queerness and comics are not portrayed as being closeted in the same space or in the same way, and even after the attentive reader notes their emergence on the page, they remain visibly distinct.

Bruce's brush with *The Haunt of Fear* is the first of two occasions on which he crosses paths with comics. The second occurs later in the same chapter, and takes place in Bruce's library when Alison is a child. As a setting, this library dominates the chapter. Bechdel figures it as a signal example of Bruce's capacity for artifice, and a testament to the power with which he projected an image of cultural respectability. She notes that Bruce "liked to imagine himself as a nineteenth-century aristocrat overseeing his estate from behind the leather-topped mahogany and brass Second-Empire desk," and goes on to speculate that "affectation can be so thoroughgoing, so authentic in its details, that it stops being pretense . . . and becomes, for all practical purposes, real. The library was a fantasy, but a fully operational one" (60.1–61.1). As in all her renderings of her family home, painstakingly restored by her father over many years, Bechdel shows the library in textured detail, noting the flocked wallpaper, the gilt window frames, the velvet curtains and the wall-to-ceiling mirror—into which, the arrangement of the room makes clear, Bruce could glance while seated at his desk, narcissistically confirming his image of himself even in the absence of onlookers (60.1).

Impressive as these details are, Bruce's fantasy of status and legitimacy is "fully operational" because the library contains actual books; when Alison has a question about geography, her father can direct her to an atlas (61.1). The power of book ownership, display and consumption is central to the chapter. Books serve as a means to exchange erotic energy, but they retain a specifically literary charge: "Part of Dad's country squire routine involved edifying the villagers—his more promising high school students. The promise was very likely sexual in some cases, but whatever else might have been going on, books were definitely being read" (61.4–5). A more censorious family historian would reverse Bechdel's phrasing, noting that, while there might have been some education going on, Bruce was definitely having sex with underage students. But with a wittily Wildean perversity, Bechdel highlights a "fully operational fantasy" of legitimation; regardless of his affairs with his students, Bruce was a literary authority who authenticated his cultural standing by directing others to follow his example and read great books.

We will shortly have to account for a book of cartoons that resided in the Bechdel home, but it goes without saying that there were no comic books in Bruce's library. Bechdel is counting on her readers to make this presumption when, at the end of "The Old Catastrophe," she presents her child self entering the library, approaching her father as he sits reading, and asking him for money to buy comics—"new MAD books," in particular (85.4, figure 4.2). While the earlier scene involving The Haunt of Fear is entirely fictionalized, this moment has an undeniable basis in fact. Bechdel has made clear in interviews that while she did not seek out many comic books as a child, and found much of her earliest pictorial inspiration in illustrated children's books, she was "obsessed" with this particular publication: "I loved MAD. I actually had a subscription, and I lived for the day it would come in the mail. I would devour it immediately" (Rubenstein interview 114).[7] When Bechdel portrays her child self taking advantage of her father's distracted absorption in literary culture to fund the purchase of more MAD comics, she affirms her own appetites, and her need to build a library much different from her father's.

Although Alison tells her father she wants new books of MAD material, a close reading reveals that she is ordering bound reprints of older issues that were initially available years before she was born, commonly known as MAD paperbacks. Deliberately deceiving her father—note the sly expression on her face—Alison is amassing an archive of MAD material extending back to the magazine's beginnings. One of the titles on offer in the advertisement she has open in front of her as she writes herself a check is Son of MAD, quite an early reprint first issued in 1959, and this sorts with Bechdel's own interview testimony (85.4, 86.1, figure 4.3). In her youth, she did in fact possess a number of early reprints dating back to the beginnings of MAD, when it was under the supervision of founder

BUT IN A WAY GATSBY'S PRISTINE BOOKS AND MY FATHER'S WORN ONES SIGNIFY THE SAME THING--THE PREFERENCE OF A FICTION TO REALITY.

IF FITZGERALD'S OWN LIFE HADN'T TURNED FROM FAIRY TALE TO TRAGEDY, WOULD HIS STORIES OF DISENCHANTMENT HAVE RESONATED SO DEEPLY WITH MY FATHER?

Zelda, Scott and Scottie on the Riviera, 1924

GATSBY IN THE POOL. ZELDA IN THE ASYLUM. SCOTT IN HOLLYWOOD, AN ALCOHOLIC, DYING OF A HEART ATTACK AT FORTY-FOUR.

STRUCK BY THE COINCIDENCE, I COUNTED OUT THEIR LIFESPANS. THE SAME NUMBER OF MONTHS, THE SAME NUMBER OF WEEKS...BUT FITZGERALD LIVED THREE DAYS LONGER.

4.2. *Alison Bechdel, page 85 of* Fun Home, *2006.*

FOR A WILD MOMENT I ENTERTAINED THE IDEA THAT MY FATHER HAD TIMED HIS DEATH WITH THIS IN MIND, AS SOME SORT OF DERANGED TRIBUTE.

BUT THAT WOULD ONLY CONFIRM THAT HIS DEATH WAS NOT MY FAULT. THAT, IN FACT, IT HAD NOTHING TO DO WITH ME AT ALL.

AND I'M RELUCTANT TO LET GO OF THAT LAST, TENUOUS BOND.

4.3. *Alison Bechdel, page 86 of* Fun Home, *2006.*

Harvey Kurtzman ("An Interview" 1012). Thus, Bechdel provides a precise record of how, as a child, she built a library of her own, one that her father would scarcely have found worthwhile, but that, as a future comics creator, was crucial for her development.

Even without her acknowledging that reading early MAD comics was "such a big influence it's invisible to [her]," it is glaringly obvious that this period of MAD was formative for Bechdel, because her compositional habits are decisively influenced by it ("An Interview" 1012). In *Fun Home*, as in *Dykes to Watch Out For*, Bechdel often tends toward crowded panels embellished with engaging, witty gags that enhance her work thematically rather than narratively, pulling at the eye and creating alternate vectors of reading and interpretation. This kind of embellishment was a favorite practice of early MAD illustrators, but particularly of Will Elder, whose mastery of what he called the "sub-gag" was unparalleled ("Damn You" 92). As Art Spiegelman points out in a recent interview, it was Elder who dubbed this cartooning practice "chicken fat," a term Spiegelman glosses as "that ladling onto an image all those extra images that slow it down. So you have to give the picture a lot of time. . . . [B]asically what MAD insisted on was that . . . you would have to re-enter deeply and decode all of the little background stuff." Yet Spiegelman also claims that chicken fat is "the guilty pleasure . . . the thing that will cause cardiac arrest eventually." Proceeding to read a single MAD cover in exhaustive detail, Spiegelman identifies this style both as that which prompts interpretation, making comics reading a dense and "literary" activity, and as that which offers "guilty pleasure" by way of an embarrassing surplus of visual enjoyment. Not surprisingly, Spiegelman then segues into a critique of the term "graphic novel" as "one of the euphemisms that people have used to say that comics are not a guilty pleasure" ("Public Conversation" 22–24). In place of this "euphemism," Spiegelman offers chicken fat as central to comics reading, and as akin to what I call autoclasm; it makes the reading of comics both richer in hermeneutic possibility and more heavily weighted with libidinous shame.

If we keep the importance of chicken fat in mind, the scene in Bruce's library invites even closer medium-specific reading than I have thus far provided. The text boxes that accompany the sequence are unconnected to the details I have been examining; they concern not Bechdel's development as a comics creator, but her sense of connection to her father on the basis of their sexuality. Noting potential parallels between Fitzgerald's death and Bruce's, and wondering whether her father timed his suicide to match Fitzgerald's, Bechdel observes that she is hesitant to face the possibility that Bruce's death "had nothing to do with [her] at all" (86.1). While the idea that her coming out caused Bruce's suicide might understandably prompt a sense of guilt, Bechdel insists: "I'm reluctant to let go of that last, tenuous bond." Just below this declaration is the final panel of the chapter: a carefully composed exterior view of the library, young Alison framed in one window as she writes herself a check for comics, Bruce framed in the other as he reads Nancy Milford's 1970 biography of Zelda Fitzgerald (86.2, figure 4.3). Taken together, the verbal and visual elements emphasize that at the level of their reading lives, father and daughter have already separated; the "bond" Bechdel might feel at the level of sexual identity, she suggests, has no exact corollary at the level of their disparate cultures of reading. Thus, at one level of interpretation, Alison's acquisition of *MAD* is a useless addition to a scene that most directly concerns queer identity. At another level, the real subject of the scene is the artistic genesis of Bechdel the comics creator and her need to establish for herself a lineage outside what was enshrined in her father's library. The multivalence of *Fun Home* is manifest at every point, and its constant gestures of expansion and qualification allow for myriad hermeneutic tracks. Yet because multiple readings are made possible by Bechdel's careful spatial arrangement of word and image, and by her elaborate panel compositions, it is fair to say that *Fun Home*'s medium-specific qualities, far more than its literary references, generate its multivalence. Its richness is inseparable from its compositional complexity—which is to say, Bechdel's penchant for chicken fat.

Thus, both the *Haunt of Fear* scene from Bruce's days in the military and the *MAD* scene in Bruce's library are autoclastic. In the former scene, Bechdel assembles a complex set of literary and biographical allusions in order to frame Bruce's self-education in heteronormativity, even as, through seemingly incidental embellishment—in the form of a comic book—she suggests that all such assemblages are imprisoning fictions. In the latter scene, the self-opposition is even more energetic. As a child, Alison appropriates economic capital acquired by her father, an amateur scholar and high school English teacher, to build a library that is very different from his. This appropriation is both validated, because readers hold one of its products in their hands, and invalidated, because this particular product seems constantly obliged to pay back its original debt in the form of literary references. And even as these references constitute the cultural capital that has, as Bechdel herself apparently anticipated, helped to bring *Fun Home* mainstream respectability, the book only exists because young Alison broke from her father's literary values in order to become a cartoonist.

A reading of *Fun Home* that places it in the tradition of literary modernism obviously runs the risk of undervaluing these kinds of complexities. And even when it is acknowledged that *Fun Home* contains a "fierce critique" of high-literary cultural attitudes, there can be a tendency to ignore the comics-specific nature of this critique by claiming that in the text itself, "the graphic novelist is presented primarily as a reader and writer and only to a lesser extent as a graphic artist" (Baetens 205). This formulation is troubling at a very basic level—it is not clear to me how a cartoonist can present herself as other than a cartoonist—and it misses the ways Bechdel addresses not only the problem of her own creative origins, but also the question of how her work might be received in a culture that has had to redesignate a subset of comics by the term "graphic novel" in order to make adult comics reading respectable.[8] *Fun Home* has entered the contemporary canon of comics that matter, at least in part because of Bechdel's impressive engagement with the literary canon as such. Yet the images of the differend that governs this engagement—unmistakable once they have been noticed—demonstrate just how fraught the stakes of such canonization remain. *Fun Home* successfully generates its own "literary" reception, and yet it expresses a strong critique of such reception that troubles any attempt to annex the work from the medium of comics or from its troubled history.

The Haunt of Fear and *MAD* were both EC publications, and while the code decimated horror comics, using provisions that seemed deliberately crafted to eliminate EC's titles, in particular, *MAD* survived the 1950s and is still published as of this writing.[9] Bechdel's affirmation of *MAD* in the pages of *Fun Home* acknowledges a major influence on the creator's style and sensibility. More broadly, Bechdel affirms what Chute calls "a register of exhilaration: the exhilaration of cartooning as a practice of embodiment that runs counter to death." In expounding this register of the text, Chute focuses on a pictographic circumflex mark, a sort of "inverted V" that is "already a form of protocomics." Bechdel created this mark as a child, and in *Fun Home* its appearances affirm her creative vitality. Chute shows how Bechdel deploys this device in two carefully composed panels, one situated below the other, on page 148; the self-invented circumflex is positioned so as to counter the image of a child's corpse that Bruce, in his sideline as an undertaker, displayed to his daughter: "The contrast of the dead body (a possible dead self, tended to by her father) with the energetic bodily marks of the inscribing body below points up the animated corporeality of writing and drawing" (*Graphic Women* 193). This page appears two chapters after the comics-centered pages I have been expounding. With Chute's reading of the circumflex in mind, we can turn again to the final panel of the scene in Bruce's library and notice how it forecasts Bechdel's celebration of the power of cartooning later in the text. If the reader flips back and forth between pages 86 and 148, staying focused on the bottom half of each page, the relationship of the panels in question is clear. On page 86, the panel's tight framing of father and daughter in two separate windows resembles the "inverted V" images that are to follow, so that the panel both materializes and symbolizes Bechdel's capacity to differentiate her own cultural trajectory from Bruce's. Here the precise distribution of pictorial images on the space of the page, crucial to the tightly designed panels of Bechdel's adult work, echoes childhood attempts at pictographic expression. Displaying artistic allegiances very different from her father's, Bechdel uses one of her earliest, crudest pictorial and design innovations to carve out space for her own creative lineage.

What I have just termed the "precise distribution of pictorial images on the space of the page" is scarcely unique to Bechdel's work; indeed, the notion of "spatio-topia"—places co-present in the same space—is fundamental to any comics page, as Thierry Groensteen has demonstrated.[10] But the meticulous care Bechdel takes with such placement, and particularly, as Chute has indicated, the attention to bodies, is highly distinctive and, again, deeply indebted to *MAD*. To understand this debt fully, we must consider the work of Charles Addams, the only cartoonist (other than Bechdel herself) mentioned by name in the pages of *Fun Home*. As a celebrated gag cartoonist, usually creating single panels with or without captions, Addams inhabited a cultural space different from *MAD*; his work appeared regularly in *The New Yorker* and had a kind of middlebrow appeal that perhaps explains why "a book of Addams cartoons" was available to Alison as a child in her parents' house (34.2). Addams is best known for cartoons of the Addams Family, a ghoulish domestic unit whose antics held up a macabre mirror to the respectable bourgeois world, and for the television show that followed, over which Addams had creative control. As a child living in a house not only associated with death by virtue of the work Bruce did as an undertaker, but also stifled by his obsession with surface and his need for control, Bechdel might well have found solace in Addams's satirical approach to middle-class life. Yet she tells us that she first perused the book "long before [she] could read," and that at this point she "began confusing [the Bechdels] with the Addams family. . . . [T]he captions eluded [her], as did the ironic reversal of suburban conformity." In Addams's cartoons, she simply saw "the familiar dark, lofty ceilings, peeling wallpaper, and menacing horsehair furnishings of [her] own home" (34.2–3).

This naïve reading of Addams's work, obviously different from the adult creator's understanding, explains young Alison's focus on "one occult and wordless cartoon" in which "a worried girl had a string running from her mouth to a trap door"; Bechdel insists that she associated this girl with herself, and compares the cartoon to a rather cadaverous childhood photograph (34.3–35.3, figure 4.4). Reading this Addamsesque take on home dentistry as young Alison must have read it, we easily intuit that it is a picture of cunningly designed parental cruelty. The physical pain the child must feel when the trapdoor is opened will, presumably, be doubled by the terror of whatever will leap out at her, and this experience is amplified in advance by the terror of anticipation. The child's stillness is part of this scenario of domestic torture, and in the context of *Fun Home*, it clearly recalls the book's opening pages, which underscore Bruce's physical and psychological abuse of his children. Watching the child in the cartoon as she sits immobile, surrounded by a décor that does in fact resemble the interiors of the Bechdel home, we may recall one of the first chapter's most devastating one-line critiques of Bruce, that he "treated his furniture like children, and his children like furniture"; the accompanying panel shows Bruce staring into a mirror Alison is grasping as he tells her, "Don't move" (3.3). Young Alison's focus on Addams's image of a trapped body, tensed with anticipation of suffering to come, expresses perfectly the powerlessness Bechdel felt as a child.

A more "adult" reading of the cartoon would understand the child to be enjoying her terror in typically Addamsesque fashion. Bechdel the creator suggests such a gloss when she notes creepy details of family life—her mother jokes that she is a vampire, her father must get rid of bats that fly into the house—and then observes that she and her siblings began to take a "cavalier attitude" toward "the family business." This observation is accompanied by two hilariously chilling panels that pay direct tribute to Addams while giving adult agency to children. In the first, we see Alison and her brother Christian in a cemetery, pretending to be corpses while their younger brother, John, looks on; in the second, John observes a grave being dug and asks the man digging it, "Can I get in?" (35.6–7, figure 4.4). Here, the children attempt to pose themselves, flouting death by assuming its attitudes at will. In their deliberate contrast to

...A WORRIED GIRL HAD A STRING RUNNING FROM HER MOUTH TO A TRAP DOOR.

THE LAMP NEXT TO HER LOOKED JUST LIKE MY LAMP. IN FACT, THE GIRL LOOKED JUST LIKE ME.

THE RESEMBLANCE IN MY FIRST-GRADE SCHOOL PHOTO IS EERIE.

WEARING A BLACK VELVET DRESS MY FATHER HAD WRESTLED ME INTO, I APPEAR TO BE IN MOURNING.

MY MOTHER, WITH HER LUXURIANT BLACK HAIR AND PALE SKIN, BORE A MORE THAN PASSING LIKENESS TO MORTICIA.

MOM, HOW COME YOU NEVER GO OUTSIDE?

I TOLD YOU, I'M A VAMPIRE.

AND ON WARM SUMMER NIGHTS, IT WAS NOT UNUSUAL FOR A BAT TO SWOOP THROUGH OUR LIVING ROOM.

BUT WHAT GAVE THE COMPARISON REAL WEIGHT WAS THE FAMILY BUSINESS...

...AND THE CAVALIER ATTITUDE WHICH, INEVITABLY, WE CAME TO TAKE TOWARD IT.

CAN I GET IN?

4.4. *Alison Bechdel, page 35 of* Fun Home, *2006.*

the bodily restriction of the Addams cartoon, these panels indicate one of Bechdel's overarching strategies in *Fun Home*: the assertion of creative power through poses.

Bechdel has long relied on photographic reference for her figure drawing. Using a digital camera and, if needed, various costumes and props, she poses herself in the attitudes she wants to render. Photoreference is a familiar technique in comics production, but Bechdel's constant use of herself as model, regardless of which figures she is drawing, is crucial; as with other aspects of *Fun Home*, such as the handdrawn documents, there is an insistence on embodying every phase of comics production, as Chute has noted (*Graphic Women* 200). Yet if Bechdel's body is the creative channel through which her images must pass at various stages of production, the act of figure drawing, once the raw materials (in this case, digital photos) have been created, also suggests a kind of meta-physicality, something akin to puppetry in its control over bodily articulation. Given the way such control allows for precise framing and careful co-articulation of figures and embellishments, it can also be seen as an extension of the *MAD* tradition, a highly refined and deeply corporeal variety of chicken fat. The Addams style of humor, with its morbid imitation of upper-crust social posturing, is folded into a larger project in which Bechdel revisits the scenes of restrictive artificiality in which she spent her childhood and animates them anew.

In a discussion of a scene from the second chapter of *Fun Home*, Chute notes how Bechdel "animates [Bruce], in the book, through her own physical, haptic acts of bearing witness to his life and death" (*Graphic Women* 197). In the book's opening sequence, the "animation" Chute describes is joined to Bechdel's concern with cultural and bodily restriction. The opening page of the first chapter shows Alison persuading her father to play "airplane" (3, figure 4.5). In the initial panel, she is literally posing her father, moving one of his legs into position. The panel is tightly framed; not all of Alison's body is visible, and we are aware that the father could easily push his child out of the frame. At the same time, Bruce's head is not fully visible either, and there is a sense that it has only come up off of the floor and into visibility within the frame because Alison has drawn her father's attention. Moments earlier, Bruce must have been lying on his back in the private act of reading. Young Alison intrudes bodily upon this moment and turns it into a different scenario of pleasure, and the adult creator capitalizes on the moment as a founding gesture for her project.

This physical animation of the prone patriarchal figure is both a

LIKE MANY FATHERS, MINE COULD OCCASIONALLY BE PREVAILED ON FOR A SPOT OF "AIRPLANE."

AS HE LAUNCHED ME, MY FULL WEIGHT WOULD FALL ON THE PIVOT POINT BETWEEN HIS FEET AND MY STOMACH.

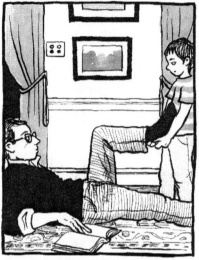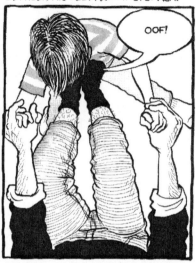

IT WAS A DISCOMFORT WELL WORTH THE RARE PHYSICAL CONTACT, AND CERTAINLY WORTH THE MOMENT OF PERFECT BALANCE WHEN I SOARED ABOVE HIM.

4.5. *Alison Bechdel, page 3 of* Fun Home, *2006.*

symbolic and a material resurrection; from the first panel of the narrative, Bechdel announces herself as bringing her father back to life, on her terms and for her own self-expression. The painful restriction of her childhood existence is answered by a return to the scene of confinement, but with a new control of its material and bodily aspects, as well as its narrative and literary elements. The scene of "airplane" ends, as all such scenes must, with the child's coming back down to earth. "Again!," the young Alison demands, but Bruce refuses, and commands his daughter to help him with cleaning and home repairs (4.2–3). Yet the adult Bechdel has the last word, using classical allusion to foreshadow her father's Icarian fall—which she amplifies by outing Bruce to the world in *Fun Home*—while demonstrating, through the precision of the way she frames and poses her father's body, the material and corporeal nature of her narrative control (4.2).

The book Bruce is reading when his daughter seizes upon his body is *Anna Karenina*, a classic on par with *Ulysses* in terms of its cultural centrality; literary reading is interrupted by another kind whose status is more unstable, to say the least (3.3, figure 4.5). Grasping this as a founding moment for the text as a whole, we can more easily see how *Fun Home* can function as a meditation on the fraught relationship between literary reading and cultural bookishness. Focusing on the latter, we note that myriad books are strewn about the space of the page, as they must have been in the rooms of Alison's youth; dozens of individual titles are visible, along with even more books whose titles are not shown, but which are nonetheless materially present as a sign of culture. Bechdel turns what she sarcastically terms her father's suffocating "still life with children" into a lively theater of poses decorated with books, transforming the latter into chicken fat even when they also serve larger framing roles (13.). While *The Great Gatsby* is a central reference for our understanding of Bruce's attempts at heteronormative respectability, and *Ulysses* becomes a founding expression of "erotic truth," both texts also take their place among many other book-images, pictorial flourishes distributed throughout *Fun Home*. At one level, the thematics and narrative structure of the work owe some debts to canonical literature; at another level, the entire category of the literary is a decorative element in the text's spatio-topia. These levels are arranged in autoclastic fashion. No larger principle resolves the fact that even as the category of "literature" is valued for its structural usefulness and its contributions to the work's themes, it is also offered for rather more immediate consumption, presented at a glance for the pleasurability of its material presence and cultural frisson. Thus *Anna Karenina* is simultaneously taken up—not least, perhaps, for its powerful evocation of domestic misery—and put down, made bookish decoration for a scene that establishes Bechdel's physical and spatial control of her work.

In her most recent long-form work, *Are You My Mother?*, Bechdel seems to turn this control against itself while retaining the pleasure it enables. An account of her relationship with her mother and with various therapists whom she casts as surrogate parents, this memoir tells of frustrated creativity, blown deadlines, and fear of maternal disapproval. The book's energy seems to come from the intense self-thwarting Bechdel experienced while creating it, which she turns inward on the page in layer after layer of self-referentiality. Despite Bechdel's typically modernist interest in psychoanalysis, the work seems less aligned with figures like Joyce and Woolf (though Bechdel references the latter in the text) than with postmodern writing by John Barth or Raymond Federman. Such metafictional leanings (Bechdel cites her mother describing the text in draft as a "metabook") are best read in light of a comics-specific lineage of cultural struggle (285.4). Rather than representing a "literature of exhaustion," to use Barth's phrase, that arrives when narrative tropes seem used up and must be self-consciously repurposed, *Are You My Mother?* is best read as the record of a recently legitimated comics creator (now even more so, as Bechdel has recently won a MacArthur "Genius Grant") experiencing creative difficulty from a newly privileged position. The tense, anxious emotional state of the narrator seems at odds with the measured and relaxed pace of the narrative, resulting in a work that paradoxically feels like a meditation on the luxury of writer's block. *Are You My Mother?* thus reminds us of what makes *Fun Home*'s creative ambition so paradoxical: it turns categories of cultural achievement into sites of pleasure.

The more clearly we see Bechdel's autoclastic practices, the less sustainable an overtly literary reading of her work becomes. In discussion of her comics, she has made clear that, like many other contemporary creators, she understands the necessity of compromise when it comes to presenting and discussing her work. While noting that "graphic memoir" is the most accurate term for describing *Fun Home*, she "refer[s] to it as a graphic novel half the time, because that's the convention" ("Life Drawing" 49). This kind of conscious compromise differs from the critical equivocations regarding *Fun Home*'s status. The sheer quantity of literary reference in *Fun Home* has been difficult for some critics to understand in terms other than those of the *Bildungsroman* discourse. But this is a case where little is gained by the urge to invent new categories or to trouble existing ones, as if a radically multivalent comic were perforce something other than itself. The more challenging path is to proceed to read this comic as a comic, and thus to see how and why it speaks of the medium's history and its cultural struggles. The soldier reading *The Haunt of Fear* behind Bruce Bechdel never says a word, nor does the text speak, in words, on his behalf. Yet, from his silent, occluded position, this reader troubles the body of literature in a way that is no less decisive for being strictly visual. It was, admittedly, the literary glamour of *Fun Home* that first drew many of its vocal supporters, or at least gave them leave to voice their support. To embrace the work as a comic, however, is to understand this glamour as merely one—and perhaps not the most compelling—of its distinct, often conflicted pleasures.

FIVE

Rolling in the Gutter

CHARLES BURNS

O f all the case studies I am considering, Charles Burns has received the least public notice. A key figure among creators who came to prominence after the emergence of the graphic novel, he has long been respected in the world of comics. Yet until his series *Black Hole* was published as a single volume, in 2005, he was little known in mainstream culture, and scholarship on his work is still sparse. The acclaim garnered by *Black Hole* has granted Burns a measure of fame, a fact that, as we will see, seems to have influenced his subsequent work. But Burns's vision remains tied to the cultural condition of comics in ways that demand a special degree of medium-specific attention. First published in regional free newspapers and in underground comics magazines (notably Art Spiegelman and Françoise Mouly's *RAW*), Burns quickly honed a distinctive vision free from any editorial or other controls, and even his commercial illustrations, key to the economic survival of many an independent comics artist, can instantly be identified. Though he has occasionally appeared in the world of the fine arts gallery, Burns has long been committed to comics as his primary medium, and while his work has been enthusiastically received in Europe, he is well aware of the cultural vulnerability and troubled history of comics in the United States.[1]

This history is, notably, a part of his creative experience; more than once, Burns's strips have been removed from newspapers because of reader outrage.[2] And as is the case with Miller and Bechdel, Burns's deliberate embrace of a troubled and marginalized medium results in a vision characterized by tension and self-opposition. Acknowledging comics as mass-produced pulp, Burns has used the "low" cultural vocabulary of precode crime, romance and horror comics in the service of a distinctive vision that meditates constantly on their cultural and political status. The ways in which Burns grasps and represents the condition of comics will require both a deep look into questions of style and a broad consideration of the social and political potentials of comics. In some ways the narrowest of the creators I am examining, Burns is also perhaps the most powerfully emblematic, as nearly every aspect of his work, from his subject matter to his shading technique, evokes some aspect of comics' cultural status.

I have observed that what Paul Lopes terms the "alternative story" of legitimation internal to comics culture in recent decades—in which comics creators, publishers and readers have found new ways to value and respect the medium—is different from the fate of comics in culture as a whole. Burns's attitudes toward matters of culture and audience reflect a clear understanding of this difference as well as of the challenges awaiting the ambitious comics creator. Too aware of the medium's status to hope for straightforward upward mobility, he has thought in terms of trade-offs: access to a wider readership could well mean a sharp confrontation with the stigma attached to comics in mainstream culture. Burns has been willing, even eager, to hazard this confrontation; in an interview given in 1992, prior to the publication of the first issue of *Black Hole*, he discussed the attractions of getting his work into the venue of the free weekly newspaper:

> Anyone could pick it up. You don't have this comic community, this comic book store crowd. Not that I have any problem with that, it's just that these papers get out to casual observers, people who just pick something up and see your work for the first time. People who would never go into a comic book store. I remember walking in New York City and seeing my comic strip rolling in the gutter. It's not the precious commodity that you're faced with in a comics shop—not a collectible or a nice book. It's a throwaway. (Sullivan interview 63)

Burns sees clearly how comics are situated in different zones of culture. While taking care not to show contempt for the "comic book store crowd" devoted to material preservation, he insists he has no investment in the "nice book" as the ideal destination for his work. The fact that a small group of buyers is committed to comics as a medium does not change—nor is it seen as adequate compensation for—the fact that a considerable number of readers, including many who read free newspapers and magazines, "would never go into a comic book store."

What is on offer in such a store is a "precious commodity," a deliberately paradoxical phrase in this context. The value of collectible comics has nothing to do with the act of reading (turning the pages of a comic book immediately makes it less valuable). Burns testifies to his willingness to forgo this kind of value, along with the cachet of subcultural acceptance, for the sake of a larger audience. But access to this audience brings the risk of "rolling in the gutter," of being perceived as every bit as "throwaway" as the comic books of the pre-code era, when there was no established culture of collection. Outside the enclave of comics fandom and collection is a world that if not as harsh as the anti-comics environment of the 1950s, is still a place where the comic book is scarcely seen as "precious." Although Burns has gradually developed a different relationship with the "nice book," his work has kept faith with a persistent tension concerning material and cultural value. For Burns, in short, greater ambition is inseparable from a reckoning with the junk status of comics in culture at large.

This interest in the truly disposable publication format, that which winds up in the gutter rather than in the library or in a Mylar bag, is matched by Burns's investment in discredited comics genres, particularly crime and horror comics. "Teen Plague," a story featuring Tony "Big Baby" Delmonto, a child living in the 1950s, shows the protagonist reading a horror comic of the kind that fueled anti-comics sentiments leading up to the formation of the code. When he read comics in his youth, Burns was already aware of anti-comics stigma, though it was less severe in his own family than elsewhere:

> [My parents] weren't encouraging, but they weren't discouraging.
> I would be able to look at stuff that I wanted to, for the most part, and
> not have it thought of as trash that should be thrown out. I mean, I had
> friends who, if a comic book was in the house, it got thrown out. The
> backlash from the '50s was still present. And I remember my father
> kind of checking out what I was bringing home. But there wasn't really
> much that you could buy that was deviant. (54)

Burns subsequently became aware of "deviant" pre-code comics, and his own work evokes a keen sense of their satirical capacities. In "Teen Plague," the horror comic that Tony reads portrays teenagers whose bodies are invaded and destroyed by an alien life form. While Tony is mistaken in his attempts to compare what he reads directly with the world around him, the plot of his comic is a satirical version of what happens to Tony's teenaged babysitter, who is infected by the plague referenced in the story's title and subsequently pursued by the authorities. In Burns's work, a belief that real life and comic books resemble one another is less naïve than it might at first appear.

Burns is thus invested in the relationship of horror comics to social reality that was part of their appeal prior to the code. In David Hajdu's popular history *The Ten Cent Plague* (for which Burns provided the cover illustration), Hajdu argues for the genre's satirical power, claiming that the most famous horror comics, which were published by EC, trafficked in "intimate, domestic terror" that focused on what was amiss in ordinary life and suggested that "the true graveyard was the living room of the American home" (179). According to Hajdu, at a time when "mainstream culture glorified suburban domesticity as the modern American ideal . . . nothing else in the panels of EC comics . . . was so subversive as the idea that the Long Island Expressway emptied onto levels of Hell" (180).[3] Burns's early work is indeed littered with domestic hells, not least in the Big Baby story "Curse of the Molemen," in which grotesque monsters form the backdrop for an examination of domestic violence. Too often, it is assumed that when contemporary comics readers interact with their history—through collection, making and reading fanzines, or attending conventions—they are either indulging an immature nostalgia for their own lost childhoods or, at most, expressing the core values of a subculture and establishing canonical texts. The way Burns uses pre-code comics is neither nostalgic nor curatorial; he asserts the direct utility of horror comics, their power to speak meaningfully to the present moment.

Burns's sense of the usefulness of discredited comics genres has, from the first, been in tension with awareness of their political shortcomings. Burns has not negotiated this tension by prizing the best examples of a given genre; in fact, he has no interest in a comics canon. He has expressed appreciation for the work of great pre-code artists, in particular the most famous illustrators at EC, but he was not exposed to their work until fairly late in his creative development.[4] His deepest interest is in the most unpolished, inept and irredeemable examples of a given genre. In Burns's view, the latter express clearly what well-executed examples might conceal:

> There are certain truths that exist in genre fiction, even though it's full of stereotypes and two-dimensional characters. I like thinking about those. . . . They're appealing at a much cruder level; they're more un-

conscious. . . . And out of that unconsciousness, I always see a certain kind of truth. . . . In a film, if you've got a fifth-rate version of John Wayne . . . [h]e's not skilled enough to pull off the Hollywood showmanship, and some kind of truth seeps out. . . . Like the woman in a movie who always runs and stumbles as the monster's coming. I'm examining these stereotypes, these archetypes, and in a way they get revealed in the most clear-cut, naïve way in some of those bad movies. Because there's no pretension, there's no sophistication . . . just the most bare-boned version of these stereotypes. . . . It just makes you re-examine it. . . . I think there's truth in some of those stereotypes. We believe those things. We believe them subconsciously. . . . No one's going to buy into that stuff anymore. It's got to be re-examined. (*Comics Journal* interview 71–72)

Eschewing nostalgia (such as the common idea that low-grade films, novels or comics are attractive because their naïveté has some intrinsic charm), Burns is concerned with how clearly a certain "truth" can be uttered by different kinds of culture.

Obviously, Burns does not mean that stereotypes of feminine weakness in the genre of horror are accurate pictures of real women; rather, he sees the basest stereotypes as reflecting ideas that exert real power. Citing the film *Terminator 2* as an example, he discusses a tendency to cover up sexist ideologies by a kind of idealized overcompensation; the weak female character, unable to defend herself, is replaced by a muscular action heroine (*Comics Journal* interview 72). In Burns's view, such gestures seem to sweep away older stereotypes, but they do not fully supplant them, in part because they do not confront them clearly. As the remarks above imply, culture in general manages to overlook ongoing sexism by taking comfort in the fact that "no one's going to buy into" the worst, most obvious manifestations of a given stereotype. Burns, by contrast, insists that persistent stereotypes have to be made newly visible, without adornment or correction, so that they can be critically "re-examined."

The need to reproduce stereotypes in all their crudeness is not, for Burns, a matter of exact repetition, or even imitation: "I don't want to do my version of an EC story, even though I've come close at times. I don't have that admiration for trying to recreate some traditional story" (*Comics Journal* interview 64). He seems to feel almost nothing of the citational urge that dominates postmodern cultural production (one thinks of the superbly executed passages of genre filmmaking in the cinema of

Tarantino, with his respect for trope as tradition). In fact, Burns has refused to inhabit the stereotypes of a given genre if doing so would run
counter to his own aims, even in cases of work for hire. In the early 1980s,
when Art Spiegelman was doing occasional work for *Playboy*, he passed
an opportunity along to Burns, who found himself unable to strike the
proper tone:

> I just never could get it. Art was trying to help me: "You've just gotta
> think about what Hugh [Hefner] would like." And I never could fig-
> ure out what Hugh would like. . . . I had a strip called "I Married a
> Maniac," about some woman who's chained to the bedpost, and she's
> washing dishes. Their response was, "Uh, Charles, you're not quite get-
> ting it. The guys who're reading *Playboy* don't want to think of them-
> selves as sexist pigs. They're not going to think that's too funny." (*Com-
> ics Journal* interview 58)

In place of the "soft" sexist stereotypes of the typical *Playboy* cartoon,
in which no harm comes to women despite their constant objectifica-
tion, Burns presented an unvarnished image of sexism—of literal domestic slavery—revealing the social reality that, in his view, *Playboy*'s cartoonists are paid to sugarcoat. Other cartoonists have spoken highly of
Hefner as an editor, praising his keen eye and ability to let artists play
to their own strengths, so when Burns claims he was unable to accede
to Hefner's wishes, he testifies to an especially strong aversion to artistic
compromise.[5]

As this anecdote shows, Burns seeks to dwell on familiar tropes, but
not to serve their usual ends. Also absent from his comics is any overt
sense of irony; Burns has rejected the notion of his work as camp.[6] Just as
his choice of the free newspaper as publication venue has carried the risk
of total disposability, so his decision to delineate cultural myths in their
crudest form, without explicit commentary or self-conscious charm, has
risked reader misunderstanding. Burns has been accused of indulging
the very stereotypes he seeks to expose, and he admits that such misread-
ings are unavoidable risks, given his decision to keep faith with stereotypes in their most illegitimate forms: "I don't think women are weak.
But I'm not trying to appease an audience" (*Comics Journal* interview
72). In his early work, Burns offers few, if any, alternatives to the stereotypes he presents; their reality is his central concern. Hence the ideological tension of Burns's early work: its satirical power derives both from
what can be said through genre stereotypes and what, simultaneously,

can be said about them. The tools of Burns's satire are, in other words, also its objects.

Although Burns is uninterested in evoking ideological realities through exact imitation, his visual style seems designed to foreground their incontrovertible givenness. Hence the unsettling familiarity he inscribes into his figures. His bland or timid women, overbearing or abusive men, and anxious teenagers all look as if one has seen them before, an effect arising from the extraordinarily accomplished, and at the same time weirdly mechanical, precision of his line. Interviewer Darcy Sullivan remarks to Burns: "Your artwork has an almost generic look of what people think comic book art would look like. . . . It's almost as if you're trying to deny your own presence in your work. When people see comics, a lot of them think that they're stamped out in a factory somewhere, and your work looks like it was." This seems like the kind of description with which an ambitious comics creator would immediately take issue, but Burns replies: "I can look at some of my earlier pieces, and the line is a little bit more fluid, showing my hand a bit more. And as I've gone on, I've been erasing any sign of my hand" (*Comics Journal* interview 77). Burns presents us with the paradoxical case of an artist whose signature style is an absence of style, a mastery of craft so emptied of the usual connotations of the term "craft," as applied to art made by hand, that it seems to be the work of machines.

Particularly important is the manner of shading, which Burns explains as follows: "In my earlier work I relied on shade patterns and cross-hatching to create a gray middle ground, but gradually I stripped it down to pure black and white" (*Believer* interview 61). In all of Burns's shading—regardless of how brightly or dimly lit a given scene is intended to be—the eye perceives a stark separation of ink from white space (even the crudest photocopy or scanning technology can reproduce one of Burns's figures accurately). Yet Burns achieves powerful dimensionality in his shading through the use of what he calls "this very thick-to-thin line that is the result of using a brush" (*Believer* interview 60). A careful examination of the shading in any figure—around a face, for example, or in the hair on a character's head—reveals examples, all uncannily precise in their execution, of this "thick-to-thin" line, a spine of sorts, extending into the white space around it. While the labor needed for these shading elements is immense (*Black Hole* was created over more than a decade, at the rate of about a page every two weeks), their final effect suggests the absence of a human laborer. This style is certainly in aid of a desire to render familiar stereotypes in paradigmatic form. Burns's figures convey a sense of maximum visibility, of an image fully revealed as it must be, without subjective perception or interpretation. Such images suggest, simultaneously, two incommensurable things: an illustrator with the patience of a classical academician training himself to delineate a stereotype, and the stereotype, as if of its own accord, mindlessly willing itself into visibility.

This style—if the term still applies—is strongly autoclastic. Most obviously, Burns's images evoke artisanal and mechanical production in a way that seems at once to emphasize and to obviate the distinction between them. These images project neither the legitimacy of the modernist auteur nor the strain of legitimacy that, as discussed at the end of chapter 3, is available to pop art and its descendants. Yet the most powerful aspect of Burns's autoclasm is the way his figures disrupt basic procedures of comics literacy. Even after one is able to discern how their effect is produced, Burns's figures seem charged with stasis, halting the eye, as it scans the page, to an unusual degree. This effect is achieved through a strong tension between the manner of shading and the overall manner of cartooning.

Leaving the shading aside for a moment, Burns's figures can best be described as strongly iconic (following McCloud's usage), though with a measure of the realistic.[7] Faces and bodies usually have perspectively accurate proportions and more or less photorealistic shapes, but steadiness and thickness of line, together with a slightly cookie-cutter regularity of feature, pull the overall effect toward the cartoonish. Using McCloud's pictorial vocabulary diagram as a guide, we would place the characters in *Black Hole* to the left of (that is, as being more realistic than) the work of Gilbert Hernandez, but to the right of (more iconic than) that of Hal Foster.[8] In other words, while tending toward the more realistic end of the spectrum, Burns nevertheless qualifies as a cartoonist in the classic sense (aside from the fact that his cartoons lack the manual traces typical of the work of most well-known creators). His command of proportion and feature is placed in the service of recognizability, and he makes his characters both distinct and quickly readable as narrative elements.

But this description is complicated by the shading. If we examine the way Burns gives dimensionality to, for example, the hair of his characters, we note how often the shading seems to float inside the lines that delineate the head, mostly or entirely detached from the rest of the image (*Black Hole* 104.1, figures 5.1 and 5.2; to the right of the original panel, a key shading element of one figure has been isolated and the rest of the panel erased).[9] If we allow our eye to be drawn to these shad-

5.1. *Charles Burns, page 104 panel 1 of* Black Hole, 1995–2004, *collected 2005.*

5.2. *Charles Burns, page 104 panel 1 of* Black Hole, 1995–2004, *collected 2005. Altered version with shading element isolated*

ing elements, they can strike us as expressive images in their own right. As such, they do not "look like" anything except themselves, and they sit firmly at what McCloud calls the picture plane, as expressive marks with no representational effect.[10] W. J. T. Mitchell describes such marks thus: "The expressive aspect of imagery may, of course, become such a predominant presence that the image becomes totally abstract and ornamental, representing neither figures nor space, but simply *presenting* its own material and formal elements" (*Iconology* 41).[11]

In the context of comics literacy as it normally functions, this kind of shading is profoundly disruptive. Whatever else is meant by "cartooning" in the classic sense of the term—the pictorial image at its most effectively iconic—it means the radical subordination of the parts to the whole. Looking at the work of the most respected and widely read cartoonists, such as Charles Schulz or Carl Barks, if we attempt to focus on specific details of a given figure (Charlie Brown's ears or Donald Duck's bill), our eye seems of its own accord to pull back to the figure as a whole and indivisible pictorial unit. Burns's shading does the reverse; it subordinates the whole to one of its parts, giving the shading its own compelling expressive sense quite different from its communicative or illustrative functions.

Insofar as the shading arrests the narrative flow, disrupting our engagement with the characters, we momentarily cease to see them as figures in a story and become acutely aware that they are assemblages of lines and spiky blobs. The more one looks at a Burns figure, the more disturbingly incoherent it seems to be. If we prompt ourselves to read on, the sense of incoherence fades, and we find our attention shifting and returning to the characters as characters and the narrative as a narrative, until—perhaps in the very next panel—we are halted again. Burns creates autoclasm through figures that prompt two incompatible kinds of visual scanning. Outside the comics of Charles Burns, these two kinds of scanning are quite differently positioned in US culture. Just as the standard developmental narrative of literacy discussed in chapter 1 is founded on the assumptions that cartoons are easily readable and that the pictorial is the place reading begins, subsequently giving way to print literature, so an investment in cartoonish pictorial styles is thought to give way to a sensitivity to the fine arts that, after modernism, prizes an interest in nonrepresentational images. Arguing that comics scholars ought "to see the graphic line" of the comics creator "in *narrative* terms," Jared Gardner observes that "art criticism remains, despite articulate challenges from within, largely grounded on the principles which two generations ago privileged abstract expressionism as 'pure art,' focusing on what was essential to visual art—marks on a flat surface" ("Storylines" 57, italics original). The difference between Burns's cartooning and his shading evokes quite precisely the difference between the narrative line and the expressive mark. In eliciting a complex reading approach that can appreciate both the directness of classic cartooning and disruption of that directness by nonrepresentational "marks on a flat surface," Burns's autoclastic iconography invites readers to leap back and forth over the gap separating so-called "early" artistic sensibility from its putatively "adult" counterpart.

This counterdevelopmental tactic sharpens our sense of the difference between two systems of artistic value. Unlike Lichtenstein, for instance, Burns does not attempt, by a change of context, to attach a new value to traditional cartooning.[12] Nor does he suggest that it is, despite cultural misconception, compatible with the fine arts. Examining his figures, we see an implicit rejection of E. H. Gombrich's well-intentioned mid-century claim that cartooning is a middle ground where high and low art can meet, a "fusion of humorous experiment and artistic search" where one might locate the root impulses that motivated both abstract expressionism and comic strip caricature (358). In fact, Burns's figures seem designed to highlight as much as possible the difference between the sequential reading of cartoon figuration and the static, frontal contemplation of expressive form. The representational and the expressive are co-present, but they are not blended; they reside in the same figures, yet each figure does not, even after repeated exposure, resolve itself into an integrated whole of the kind that is essential to traditional cartooning.

Burns thus designs his figures so that they remain other to themselves, damaging both the narrative value they might have if they were more traditionally effective as cartoons and the stylistic value they might have if their expressive elements were not being placed in the service of shading figures in comics. In opposing aesthetics to narrative, "Art" to iconic cartooning, and in forcing these oppositions to play out at length, Burns turns his figures into pictures of the differend that governs both the relationship of comics to the fine arts and—to turn to the matter most central to *Black Hole*—the way in which comics are situated in culture as a whole.

Black Hole is the most powerful work Burns has created to date. A twelve-issue series released between 1995 and 2004, its rapid legitimation after its publication as a graphic novel in 2005 testifies to the link between the *Bildungsroman* discourse and the book-length comic. Despite the move to a new format of self-enclosed single issues leading to a collected edition, *Black Hole* represents not a departure from the vision of comics Burns had from the first, but an intensification of that vision.[13] While characters in his early work were, in Burns's own words, "ciphers," rather than "real whole people," the teenage protagonists of *Black Hole* are much more individuated, and evince considerable psychological depth (*Comics Journal* interview 70–71). Yet Burns uses this depth not to overcome or leave behind his interest in generic stereotypes, but to emphasize even more strongly the dynamic tensions that are central to his work.

The story's four protagonists, two male and two female, all have specific personalities, desires and fears, and while they share a sameness of feature that is part of Burns's uncannily automated style of cartooning, readers can quickly differentiate them. The cartoon's power to strengthen our sense of attachment to a figure is intensified when placed in the service of an emotionally complex character (Schulz's Charlie Brown being an obvious example). The narrative investment that grows as readers follow the characters in *Black Hole*, however, only amplifies the unsettling effect of Burns's autoclastic style. More than with any of Burns's early works, we perceive how the experience of getting to know characters emotionally is also the experience of being alienated from them visually. At the same time, such an effect highlights the particular stereotypes of teenage alienation Burns explores in *Black Hole*. The characters feel strangely other to themselves, in a manner at once immediately familiar and perpetually disturbing, and this otherness is what they have in common, despite their different experiences. All four protagonists are, in one way or another, in crisis, but the notion of crisis itself is normalized and made to seem mechanically inevitable. Thus, Burns deploys his style in a narrative that simultaneously normalizes the stereotypes he wants to examine and underscores the destructiveness of the social "truths" they express.

The stereotypes Burns pursues in *Black Hole* are taken not from pre-code comics or the culture of the 1950s, but from broader notions and images of teenage angst. The social "truth" or reality he explores through these stereotypes is, not surprisingly, that of exclusion. What distinguishes *Black Hole* from countless other works on this topic, aimed at and/or about young adults, is the degree to which Burns is able to focus not on this or that form of exclusion, or on the particular social phenomena (race, class, gender, sexuality) that are often its basis, but on exclusion as such, regardless of the means by which it operates. Set in a white, middle-class, suburban environment in the 1970s (roughly the place and time in which Burns was a teenager), *Black Hole* follows its protagonists as they become infected by a disease, which seems specific to their age group, known simply as the Bug. Typically transmitted through sex, the disease causes various kinds of physical deformity, some more visible than others. If their symptoms are too obvious and grotesque, infected teenagers run away from their parents and friends and live in the woods near the suburbs in which the story takes place, hiding from the uninfected and struggling for food and shelter. Burns thus connects emotional isolation and shame, which is the portion of many a teenage outcast, to material disenfranchisement and permanent homelessness.

Black Hole portrays these experiences of exclusion without recourse to the devices that usually organize stories of disenfranchisement. Burns has noted that the story of the Bug has parallels with the AIDS crisis, but no particular emphasis is placed on this connection in the text.[14] Unlike most AIDS narratives—for which, as Susan Sontag pointed out in 1988, the way the illness is often contracted is crucial to its meaning—Burns's story is arranged so that sex, the specific mechanism of transmission, is not linked to the social significance of the Bug itself (though it is obviously relevant to the book's pervasive sexual imagery, which we will consider briefly).[15] Very little about the Bug, as a disease, seems significant, other than that its symptoms are visible and usually grotesque, and that being infected brings the threat of exclusion, regardless of how infection occurs.

Burns manages to portray the Bug in this way partly by avoiding or downplaying a host of standard tropes of contagious illness. Little space is given to themes of trust and betrayal, either personal or communal. *Black Hole*'s protagonists—Keith, Eliza, Chris (who is female) and Rob—are, as the story progresses, organized as two heterosexual couples, and within each couple the Bug is transmitted from one person to the other. Keith knows Eliza to be infected when he first has sex with her, while Chris is initially unaware of Rob's infection. In the latter case, there is a misunderstanding; Rob thinks Chris already knows he is infected, though she is not actually aware. Yet, after Chris contracts the Bug from Rob, she is distressed without feeling betrayed. Likewise, Keith seems to have no fear of contracting the Bug from Eliza despite the obvious nature of her symptoms, and he is neither more nor less drawn to her after his own symptoms manifest. Among the protagonists and minor characters alike, no pattern emerges in the ways the infected confront their fate. Some form semifunctional communities, others live alone, and still others manage to keep living as before, attempting as best they can to "pass" as normal (123.2). While Keith and Eliza stay apart for some time after their first sexual encounter, Chris and Rob rapidly become more intimate, and when Chris decides to flee to the woods, Rob, who is still passing, cares for her. These varied reactions emphasize the core experiences the infected must confront—stigmatization and exclusion—without limiting their meaning by tying it to questions of sexual shame or personal trust.

Likewise, Burns assigns no causal logic, moral or otherwise, to the choices *Black Hole*'s characters make as they deal with the Bug. Neither Rob's decision to continue living a normal life, despite the fact that his infection is known to at least some of his peers, nor Chris's decision to live in the woods, despite the fact that her symptoms are less remarkable than Rob's, is ever explained; Burns emphasizes the arbitrary nature of infection and exile. Also absent from the story is any logic of injustice or punishment. While the Bug is understood as a horrible misfortune, the infected do not ask "Why me?" And neither they nor anyone else suggests that their illness is deserved, regardless of circumstance or gender. Chris initiates unprotected sex with Rob, something for which she later castigates herself as "stupid," but she stops short of criticizing her actions as promiscuous or otherwise wrong (52.1–2). Burns provides only enough detail to make it plausible that the infected might choose to leave their homes; there are indications that they are usually shunned by their parents and most of their peers (192–195). Beyond these hints, however, *Black Hole* constructs no stable economy of meaning to which illnesses, as they are socially constructed, so often give rise.[16] In contrast to "Teen Plague," in which teenagers infected with a mysterious disease are apprehended by government agents, *Black Hole* shows no news reports, no school assemblies, and no institutional efforts to respond to the Bug. In the absence of any official descriptions, even condemnatory ones, carriers of the Bug face a stigma whose reality is certain, but whose boundaries are unfixed; the disease is at once distressingly amorphous and painfully personal. Each infected person knows herself or himself to be part of a larger phenomenon, but its mysteriousness seems only to increase both the individual distress the infected feel and the power of the stigma by which they are marked.

This sense of collective yet isolated suffering is underscored by the formatting choices Burns made for the graphic novel. When *Black Hole* was first released in single issues, each opened with two splashes on facing pages; on the left was a portrait in the style of a school photograph, and on the right was a picture of the same person manifesting symptoms of the Bug. When the twelve issues were collected as a graphic novel, these images were assembled together in the endpapers after the fashion of a high school yearbook, the "before" images at the front and the "after" images at the back. This reassemblage emphasizes the form of the distress the Bug inflicts in the story; the illness is happening on a large scale, yet each person who contracts it is confined to his or her own experience. Accompanying the portrait images in the original issues was a brief monologue, often related to the Bug, in some cases spoken by the teenager whose portrait we see. A few of these monologues hint at larger public discourse or institutional realities (in issue 2, there is a mention of the infected being "quarantined"); others are musings on the teenage experience in general; and the monologue featured in the final issue suggests that symptoms of the Bug may eventually go away of their own accord. When *Black Hole* was collected, none of these monologues were retained; as far as first-time readers of the graphic novel are aware, the infected are subject to no official institutional attention but nevertheless are potentially marked for life. In comparison to the original frame narratives, the assembled yearbook pictures constitute a schematic representation of suffering, at once general and segmented, that gives the meaning of the Bug a topical focus, but not a limit.

The most subtle, and perhaps also most powerful, creative choice Burns makes is to conflate bodily sensation and social stigma. Take the indelible image of Chris, who occasionally sloughs off her skin, pulling at her own face as another round of shedding begins (33.4, figure 5.3). Her expression and her cry are equally interpretable as signs of shame or of physical distress. Even when infected characters have symptoms that must certainly be painful to bear, they never say anything that indicates physical discomfort alone. We do see Keith in pain as he tries to remove his symptoms, which are growths on the right side of his ribcage; but after his attempt to cut them off is unsuccessful, he conceals them with an elastic bandage under his shirt (275.2–3). The perfunctory way Keith describes this as a daily ritual ("[doing] my whole thing with the Ace bandage"), together with the image of the ritual itself, clearly binds physical discomfort to social anxiety (263.2, figure 5.4).

Symptoms as they are experienced in isolation are not portrayed as

5.3. *Charles Burns, page 33 panel 4 of* Black Hole, *1995–2004, collected 2005.*

5.4. *Charles Burns, page 263 panel 1 of* Black Hole, *1995–2004, collected 2005.*

separate from either the experience or the threat of stigma, and characters who pass, such as Keith and Rob, are not seen by other infected characters as somehow more fortunate. They may have opportunities the more visibly infected do not (Keith is able to stay employed), but the struggle to conceal one's symptoms and the distress of being unable to do so are not differentiated. This neutral presentation of characters' fates corresponds to the offhand way Burns eventually reveals that the Bug can be contracted through any transfer of bodily fluids, not just through sex (291.1–3). The question of transmission is, as far as possible, divorced from the meaning of infection, even as infection's sensory and social aspects are made inextricable.

I have delineated *Black Hole*'s narrative tactics, paying close attention to what Burns does *not* do, to emphasize the distinctiveness of his project. To unfold its radical nature in full, we must dilate further, glancing momentarily at the long tradition of the *Bildungsroman*. As a coming-of-age fiction, *Black Hole* is a strong departure from the usual procedures of this literary genre. Scholarship has long emphasized that in telling the story of the development of an individual, the *Bildungsroman* reflects on the conditions surrounding him or her. If there is a common thread we can trace through the various manifestations of the genre, it is a diagnostic tendency, an urge to identify problems, either in society or in the individual, that interfere with development.

This tendency works itself out differently in various times and places. Early in the history of the *Bildungsroman*, as Franco Moretti argues, the predominant idea is that whatever stops the protagonist from developing is simply a youthful and unfortunate misperception of existing conditions; what is needed is a new way to phrase, and then to embrace, what is already common sense for fully developed citizens.[17] In the era of modernism, Gregory Castle explains, there is a more self-reflexive urge to critique institutionalized and ossified models of development. Protagonists of the modernist *Bildungsroman* forge alternate paths, both by inventing new models and by returning to classical ideals. And as the *Bildungsroman*, like the novel as a whole, has diversified during its global travels over the course of the past century, its diagnostic functions have become increasingly complex. Joseph Slaughter contends that in the postcolonial *Bildungsroman*, "the genre retains its historic social function as the predominant formal literary technology in which social outsiders narrate affirmative claims for inclusion in a regime of rights and responsibilities" (27).

The way in which this narration unfolds, however, is multifaceted.

The postcolonial *Bildungsroman* often critiques existing models of development and, more affirmatively, points to conditions that can be altered in order to allow human rights to advance:

> Contemporary postcolonial examples . . . register the discrepancy between an international human rights ideal and actual social practice. Therefore part of what these . . . Third World *Bildungsromane* make legible are some of the exclusions, disparities, and inequities enacted when the *Bildungsroman* is canonized as the compulsory genre for incorporation into an international human rights society of readers and when its idealist image of human sociality is taken as the necessary paradigm for human personality development. . . . Thus, we should recognize these novels not primarily as gauges of the triumph of human rights globally. . . . [W]hat they make legible in their depiction of the ruptures between the ideal and the real and in their registration of human rights claims is the current state of the human rights promise— the location where (and the condition in which) the "not yet" of human rights universalism now stands. (316)

If Slaughter is correct, the postcolonial *Bildungsroman* both testifies to the way human development is restricted by inequities in the current order of things and self-reflexively critiques problems in the standard narratives that claim to offer a way forward.

Whether we examine nineteenth-century models or contemporary ones, we see that while the ultimate ideals driving the *Bildungsroman* may be collective, even (putatively) universal, its diagnostic procedures are necessarily particular. There is no general, unfixed problem of exclusion as such, only specific instances with specific causes, which can or cannot be cured by specific means in this or that instance. Even in standard young adult classics in the United States, such as *The Outsiders* or *Catcher in the Rye*, what might initially appear to be an existential picture of exclusion as a part of the natural order of things turns out, upon closer examination, to articulate more specific causes, such as class division, inadequate nurture, or the stigma surrounding mental illness. If in its earliest and most optimistic phase the *Bildungsroman* offered what Moretti terms "the comfort of civilization," its long history reveals a lesser (though apparently quite durable and possibly more productive) consolation: that of diagnosis (16).

I do not offer this analysis of the *Bildungsroman* as a critique; in fact, I follow Slaughter's lead in affirming the ethical and political potential

of the genre, particularly its contributions to the growth, however uneven, of human rights. But the *Bildungsroman*, as it has long been written and read, cannot easily express the fact that some form of exclusion
or marginalization, regardless of its specific instantiations or justifica-
tions, seems to be one of the default certainties of modernity. In its drive
to particularize the problem, to subject it to diagnosis and consider possible cures, the *Bildungsroman* keeps faith with a notion (however fraught
or subject to critique and revision) of legitimacy. Under the rubric of this
genre, there are always particular *kinds* of inequity that make a given
state, or legal regime, or instantiation of human rights, less legitimate
than it could be if the inequities were removed.

In *Black Hole*, by contrast, various aspects of the Bug, from its mode
of transmission to its social effects, are presented not as manageable
causes but as ineradicable contingencies. Joining a discontinuous lineage whose most prominent twentieth-century representative is Franz
Kafka, Burns refuses to explain the problems he is attempting to confront. His diagnosis of social exclusion is that there is no diagnosis; exclusion is *given*, regardless of the specific causes that might serve as its alibi.
Thus, characters' fates are not distributed according to some identifiable
pattern; the forces of exclusion place and displace subjects without reference to their original social position (if some who were already marginalized are exiled to the woods, some "popular" individuals, such as Chris,
end up there as well). Further, while some infected characters exercise a
degree of resistance by passing or by clinging to their ordinary lives even
if they cannot pass, Burns does not equate agency with merit. Infected
teenagers do not mobilize or protest their conditions; indeed, in the absence of official discourse that spells out exactly why they must run away
from home and be shunned by their peers, there is no target for dissent.
These contingencies strengthen the forces of exclusion; those infected
with the Bug are victims of social effects that are experienced as onto-
logical because they have neither an identifiable cause nor a predictable
pattern.

Part of what makes the usual diagnostic procedures of the *Bildungsroman* feel ambitious, rather than limiting and reassuring, is some implicit claim to analytical depth. A coming-of-age story often seems to
take us past the surface features of a given conflict or frustration to its os-
tensible source. In pursuit of the problem of exclusion on a large scale,
Burns avoids depth; his lack of interest in causes prompts him to keep
faith with symptoms. And while this approach, like the precision of his
pictorial surfaces, might initially seem to give too much weight to style, it

enables a formidable ambition to critique developmental models of subjectivity. Insofar as *Black Hole* specifies any source to which we might
trace its characters' woes, that source is the idea of development itself. In
a 2008 interview about how he began to conceive of *Black Hole*, Burns
says: "I started . . . wanting to do a story about adolescence, thinking of
adolescence as this disease that some people get over, some people don't
get over" (*Anthem* interview n. pag.). To recast a key stage of human development, a stage now largely identified with the *Bildungsroman*, as the
progress of a disease is obviously to cast radical doubt on typical ideas of
maturation—and of the legitimacy it ratifies. Diseases develop and grow,
have stages and phases, but they do not mature. While those who survive an illness may sometimes believe their suffering provides experi-
ential gains, the illness they have survived is seen as destructive. What
the diseased/adolescent characters of *Black Hole* discover is not how to
find their place in society, but rather the harsh fact that growing up is
defined by—in fact, is more or less synonymous with—the threat of exclusion. Teenagers enter a society that places and displaces them arbi-
trarily; some people get excluded, some don't, some of the excluded recover from the experience, some don't, and beyond this there is little to
say that will not reduce the scope of the reality Burns is attempting to
picture.

Reading with the grain of Burns's broad, symptomatic approach to
the problem of development, perhaps I offer too generous a gloss to a
universalizing tendency that claims to see exclusion in terms of some
"human condition" but whose perspective is quite specific. Admittedly,
the tendency to think of suffering and exclusion as broad and undiffer-
entiated phenomena might be an effect of Burns's own position as white,
male and middle class. Burns himself has never claimed any universal stance, and he speaks bluntly about the specifics of his identity: "I
don't feel comfortable taking on other stereotypes. . . . I'm a middle-class
white" (*Comics Journal* interview 73). I suggest that the particular kind
of universalism (if that is the best descriptive) Burns practices is a matter
of his position as a comics artist, especially an artist interested in illegitimate comics genres. When a novelist writing a *Bildungsroman* turns to
issues of social exclusion, those issues can be differentiated and weighed
carefully and authoritatively, because the valuation is carried out in a legitimate literary discourse that has the power to discriminate among various conditions of justice and injustice. When a comics creator takes up
the very same issues of exclusion, they immediately assume more fluid

valences because they have something new in common: the illegitimate medium in which they are being represented.

If any figure shapes the problems of exclusion Burns takes up in *Black Hole*, it is comics as a censored and illegitimate medium. While the Bug is stripped of most of the associations with which a portrayal of an epidemic illness is usually freighted, Burns deliberately connects it to the genre of horror comics. The symptoms of the Bug are always grotesque, and they usually suggest one or more of the categories of bodily transformation that are key to the tradition of horror in general and to styles of pre-code examples of the genre in particular. Some bodies seem to be decomposing, such as the boy whose "after" yearbook picture shows that his lips are gone, leaving his teeth exposed; some are monstrous, like Rick, a social outcast whose symptoms make him look subhuman; and some are bestial and/or demonic, such as Eliza, whose symptom is a tail that, like a lizard's, grows back when it is broken off. The social exclusion and oppression of these individuals thus figures, at every appearance, the suppression of the genre from which Burns is drawing.

The parallel is especially strong in the character of Eliza, an artist whose work is suffused with grotesque images. Slightly older than the other infected characters, she lives in the basement of a house rented by some college-age men. During a party, they and some of their friends enter her room and proceed to mock and deface her art. When she fights back, they beat and rape her, and then write "ugly, nasty stuff" on her body (313.2). Eliza is thus identified with grotesque images, and is literally marked as if she herself were such an image, fit only to be degraded and violated (this conflation of gender and genre will require further attention). Again, Burns figures the physical experiences of infection and its social consequences as inextricable. By associating infection with the genre of horror, he further conjoins the corporeal to the discursive. Bodies physically and socially marked as other become synonymous with a comics genre in which such bodies often appear.

The most powerful and complex fusion of social content with genre and medium occurs in a passage where Chris first discovers that she has the Bug (136–137, figures 5.5 and 5.6). The realization unfolds as a two-page spread consisting of ten panels. They are arranged so that the panel divisions mirror each other; each page consists of four square panels atop a fifth rectangular one (the wavy panel borders, it should be noted, indicate a flashback). On the left-hand page, Chris is experiencing her first taste of the alienation the Bug produces. She discovers her symptoms

5.5. *Charles Burns, page 136 of* Black Hole, *1995–2004, collected 2005.*

5.6. *Charles Burns, page* 137 *of* Black Hole, *1995–2004, collected* 2005.

with the aid of two mirrors, seeing for the first time how she will henceforth appear to others. The mirrors enable Chris to realign her view of herself in accordance with the social stigma that awaits her (suggested by her friend Marci's horrified reaction), but this change is marked by occlusion and division. In the first two panels, the mirror Chris holds obscures part of her face, and in the third panel the framing suggests that even as she flinches at the sight of her symptoms, her new, visibly infected self is pushing aside her previous sense of identity. In the fifth panel, half her face is covered once more, as if she is no longer able to look at the reality of her situation, yet her defeated posture suggests resignation. The link between self-image and social reflection is now formed.

As he explores social and psychological experience in bodily terms, Burns connects Chris's experience to the material form of the comic book. The lines denoting the "loose tear" of skin "running up [Chris's] spine" in the second and third panels strongly resemble the panel borders that surround the image.[18] Chris's manual manipulation of her skin, together with the book-like associations evoked by "tear" and "spine," figure her body as a book and suggest that *Black Hole*, the printed object in which Chris appears, is a grotesque physical body that incarnates and partakes of the social exclusion it represents. At about the time he began work on *Black Hole*, Burns produced a self-portrait for the cover of *The Comics Journal* (figure 5.7). The image shows him in his studio, his body monstrously transformed, pen in hand, as he stands over his drawing table. The pen itself has a tube attached to it, like a tattoo gun, and on the table is not a sheet of paper but some sort of hide or skin, stretched flat with pins: a vivid image of comics creation as grotesque bodily signification.

The left-hand page of the spread we are examining in *Black Hole* establishes a link between persecuted body and illegitimate book. On the right-hand page, Chris comes to terms with her infection in a larger context as Burns explores the suppression of horror comics as a genre. The mirroring of panel layouts suggests that this spread as a whole will reward reading that does not simply move from left to right and top to bottom; and the right-hand page, in particular, opens up other reading vectors. If we examine the top four panels of this page, we can see a vertical separation of legitimate and excluded characters. The first panel focuses on Chris (still passing for the moment) and Marci as they consume fast food, and the second panel shifts the focus to the visibly infected teenagers nearby, who are eating what others have discarded. In the third and fourth panels, the same division is repeated and amplified; the visibly in-

5.7. *Charles Burns, detail from self-portrait for the cover of* The Comics Journal *issue 148, 1992.*

fected are outside the frame in the panel on the left, and the uninfected are not visible on the right. The infected male teenager whose face is in close-up in the fourth panel is especially grotesque. His misshapen skull, ragged teeth, maimed features and clawlike hand all strongly evoke pre-code horror, while the tight visual framing of his head in the panel underscores both the stigma his appearance bears and the isolation resulting from it.

Pre-code horror comics usually showed an uncanny or monstrous force breaking into and terrorizing the ordinary world, but in this scene the emphasis falls much differently. The infected pose no concrete threat; Marci simply remarks that they are "disgusting" and complains, "Why do they have to come here and ruin everybody's good time?" (137.2–4). Chris's interior monologue is more perceptive, contemplating "the awful reality" of social exclusion. Chris compares herself, "sitting there eating food [she isn't] hungry for," to the infected, who are "out there eating garbage" (137.3–4). This last line is positioned in a narrative box above the close-up of the infected male teenager, so that the phrase "out there" takes on a number of meanings, evoking the homeless state of many infected characters, their social exclusion, and also the visual isolation Burns creates through framing, panel divisions and page design. Here Burns makes clear both that the genre of horror is present in

Black Hole because of what it has the power to say about the cruelty of social norms and that the genre's history of marginalization is one of the things it must utter. The infected characters are subject to an implacable discourse of social marginalization, and at the same time they embody a suppressed comics genre.

Burns wants simultaneously to activate the satirical power of horror comics and to show how that power has been suppressed in culture at large. Note the economy of consumption evoked by the fast-food restaurant, Herfey's, that Burns invents. In an earlier scene, we see Chris drinking beer from a Herfey's cup. Printed on the cup is an image of "a big dumb cow ready for the slaughterhouse." Chris thinks, "What a weird logo for a drive-in. . . . [I]t's like he's saying . . . "—and there is a sudden switch from interior monologue surrounded by a narrative box to dialogue in a speech balloon—"'Eat me'" (38.3). The logo is an image of abjection, of an oppressed victim that seems to collude in its own victimization. The fact that Chris speaks the words "Eat me" aloud becomes a joke (her friends overhear and mock her), but it is a decidedly uneasy one, given that, after she is infected, Chris does in fact become a victim who accepts her status and moves to the woods. In the two-page spread showing Chris's first thoughts about her infection, Burns uses fast food as a way to trace the economy produced by the Bug. The uninfected purchase and eat Herfey's hamburgers, and the infected then salvage their discarded food from the trash and consume it; legitimate consumption is followed by illegitimate scavenging, which Marci calls "disgusting" (137.4). The infected are thus consumed by a normative gaze that fixes them as deserving victims, fully complicit in their consumption.

For a character like Marci, this dynamic keeps the normal world separate from its excluded others. But Burns wants us to notice that if eating recently discarded hamburgers is viewed as repulsive, the food in question is probably repulsive to begin with. Like the facing page, in which Chris discovers that she is infected, the right-hand page shows how unstable distinctions between normal and marginalized can be. Legitimate consumption and illegitimate consumption of Herfey's food mirror one another just as ordinary teenage social anxiety and the shame of infection do. The world of acceptable subjects suppresses this mirroring through displacement (it is the infected, not the normal, who are marked as repulsive), but on the right-hand page, such displacement is not wholly effective. While the ordinary world in the first and third panels manages to displace its discomfort to the infected in the second and fourth panels, both sets of panels lead to the fifth panel below them, in which Chris is positioned precisely between the two worlds (legitimate and illegitimate) as she thinks, "I was one of them. It just didn't show as much" (137.5). The economy of consumption Burns creates is unstable; that which is displaced onto the excluded flows back into the normal world. Yet, even as he shows how this system of persecution is unsustainable, Burns makes clear that it still works to create and enforce categories of exclusion. It possesses no final legitimacy, yet it effectively marks those with the Bug as illegitimate. The normal world is porous, constantly subject to infection, yet it manages to avoid any real reckoning with this fact. The mechanisms of displacement may be glaringly illegitimate, but they manage to displace this reality as well. Burns thus creates an autoclastic image that simultaneously activates the power of horror comics to critique normative social reality and demonstrates how fragile and prone to suppression such a critique is.

Key to this autoclastic approach to horror is *Black Hole*'s pervasive phallic and yonic imagery, with the latter as the dominant element. Instances of such imagery appear on almost every page, and sometimes every panel, so that the work seems constantly to offer itself as a series of openings, sexual and erotic in some cases, conceptual in others. In either case, they seem designed to evoke attraction and repulsion, vulnerability and aggression, melancholy and rage (as does the work's title). It would be possible to trace these openings in their connections to pornography, another despised pictorial genre in which Burns has some interest, but in the context of my discussion of horror, what stands out most vividly are the characters' mouths. Relative to the rest of a given character's face, a mouth drawn by Burns often seems mobile and expressive, and this allows for it to evoke and contain paradoxical affects. In the example I have been discussing at length, the mouth of the infected character at the garbage bin seems at once to be eating and spitting, the action of consumption visually reversible as disgusted, and disgusting, excretion. Moreover, the open mouth is readable as both a threat to the viewer—the menacing, jagged teeth, in particular—and a cry of pain, perhaps a protest against disenfranchisement (137.4). Each such autoclastic opening in *Black Hole* presents the characters and the book itself both as a threat, something that might swallow, tear or crush the social order, and as a vulnerable breach subject to violation.

Moments like the ones depicted on the two-page spread on which I have focused take their place within a larger narrative structure that does not privilege any particular outcome. Some characters, including Rob, are murdered by others who are infected. Chris is eventually trapped in an isolation from which—as the nonlinear arrangement of the book's chapters implies—she may never escape. Keith and Eliza leave their homes behind and seem to attain a kind of self-acceptance and intimacy that may allow them to heal; these are the characters who "get over" the "disease" of adolescence, to return to Burns's own phrasing (*Anthem* interview n. pag.). As with the novel's spectrum of social differentiation, so with these narrative destinies: none seems deserved or earned. While refusing diagnosis, Burns shows that the conditions his characters do, or do not, manage to survive represent no absolute "human condition"; it is evident that any given narrative thread could be otherwise, even when it is not always clear how. *Black Hole* thus achieves a complex critique of the question of legitimacy that operates, usually in obscurity, at the center of the *Bildungsroman* as a literary genre, and at the center of the *Bildungsroman* discourse in which comics have been entangled in recent decades. Counter to this discourse, Burns uses the precision and decisiveness of his craft to realize a powerfully unbounded vision of disenfranchisement. In *Black Hole*, the question of why some subjects, genres and media are or are not granted legitimacy—a question we prefer to approach in causal, diagnostic terms that allow us to speak of earning or deserving an improvement of status—expands beyond the limits of hegemonic notions of development. The distinctiveness of Burns's most ambitious work to date lies in its commitment to exposing the vertiginous depths of the problem of illegitimacy, which no upwardly mobile ambition can address in full.

Burns grounds his vision, self-reflexively, in a commitment to one of the most despised genres of comics, a choice that enables him to express the violence at work both in the disenfranchisement of human subjects and in the marginalization of "low" media. To make comics themselves the central figure of disenfranchisement is to connect disparate kinds of suffering in ways that might distort their significance. An obvious case in point is the aforementioned conflation of genre and gender. Burns associates the rape of Eliza with the defacement of her art, and this association arguably enacts its own kind of violence. However, distinctions among various kinds of injustice or inequity—for example, the separation of the category of creative effort, or medium, or literacy from that of gender, race, class, ethnicity or religion—are easiest to make when each already possesses its own kind of legitimacy. When Burns uses horror comics as a ruling figure for social persecution and other forms of violence, he asks where exactly the question of comics creation and literacy might reside in our understanding of such violence. The parallel that *Black Hole* establishes between the rape of Eliza and the destruction of her art calls out for a sharper sense of how these two (quite obviously different) kinds of harm might be articulated, whether separately or together.

Although such articulation is not provided in *Black Hole*, Burns's recent work has traced relations among various social and cultural categories more precisely. *Black Hole* was canonical in comics culture well before its completion—six of its twelve issues had been released when it was included in *The Comics Journal*'s 100 Best Comics of the Century— but Burns achieved much wider fame when the collected graphic novel was published in 2005.[19] The subsequent three-volume series released in the second decade of the new century, *X'ed Out* (2010), *The Hive* (2012), and *Sugar Skull* (2014), shows how Burns has reflected on his changed circumstances.

There is, as one would expect, little conviction that the essential condition of comics has altered, as well as an ongoing interest in representing these conditions on the page. Doug, the protagonist of the three volumes, is both a comics maker and a symbol for the medium's marginalization. However, while keeping faith with the condition of comics, Burns opens up a more nuanced consideration of how various social and cultural lines of force interact. Following Doug from his youthful creative struggles with artistic expression and with family and romantic relationships to his adult realization of his failings—not least as the father of a child he takes no part in raising—the three volumes move from a sympathetic examination of teenage angst to a frank indictment of what readers, and possibly Doug himself, realize has become a false sense of victimhood. While *Black Hole* speaks of, but also from within, the tradition of horror comics, the new series brings in a range of cultural expressions across the high/low divide and uses them to frame the relationship between Doug and his girlfriend, Linda, whom he abandons when she becomes pregnant. Authentic and inauthentic expression, early and late periods of artistic work, private and public visions of artistic value: these become the ground on which Doug's personal development can be staged and, ultimately, found wanting, and on which the protagonist's struggles as a comics artist can be distinguished from, and implicitly subordinated to, other aspects of his character. The fact that Doug is a struggling artist in the early part of the narrative seems far less important once we see his abandonment of Linda and his child. While not claiming his present position as indicative of his medium as a whole, Burns seems to have taken his newfound cultural authority into account, and thus limited the degree to which comics as a suppressed medium can stand for other kinds of injustice or marginalization.

It is tempting to say the new work is simply more mature than *Black Hole*. But this judgment would underestimate the paradoxes of legitimation that Burns now confronts from a new perspective. The danger of operating from a position of respectability is that it grants the authority to assign or withhold degrees of status, to establish overlaps or make distinctions among varieties of experience, kinds of injustice, or degrees of suffering, without much transparency in the way such differentiations are made. Legitimate discourses can easily generate the appearance, and the rhetoric, of careful adjudication. Yet, in so doing, they create the possibility of a differend, or of other limiting standards of value, in a way that *Black Hole*'s more obvious tactics of association do not. The association of Eliza's rape with comics is problematic, but it is certainly not hidden. By contrast, in the new series, it is not as easy to notice that the link Burns suggests between Doug's lack of growth as an artist, compared to Linda, and his abandonment of the child he fathers with her, is a false parallel, and does justice neither to questions of artistic development nor to those of parental responsibility. Throughout the three-volume series, we piece together an elaborate dream world that Doug constructs in order to hide from his obligations and distort the facts of his life. But this fantasy realm is not so easy to dismiss; it can also be read as the place where the radical energy of *Black Hole*, which merges all forms of violence and exclusion in the image-nexus of the comics page, is contained and disciplined.

Thus, Burns still confronts the ways in which the status of art can frame other kinds of social conflict, although when the art in question is legitimate, how this happens is more likely to be obscured by the hegemonic nature of the forces at work. The specific tactics that he uses to address the challenges of his new position lie beyond the scope of this study. In the context of my focus on *Black Hole*, what Burns's recent work highlights is that in the very act of taking up serious social concerns and addressing them with authority, legitimate culture all too easily learns to forget, on its own behalf, the paradoxes it remembers readily enough when confronting its less respected counterparts. Self-aware of all that is implied in problems of status to a degree that is unusual even among his generation of creators, Burns remains a signal example of the clarity with which comics creators have come to articulate not only the medium's subordinate cultural position, but also the tensions inherent in any system of cultural inequity.

SIX

Blood and Fire

GILBERT HERNANDEZ

As with the other creators examined in this study, Gilbert and Jaime Hernandez began their careers at the start of what is now understood as the era of the graphic novel. Despite the distortions that accompany this term, the moment of its emergence certainly opened new possibilities for ambitious comics creators. In 1981, the brothers self-published a single comic book entitled *Love and Rockets*, and the following year, Fantagraphics Press—which had begun to champion the legitimacy of comics a few years earlier through *The Comics Journal*—republished it with some new material added. This second release led to an ongoing series that lasted until 1996 and that featured the work of both Gilbert and Jaime in each issue, together with occasional contributions from Mario, their elder brother. Though *Love and Rockets* (hereafter *L&R*) would shortly be joined by other successful creator-run titles, such as Dan Clowes's *Eightball* and Peter Bagge's *Hate* (both also published by Fantagraphics), the Hernandez brothers were the first to take full advantage of a new model of production quite different from that of previous decades, and also different from the career beginnings of Miller, Bechdel and Burns. *The Dark Knight Returns* became possible for Miller only after he had proved himself through a kind of factory apprenticeship at Marvel, during which time he had no final say over the direction of the storylines he wrote, much less complete ownership of his work. Bechdel and Burns, by contrast, had wide creative latitude in their early years, but often lacked economically stable avenues of publication. Fantagraphics provided Gilbert and Jaime with steady distribution to many comics shops but imposed no editorial constraints; *L&R* belonged to the Hernandez brothers, and so long as it garnered an audience, it would continue to run.

The Hernandez brothers' single issues were routinely followed by graphic novel collections that, by the late 1980s, allowed for some distribution in bookstores as well as comics shops.[1] The fact that this particular combination of distribution options, a steady system of remuneration, and creative freedom only became possible for some creators in the late 1970s and early 1980s is a reminder of how different the history of comics has been from that of print literature.[2] Insofar as the Hernandezes themselves have sometimes struggled to maintain an audience large enough to allow them to make comics full-time, their story underscores the fact that the era of the graphic novel has been, at best, a period of very gradual change.

The challenges faced by comics creators are thrown into particularly sharp relief when we consider the work of Gilbert (in critical and fan discussions, each brother is usually referred to by his first name), whose reception over the years has been quite uneven. Although he has often been widely read in comics culture and is still attracting new readers now, some of his attempts at complex storytelling did not succeed with his audience upon first reading, and the variety and popularity of his most recent output was preceded by a number of failed experiments. Early in the publication of *L&R*, readers responded positively to his tales of Palomar, a fictional Latin American town populated with memorable characters and explored through a number of long-running narrative arcs. As these storylines became ever richer and more tangled, readers found them increasingly difficult, and in the later years of *L&R*, Gilbert struggled to keep his audience engaged. While paying some attention to the entire course of Gilbert's long career, I will focus on the fifty-issue run of *L&R*, and particularly on the Palomar stories, in which Gilbert has most fully expressed his vision of the cultural fate of comics.

What we see in *L&R* is that even before Gilbert had to struggle with uneven reception, and thus reexamine his creative strategies in order to keep attracting an audience, he already conceived of comics as an embattled medium. Rejecting the cultural demotion of comics as cheap, easily consumed commodities, he was nevertheless deeply skeptical of an optimistically progressive vision of comics as destined for legitimacy. He registered the violence done to his medium at the basic level of his pictorial vocabulary and, increasingly, in his larger thematic and narrative designs. His autoclastic tendencies emerged precisely with his earliest success, intensifying as his work grew in complexity, even before readers began to complain of its difficulty. In later stages of Gilbert's career, there have been further attempts to wrestle with a concern that was

central to, and highly visible in, the Palomar stories almost from the beginning—and that, as I have been arguing throughout this study, is a
birthright for many comics creators in the United States.

Gilbert's awareness of status concerns is particularly striking because it was not, by his own testimony, part of his earliest childhood perceptions of comics. From the viewpoint of a comics reader, the early
cultural experiences of the Hernandez brothers look nearly utopian. Gilbert has testified that his mother was an avid comics fan who retained
strong memories of the comic books she had read in the 1940s, memories that were all the more important because they were marked by
loss: "Our mom collected comic books . . . and it's the old story, her
mother—our grandmother—threw them out, so she didn't have any
left" ("Pleased" 63). Mario, who began collecting comics at age five,
has noted that "comics were everywhere [in their home]. You'd go to the
bathroom with comics, you'd eat dinner with comics. . . . You could get
away with something like that, just be reading all the time" ("Pleased"
63). Gilbert adds, "I imagine our mother let us read comics because she
[read them]. . . . [C]omics were always normal to us, it was an everyday
thing. It wasn't until school that we realized we were abnormal. . . . [I]
t didn't click with any of the other school kids" (63). Gilbert claims that
he had little sense of the cultural hierarchy that subordinates some media and narrative genres to others. He experienced the cinema to which
he was most attracted as a heterogeneous assortment of "strange movies with strange plots," watching monster films, noir films and European
arthouse cinema indiscriminately (Sobel interview 130). Gilbert's adult
career as a comics creator can be understood as a decades-long conflict
between this pluralistic sensibility, learned intuitively in childhood, and
the larger realities of cultural hegemony.

This conflict first becomes visible in Gilbert's approach to the fine
arts. I turn to *L&R*'s treatment of Frida Kahlo, whose status as the pre-
mier Mexican painter of the twentieth century was established by the
time Gilbert began his career in comics. Gilbert reveals his love for
Kahlo in the story "Frida," a twelve-page biography that is inspired—
as noted at the end of the story—by Hayden Herrera's 1983 study and by
a catalog accompanying a museum retrospective held in 1987, a year or
so before Gilbert's story was published.[3] As William Nericcio notes in a
close reading of several panels from this story, Gilbert situates Kahlo's
life against the background of a staggeringly diverse cultural tapestry. He
surrounds his titular figure with references to a wide-ranging spectrum
not only of visual art, from the expressionist canvases of Wassily Kandin-

sky to the cartoons of Chester Gould, but also of film, from low-grade, double-billed science fiction cinema to the surrealist works of Luis Buñuel. Noting the ways Gilbert weaves references to his chosen medium into the story, so that it is autobiographical as well as biographical, Nericcio argues that "Frida" represents a profound breaching of national and cultural barriers: "The borders dividing and defining Mexico and the United States as well as those no less real borders dividing high culture and popular culture cannot stop the surging of ink, the dance and coupling of photons as they bounce off canvases and comic book pages into the willing and willful eyes of readers and viewers" (204). It would be difficult to summon a more powerful affirmation of the democratic vision of culture projected in "Frida."

But whose vision is it? I do not think the heterogeneous array of culture present in "Frida" is something Gilbert claims for himself. Notably, the range of references appearing in this story is matched by the almost limitless variety of its pictorial vocabulary. A formidably gifted cartoonist often recognized as one of the greatest of his generation—even the masterful and demanding R. Crumb has bowed to the Hernandez brothers' genius in figure drawing—Gilbert tends not to deploy more than one or two styles at a time (though presently we will observe the way his autoclastic tendencies trouble our sense of how a given style functions).[4] His relatively realistic cartooning, used for the majority of his Palomar work, is generally kept separate from the livelier mix of hypericonic and hyperexpressive work in other stories less grounded in daily life. In terms of its pictorial vocabulary, "Frida" is easily the most diverse story Gilbert has ever produced, and there is a clear connection between its plurality of styles and its subject. This story presents not the world as it can ordinarily be accessed and expressed by a comics creator, but the world as it could be encompassed by a figure like Kahlo; Gilbert portrays her as an artistic, erotic and cultural adventurer who joined disparate artistic traditions as forcefully and confidently as she crossed national boundaries. "Frida" is a vision of the freedom the cartoonist wishes he could possess, but it is represented as the freedom of another, more firmly established artist. As with Bechdel's vision of cultural hierarchy, there is some oversimplification in Gilbert's vision. The style of "Frida" marks Kahlo as proleptically legitimate, somehow inspired from the first by an authoritative status that, in reality, she gradually attained toward the end of her life and career. Accurately or not, Gilbert imagines Kahlo's status as utterly different from his own.

Though "Frida" is understood to be a stand-alone story, it actually overlaps for a moment with the universe of Palomar. One panel reads: "[Frida] begins to drink too much and makes no effort to hide her bisexuality" (180.1, figure 6.1). This panel runs the vertical length of the page. At the top, just below the narrative box, Kahlo sits on a high wall and calls out to a woman walking below her who is carrying a basket on her head; a second woman atop the wall sits next to Kahlo and looks on. The woman below, wearing a confused expression, is Tonantzín Villaseñor, a resident of Palomar who, by this point in *L&R*, is a nearly universal object of desire for the men and women around her. Tonantzín's fate will be central to my later discussion of Gilbert's autoclastic strategies, but for the moment I note the lopsided nature of the exchange the creator imagines between himself and Kahlo. This moment is not intended to ground Palomar in actual history; Gilbert's timeline for his fictional town is more than precise enough to let us know that, in 1934, the date of this fictional encounter, Tonantzín was not yet born. This is an encounter between two artistic universes, which Gilbert stages so that his work is somewhat appreciated, but ultimately slighted. Gilbert presents Tonantzín as so attractive that Kahlo herself would instantly find her beguiling, but the panel stages the painter as controlling the encounter, hailing the object of her desire from an elevated position of leisure while the gaze of Tonantzín, a boundlessly generous and hardworking member of her community, is limited by the burden she bears. In the Palomar stories, Tonantzín, like almost all of Gilbert's characters, is both subject and object of the gaze; as we shall see, she is also an agent who acts on her own desires. Yet in this brief encounter, when Palomar crosses paths with the life of Kahlo, Tonantzín is merely a bemused prop.

This discomfiting moment foreshadows the strange role Kahlo's work plays in "Poison River," the longest and most complex of the Palomar story arcs—begun, perhaps not coincidentally, just after "Frida" (the latter was published in issue 28; "Poison River" ran in issues 29–40). This arc shows the early history of Luba, the character who is closest to being a central protagonist in the Palomar stories. Tracing her development from infancy to early adulthood, "Poison River" explores how Luba absorbs culture in her youth, and especially how she learns to read. Under the supervision of her cousin Ofelia, Luba reads comics featuring Pedro Pacotilla, a racist caricature modeled, in all likelihood, on the Mexican comic book character Memín Pinguín.[5] In the words of Gina, a progressive, leftist character, Pedro is "the good little black boy who's happy to be poor and uneducated," a disenfranchised victim who embraces his own disenfranchisement (36.1). A leftist herself, Ofelia agrees with Gina

6.1. *Gilbert Hernandez, page 180 panel 1 of "Frida," 1988, collected in* Love & Rockets Library *edition, 2008.*

6.2. *Gilbert Hernandez, page 37 panels 3–4 of "Poison River," 1989–1993, collected in* Love & Rockets Library *edition, 2007.*

when she suggests that Luba should be exposed to fine arts work, such as Kahlo's, as a corrective to Pedro comics. But Kahlo's work terrifies Luba, who continues to make progress in literacy with Pedro comics, despite their offensive content (37.3–4, figure 6.2). Here, as in some of the other case studies I have examined, the horizon of literacy is separated out from others—quite sharply in this instance, as we find ourselves caught between two incommensurable readings. Given their political import, Luba should not be reading Pedro comics, but given their role in the development of her reading, she certainly should.

This tension impinges most painfully upon the comics creator himself. Committed to progressive representations of Latina/o culture, Gilbert is in some sense aligned with Kahlo, but as a comics creator, he is aligned with the nameless, and presumably highly constrained, makers of Pedro. Much later in the Palomar timeline, we see Luba remarking to her sister Petra, "I learned to read from comic books. . . . Do they still make them?" Petra responds, "Yes, and although most of them are very bad, the best ones are as compelling and enriching as any other art form." Petra's daughter Venus, a proud comics fan who is often seen visiting

6.3. *Gilbert Hernandez, page 222 panels 5–6 of "Venus Tells It Like It Is!," collected in* Love & Rockets Library *edition, 2014.*

comics shops, chimes in and declares: "Anybody who doesn't believe in the infinite artistic possibilities of the comic book medium just can't see the forest for the trees!" ("Venus Tells" 222.5–6, figure 6.3). At first glance, this panel feels propagandistic; Venus faces the audience and seems to serve as her creator's mouthpiece. But standing behind Venus are, among others, Luba and Ofelia, a reminder that the child's claim must be seen against the background of a long and difficult history. Venus may be able to view Kahlo and read comics on equal terms, but her childhood optimism about comics' "infinite possibilities" does not yet carry the weight of Luba's experience with comics and the fine arts. At this intermedial moment in US culture, we must attend to the ways in which various media "see" one another—for instance, how Kahlo, as a representative of the fine arts, appears from the point of view of a comics creator. Venus seems to envision a progressive, intermedial future, but the comics in which she appears see their position much more guardedly.

As we have seen in previous case studies, medium-specific awareness of cultural division can influence many aspects of a creator's work, including features of style that might otherwise seem incidental. Different creators can respond differently to the same conditions, as evidenced by the contrast between Gilbert's pictorial vocabulary and that of his brother Jaime. I want especially to focus on the brothers' depictions of violence.[6] In the work of both, violence is usually iconic, to use Scott McCloud's term, conveyed through prominent sound effects and motion lines.[7] In Jaime's case, this iconic quality is tempered and made a specific element in a controlled narrative language. For instance, bloodshed appears infrequently and is represented with restraint. If we inspect the blood Jaime creates, we see there is a strong sense of its being applied to a preexisting image with careful respect to the proportions of objects and figures. The latter take special priority; figures often retain an elegant completeness that is embellished, but not marred, by a modicum of additional ink ("Mechanics Part 6" 63.5, figure 6.4). Given this controlled aesthetic, it is perhaps not a coincidence that Jaime's stories often feature professional wrestling. A bounded realm of methodically and ritually performed movements, in which events are expressed through poses, sorts well with his overall pictorial vision.

If we apply careful visual forensics to Gilbert's depictions of violence, we arrive at quite a different aesthetic. Frequently, poses are secondary to actions, and figures are more likely to be visually distorted in and through violence. Bloodshed can be copious and gestural; ink is, in some cases, applied so heavily that figures are largely obscured. Note the profusion of gore in Gilbert's representation of Chancla, the victim of an attempted murder, in "Human Diastrophism," one of the central narrative arcs of the Palomar stories (80.8, figure 6.5). Blood nearly overwhelms the figure; Chancla seems not so much drawn over as nearly blotted out. An essential material element of most hand-drawn comics

6.4. *Jaime Hernandez, page 63 panel 5 of "Mechanics Part 6," 1983, collected in* Love & Rockets Library *edition, 2007.*

6.5. *Gilbert Hernandez, detail*
from page 81 panel 4 of "Human
Diastrophism," 1987–1988, collected in
Love & Rockets Library *edition, 2007.*

(and of all printed ones), ink can have a usefully metaphoric relationship to blood as a pictorial element; they both flow, drip, spill and run. In Gilbert's work, such metaphorics attain extraordinary resonance and force, and the moments of violence make us newly aware of comics' material elements. Given the lavish inventiveness and beauty Gilbert expresses in much of his cartooning, we also become aware of a deep ambivalence in his line, a sense that the very element that coalesces to form his memorable and resonant figures can, at other moments, manifest as destructive marks. In fact, for Gilbert, violence functions not simply as one narrative element among others, but as a lynchpin in the dynamics of comics making and reading.

A signal instance of copious, gestural blood appears toward the end of the story "An American in Palomar" (first published in *L&R* issues 13–14), which, not coincidentally, shows how Palomar as a narrative space is connected to the creator who renders the town visible as well as to the readers who see the images he makes. The creator-surrogate, US photographer Howard Miller, visits Palomar with hopes of producing an award-winning book featuring the town's inhabitants. He seduces Tonantzín with false promises of fame in Hollywood, and when some of the young men of the town learn that Miller has broken her heart, they assault him. The assault, and Miller's callousness, are neither condemned nor justified by the story as a whole, which portrays all parties to the conflict as ethically ambiguous. The young men who assault Miller have repeatedly harassed and stolen from Tonantzín themselves, and her friend Carmen believes that Tonantzín exploited Miller as much as he exploited her (169.1–4, 188). While the circumstances surrounding the assault are complex, the depiction is brutally simplified. Gilbert shows us one panel in which the assault begins, and then a cluster of blotches, as if he has splashed ink onto the page (189.4–5, figure 6.6). At one level, this depiction condemns violence as an oversimplified reaction to ethical complexity. The assault on Miller does not solve or balance the conflicted relations between him and those whose images he has taken; nor does Miller seem to learn much from the experience, as his self-aggrandizing internal ramblings indicate (190). The assault changes nothing. None of the residents of Palomar end up feeling differently about Miller's visit as a result of it, and Miller himself moves past the moment and produces his book as intended from the first. Yet this "bloody" panel underscores violence as a key part of depicting, seeing, and being seen.

No discrete cause seems fully adequate to explain such a reduction of visual and narrative complexity to splashes of ink. As Gilbert arranges

6.6. *Gilbert Hernandez, page 189 panels 4–5 of "An American in Palomar,"* 1985, collected in Love & Rockets Library *edition,* 2007.

his work, there is no prime mover for such a moment, be it a failure of communication, ethics or vision. Whatever is at work is more pervasive and more strongly rooted in the dynamics of comics as a site of image production and consumption. As a visual device, the bloody assault on Miller strikes in all directions at once. Most obviously, it is a self-critique on the creator's part. Visually alluring female characters like Tonantzín are central to the Palomar stories, and here Gilbert attacks himself as the maker of their images, subjecting himself, by proxy, to violence that seems to come from outside the representational. At the same time, there is a critique of the viewer, that ever-present "American in Palomar," whose desire to consume the artist's images is affronted by splashes of ink in the place of figures. Further, there is a critique of some of Palomar's residents, whose violence makes them (at least momentarily) unrepresentable; their assault on the interloper is a breakdown of effective communication across lines of difference. In theory, each of these forms of violence is separate, though some are narrative consequences of others. Yet Gilbert's radically simplified, gestural bloodiness acts as if all vectors of force are connected at some level other than the causal. The panel, even the page itself, seems to bleed as a symptom of an encompassing destructive energy.

Gilbert's work can not only bleed, but also burn, and images of combustion are prominent throughout the later issues of *Love & Rockets*. At the end of "Human Diastrophism" (issues 21–26), Tonantzín, now a political activist, immolates herself (121.1–4). Her companion, Khamo, is badly scarred in an unsuccessful attempt to save her life, and his disfigurement becomes a recurring visible reminder of her death. Once it is introduced in this dramatic way, the motif of burning resonates backward and forward along Gilbert's exploration of the entire Palomar timeline. At the beginning of the narrative arc "Poison River," Luba is nearly scorched by a cigar while in infancy (7.4–6), and much later in the timeline, her daughter Casimira—fathered by Khamo—sets her own prosthetic arm afire with typically exuberant mischief and becomes a sort of self-immolating torchbearer carried on her father's shoulders ("Farewell" 139.5). Consciously or unconsciously, this motif aligns Gilbert's characters and the medium in which they have their being as similarly imperiled. Burning is the kind of destruction that most readily can happen, and has happened, to both flesh and paper. Thus, it makes visible two overlapping kinds of vulnerability: that of the denizens of Palomar—whose lives and dignity are often threatened as they interact with each other, with their own histories, and with the outside world—and that of comics, subject as the medium has been to marginalization and suppression, including, in the middle years of the twentieth century, repeated acts of immolation.[8]

Burning means more than simple death or disposal. Combustion paradoxically implies a release of energy resulting from annihilation, a revelation of potential that obliterates what is revealed. Gilbert exploits this dynamic in a way that is specific to the fraught condition of comics making and reading. The burning of Tonantzín might initially recall current theories about the expression of trauma in narrative, but a glance at the precise logic of contemporary trauma theory suggests some key differences. In an extended reading of Sigmund Freud's well-known case of a parent dreaming of his burning child, Cathy Caruth discusses trauma under the heading of ethics, emphasizing the relationship between self and other as that of witness and victim. Awakening from his dream to discover the reality of his dead child (awareness of which has been both announced and delayed by the dream), the parent illustrates for us "the trauma of the necessity and impossibility of responding to another's death" (100). The paradox Caruth unfolds requires a very specific scenario in which the victim has already been destroyed while the dreamer/ witness is caught impossibly between engagement and disengagement with the victim's destruction. Tonantzín's death is markedly different from such a scenario. Exploiting the paradoxical valences of combustion, Gilbert uses the motif of burning, like that of bloodletting, to underscore agency along multiple vectors. The death of Tonantzín is, importantly, a suicide, and it indicates not her victimhood but the strength of her moral conviction and political passion; neither is precisely specified, but each is characterized as concerned with social justice.

Equally important is the fact that Howard Miller is an unwitting witness to the suicide; he learns of it from a report on television, and he responds philosophically without knowing that Tonantzín is the one who has killed herself. In this instance, Miller is positioned even more ambiguously than he is in "An American in Palomar." There is a distance from the singularity of what Tonantzín has done—"That kind of thing happens all the time," Miller observes—and a partial understanding of her motives, as when he claims that "there comes a point for some of us where talk or art or propaganda just isn't enough" ("Human Diastrophism" 121.2–3, 6). Miller's position is both more ethically distant and more interpretively engaged than that of Freud's dreamer. By turning Miller into a commentator on the suicide, Gilbert points to his own agency as his character's destroyer even as he affirms that his agency partakes of an ambiguous political impulse that goes beyond the artistic. The presence of Miller, the outside observer who is never more than a tourist when he visits Palomar, also involves us as we consume images of Tonantzín, one of several characters intended to seduce the viewer as much as she attracts the desires of men and women in her town.

Repetition, which is central to most theories of trauma, redounds here upon the reader, not as witness or survivor, but, in more complex fashion, as co-participant in an irrevocable act of consumption. Thus, in the Palomar stories, burning can be, simultaneously, something characters do to themselves as they determine their own destinies, something the comics creator does to his characters as he directs their fates, and something comics readers do to characters by consuming images of them. Burning pervades and surrounds the death of Tonantzín in a violent dynamic of agency and destruction, recognition and alienation. Gilbert creates a narrative moment that is inseparable from the act of making comics, from the act of reading them, and also, perhaps most disturbingly, from the act of destroying them.

These autoclastic dynamics are at odds with much of what has been assumed about the early work of the Hernandez brothers. Initial responses tended to see their work as achieving a new visibility both for Latina/o characters in English-language comics and, together with other titles emerging at the time, of alternative comics as a viable entity. The unfolding of both Gilbert's Palomar stories and Jaime's Hoppers stories in L&R was also seen as a new expansion of narrative possibilities— again, for Latina/o comics and for US comics as a whole.[9] Many aspects of L&R justify the initial responses. Visibility is a crucial category for the Palomar stories; even apart from their intrinsically visual nature as comics, they demand constant attention to categories of sight. The case of Howard Miller is one of many that raise issues of perception and the gaze with keen attention to responsible depictions of Latina/o culture. The idea of narrative expansion is likewise appropriate; early in L&R, both Gilbert and Jaime removed most of the science-fictional and superheroic elements from their stories and focused on realistic depictions of daily life, a narrative direction that had few precedents in comics at the time. However, even as Gilbert explores the lives of his Palomar characters through an extensive and consistent chronology, and with increasing psychological and social realism, he introduces autoclastic elements that frustrate impulses toward visibility and expansion. The way these elements have been overlooked in critical discussion points us again to the influence of the *Bildungsroman* discourse, of which the standard critical line concerning the significance of the Hernandez brothers is yet another example.

In Gilbert's work, the implosive violence of bloodletting and burning constitutes a key visual and thematic nexus. Here, the concept of lack—lack of safety, of meaning and of legitimacy—manifests in various ways. The pervasive dissolution circulating among the creator, his comics, and his readers in L&R declares the troubled conditions of comics production and consumption. The extremity of Gilbert's visual and thematic tactics indicates a need to address deep problems for which, in Howard Miller's words, "talk or art or propaganda just isn't enough." Yet these tactics do not express despair. What might seem at first to be gestures of simple negation—as if Gilbert were doing to his work what was long done to US comics as a whole—turn out to announce the power of comics to manifest the medium's travails, and to allow them to resonate with other historical experiences in which progress and growth, either personal or cultural, are thwarted.

The resonances among the aesthetic, the cultural, the personal and the historical are critical and open-ended, rarely suggesting a clear path to healing and progress, yet the violent expressiveness of Gilbert's aesthetics—even when what is expressed is a blotch of ink—contains an affirmative element. In her study of contemporary autobiographical comics by women, Hillary Chute persuasively urges an understanding of comics as having a positively representative function in relation to trauma:

> The stories to which women's graphic narrative is today dedicated are often traumatic. . . . However, the authors do not project an identity that is defined by trauma: they work to erase the inscription of women in that space. . . . [T]he force and value of graphic narrative's intervention, on the whole, [attach] to how it pushes on conceptions of the unrepresentable that have become commonplace in the wake of deconstruction, especially in contemporary discourse about trauma. Against a valorization of absence and aporia, graphic narrative asserts the value of presence, however complex and contingent. (Graphic Women 2)

The avoidance of "an identity . . . defined by trauma" in the women's life narratives that Chute discusses recalls an exchange between Gilbert and one of his readers in issue 31 of L&R (December 1989). The reader inquired, "Do you think you could develop a character whose life *wasn't* pure misfortune? Someone who didn't have a miserable, depressing life? Someone I could care for, but *not* pity?" Gilbert responded, "*None* of my characters has had a 'miserable, depressing life.' None. And I don't do requests" (Harris 33).

Coming as it did after Tonantzín's suicide, Gilbert's terse declaration affirmed a principle of vitality over and against that of abjection, and its coda announced a commitment to challenging readerly satisfaction. The dynamics of Gilbert's work depart, in some ways, from what Chute describes; in *L&R*, "presence" itself is a fragile category, and the medium is likewise fragile and given to destruction. There is, furthermore, radical insistence on consumption (reading) as a practice of destruction; this insistence violently interrupts a straightforwardly affirmative relationship with Gilbert's characters. Nevertheless, there is a strong sense that the fragility of comics, and the looming destruction attendant on the very act of reading them, can be made powerfully manifest, and that comics are sufficient to address their own and the world's threatened condition, however violently self-opposed the tactics needed for such a task. As these tactics manifest in the Palomar stories, narrative as well as visual elements are transformed. Gilbert sends his Palomar stories along trajectories that depart both from the narrative models of many serial comics and from the closure-oriented (and culturally legitimizing) tactics of the novel.

The first Palomar arc, "Heartbreak Soup" (issues 3–4), ends in conventional tragic closure with the death of Manuel (though, unconventionally, the love triangle of which Manuel is part is not strictly heterosexual), but later stories discover new kinds of endings that leave characters in states of suspension or exile. "Holidays in the Sun" (issue 15) is a prime example. The story follows Palomar resident Jesús, who has been imprisoned for assaulting his wife, Laura, as he serves his sentence. Incorporating flashbacks and fantasy sequences, Gilbert portrays Jesús as internally imprisoned by conflicting desires as surely as he is physically confined on a remote island. The two fantasy figures that reappear in the story, Luba and Tonantzín, first present themselves as an escape, both from the reality of daily life in the prison and from guilt-inducing memories of Laura, who seems to push her way into the fantasies (203.4–5). By the story's end, it is clear that Jesús's desires are compromised by their fragmentation into irreconcilable fantasies and by their alienation from his actual life—in which, notably, he has a sexual relationship with a fellow prisoner.

The story's final page is a five-panel sequence in which Luba, Tonantzín and Laura call out to Jesús in rapid succession as he works in a field. Each figure interrupts extended engagement with the others,

6.7. *Gilbert Hernandez, page 212 of "Holidays in the Sun," 1986, collected in* Love & Rockets Library *edition, 2007.*

and in the story's final panel, Jesús appears pensive and trapped (212, figure 6.7). This sequence generates narrative and visual autoclasm. Jesús's perpetually disrupted, unfocused desire is paralleled by disruptions in readers' attempts to participate in this desire. As characters and as visual elements, the various female figures differ too much to become aspects of one another, but they displace one another too quickly to allow for some choice among them. Together they convey a sense of Jesús's suffering as an experience that cannot be resolved either into serial enjoyment (one fantasy after another) or into closure (desire reconciled or relinquished). To dismiss the lure of Jesús's fantasies would be to underestimate their meaningfulness; yet to invest in them as viable answers to his suffering would also be a mistake. Here Gilbert positions readers much more precariously than he does in the panel in "Frida" where Tonantzín crosses Kahlo's path (figure 6.1). In that panel, the reader's view of Tonantzín is troubled by the cultural division between comics and the fine arts, but the reader is still allowed to see this problem in parallax (either from Gilbert's own view or from Kahlo's). Not so with the conclusion of "Holidays in the Sun"; just as Jesús is caught between the lure of fantasy and the crushing weight of reality, so readers are positioned so as to experience a clash between a libidinal investment in the story's images and a rejection of them as destructive illusions.

The suffering Jesús undergoes is not part of any moral economy; in interviews, Gilbert has made clear that he does not punish his characters for their desires, or for the ways they act on them ("Pleased" 91–92). What does emerge from "Holidays in the Sun," and from other early Palomar stories, is a critique of restrictive gender roles and a call for new possibilities. The machismo of the men of Palomar is a particular target, not only for its oppression of women (Sherriff Borro's bullying of Chelo and Luba, Jesús's violence against Laura, the routine abuse Gato inflicts on Pipo during their marriage), but also for its inability to provide a coherent model of masculinity. As one humorous panel in the story "The Reticent Heart" (issue 12) makes clear, most teenage boys of Palomar feel that there are only two options open to them: they must become either "virile, stud-like men" or "hopeless geeks" (157.3).

Gilbert takes care to show that this model of development is insufficient to account for the reality of adult social roles and desires. Of particular interest is the character Israel, who is presented as the exemplar of Palomar's "virile, stud-like men"; he is fiercely loyal and brave (as when he singlehandedly wrestles a panther attacking his friend Heraclio ["Laughing Sun" 123.3–5]). Yet Israel is bisexual, a fact Gilbert reveals casually in "The Reticent Heart," where we see that Israel's romantic fantasies include both men and women (156.2). The contrast between Israel's imagination and that of the other boys indicates a desire to broaden available roles for Latino men, and for Gilbert's male readership more generally, and in so doing to push past incomplete stories of adult manhood.

Although Gilbert engages in a progressive critique of limited gender roles, he refuses to provide finished, easily accessible alternatives. In the case of Israel, adult discovery of a range of desires does not lead to a stable or coherent identity. In the story "Bullnecks and Bracelets" (issue 19), Israel is another figure of suffering in exile. Unable to return to Palomar because he has had an affair with Heraclio's wife, Carmen, he is also haunted by the sudden loss of his twin sister, Aurora, in early childhood. The sister's disappearance occurs during a solar eclipse, and the image of the sun obscured, its corona visible, recurs in the story as a figure of revelation through visual occlusion. The shape of Israel's vitality is defined by the connection he lacks, and his apparent strength becomes a reminder of his vulnerability, as when one of his lovers advises him not to exercise too energetically: "Careful . . . you don't want to hurt your shoulder again" (271.1). Unable either to maintain or give up life as a gigolo, Israel moves aimlessly from one sexual and emotional attachment to another. His desire to form bonds with others conflicts with his anger at the fact that such bonds do not sustain him.

At the climax of the story, shortly after experiencing another disappointment in his attempts to find his sister, Israel finds a way to express rage against his life: he instigates an orgy. This event takes place at a decadent bohemian party attended by the kinds of wealthy men and women whom he services. In a modified version of the same tactic used in "An American in Palomar," Gilbert shows six panels in which only dialogue, screams, sound effects, and fragments of images (generally suggestive of sex and violence) are visible, followed three panels later by an image of the eclipse (283, figure 6.8). The visual/metaphoric pun is unavoidable; Israel's rage eclipses both its origins and its ends, and registers suffering by refusing coherent representation. The autoclasm here comments on pressing social and political topics, particularly the relationship between sexual identity and class. Yet it goes beyond or beneath these topics toward the broader question of an unfinished or unrequited existence—a question Gilbert manages to ask, through autoclastic images, without suggesting an answer. Notably, the next-to-last panel of the page shows Tonantzín walking away from the orgy, leaning forward in a way that propels the eye toward the image of the eclipse; symbolically, she moves toward her own immolation. For both her and Israel, no specific horizon of injustice or suffering can fully encompass their narrative trajectories.

Israel, like Tonantzín, is both a subject and an object of desire, and in this he is typical of the carefully balanced characterization that Gilbert refines over the course of the Palomar stories. In revisions of major L&R arcs for collected publication, Gilbert adjusts his characters' devel-

6.8. *Gilbert Hernandez, page 283 of "Bullnecks and Bracelets,"* 1987, *collected in* Love & Rockets Library *edition,* 2007.

opment to allow for equal measures of agency and victimization. In "Human Diastrophism," Gilbert alters the appearance of Tonantzín, together with a few details of her story, to emphasize both the trajectory of her fate and her own role in it. While the main thread of "Human Diastrophism" concerns a serial murderer who turns up in Palomar, Tonantzín shows us a differently focused story of how the town interacts with the

outside world. Thanks to the influence of letters, first written by the imprisoned Geraldo and later forged by Maricela and Riri, Tonantzín becomes concerned with the critical state of global affairs. She tries various ways of acting on her new concerns, including a period in which she
dresses in indigenous clothing. In the original serial comics, this clothing is very revealing, leaving her almost naked. Revisions make the garb
more substantial, de-eroticizing her figure to some degree ("Human Diastrophism Part 3" 5.7, *Human Diastrophism* 50.7, figures 6.9 and 6.10).

This shift in appearance is not a matter of chastening her sexuality. It does, however, emphasize Tonantzín's transformation from a flir-
tatious woman who wants to be appreciated for her beauty to a political subject who wants to change the world. Neither of these identities
is presented as better or worse, but the difference between them, and
Tonantzín's agency in moving from one to the other, are paramount. If
the choice to become an activist is influenced by forged letters, which
Maricela and Riri create out of a desire to be close to Tonantzín, it is
nevertheless a choice Gilbert allows her to own. Such balancing gestures ensure a measure of dignity for Tonantzín's choice to commit suicide while, again, making that suicide the meeting place of multiple acts

6.9. *Gilbert Hernandez, page 5 panel 7
of* "Human Diastrophism Part 3," 1987,
Love & Rockets *issue 23, 2007.*

6.10. *Gilbert Hernandez, page 50 panel
7 of* "Human Diastrophism," 1987–1988,
collected in Love & Rockets *Library
edition, 2007.*

(perpetrated by creator, character and reader) of destruction. This sense of agency in the face of fundamentally destructive conditions is central to Gilbert's creative sensibility.

Turning to the broad political horizons of Gilbert's work, we should note that Tonantzín's story concerns both the fate of an individual engulfed by forces she struggles to comprehend and the fate of the world itself in the grip of insoluble crises. This latter, larger horizon is more persistently visible in "Poison River," the lengthiest, most complex and most heavily revised of the Palomar arcs. Tracing the childhood and early adulthood of Luba through tumultuous political struggle and the violence of organized crime, the story allows Gilbert to realize his vision of comics in a more complete and overt form, partly by expressing more clearly what kinds of narratives he rejects as inadequate.

Most obviously, he rejects stereotypical, genre-driven serial narratives, which he represents through Pedro Pacotilla. As previously discussed, Gilbert indicates some value in Pedro comics *as* comics; at a broader horizon of the narrative, however, he critiques them as the kind of comics he seeks to avoid making. As images of Pedro recur throughout the years of Luba's life in "Poison River," it becomes obvious that Pedro never ages or changes; he represents comics driven by genre and ideology, unable or unwilling to protest an oppressive status quo. These kinds of comics contrast strongly with Gilbert's stories of Palomar, which allow for decay and transformation and which at times boldly critique social and political norms. Charles Hatfield suggests that the recurrent presence of Pedro sometimes rhymes with Gilbert's own narrative project, and thus "opens a self-reflexive dimension, a space for auto-critique" (102).[10] Pedro's frequent non sequitur appearances are, admittedly, a comic appearing within a comic, and they invite us to interpret the main action in their light. But despite this fact, and despite the early clash between Pedro and Kahlo, this reflexivity is governed by a sense of the difference between comics about Pedro and Gilbert's own comics about Luba—the latter being open to the possibility, however fraught, of transformation. Each time Pedro interrupts the flow of the narrative, his presence indicates the intransigence of the kinds of comics he represents—their inability to change, their unwillingness to speak meaningfully of the world outside their own images, and the aesthetic violence necessary to appropriate them for more productive ends.

While this violence does, in Gilbert's view, liberate comics from the deadening strictures of the commercial and the propagandistic, it does not clearly indicate a way forward. Hatfield observes that in "Poison River," as in US history, voices criticizing comics can be heard all along the political spectrum (*Alternative Comics* 100). It is therefore significant that while "Poison River" clearly distances itself from comics driven by stereotypes, it also rejects narratives of progress preached by both the left and the right. In "Poison River," the latter are most obviously condemned through the figure of the criminal boss Garza, a right-wing mouthpiece who spouts clichéd patriarchal and nationalist sentiments. He relentlessly persecutes Peter Rio, Luba's first husband, out of feigned concern that Peter is a communist, but his real motivation is a jealous grudge that has little to do with politics. As Hatfield notes, Pedro becomes identified with the story's gangland characters (*Alternative Comics* 100–101). This alignment indicates that the unchanging world of Pedro and the false promise of Garza's rightist vision are two sides of the same coin.

Gilbert is not as overtly critical of leftists, who are sympathetically represented by Luba's cousin Ofelia and her comrades. However, even these characters' progressive agendas sometimes fail to grapple with the realities they are attempting to alter, as when Ofelia's attempt to expose Luba to Kahlo's art fails; the model of development imposed on Luba proves to be no less unworkable for being progressive. Ultimately, what Gilbert observes of almost all his politicized characters is that their visions of progress impose oversimplified models of growth on complex realities where development is frequently uneven and haunted by lack.

In "Poison River," the critique of both left and right becomes more intense, and the competition among progress narratives explodes in violence. One such instance is a gangland shootout, provoked by Garza, in which he and several others die. At the conclusion of this scene, after two panels of copious bloodshed, Gilbert includes one of Pedro's many non sequitur appearances (114.6–8, figure 6.11). In this case, the juxtaposition allows for a mutually reinforcing critique of propagandistic comics and destructive ideologies. Pedro comics abet right-wing class oppression, so it is no accident that the emptiness of Pedro's smile mirrors the hollowness of Garza's anticommunism. Both are façades concealing what is, at best, a lack of complex and productive social vision, and at worst a brutal cynicism.

A similar moment, this time aimed at both left and right, occurs late in "Poison River" when three men are publicly burned alive (178–181). Gilbert refuses to make clear whether the men are soldiers of the rightist government or rebels of the leftist insurgency. The fact that either is possible (and neither is guaranteed) is key to the burning itself. Just be-

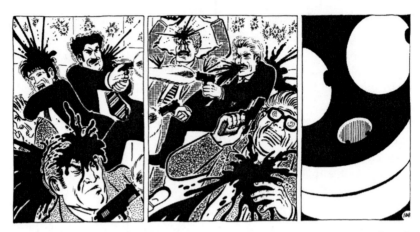

6.11. *Gilbert Hernandez, page 114 panels 6–8 of "Poison River," 1989–1993, collected in* Love & Rockets Library *edition, 2007.*

fore the burning commences, Ofelia, who was once brutally raped and beaten by rightist thugs, and hopes the victims are soldiers, scans the crowd and spots Luba's lover, Antonio, an ex-soldier who seems to identify with the victims (181.1–3). Antonio's presence seems to alter Ofelia's response to the burning. Though it prompts her to grieve, it provides no closure; it manifests her trauma without furnishing either a panacea or a scapegoat (182–183).

This unstable dynamic is enacted in miniature in the three-panel sequence that shows the burning itself, beginning with an image of the unburned victims and ending with an image of their living bodies aflame; the middle panel shows the fuel and the match that start the fire (181.4–6, figure 6.12). Interrupting as it does the story of Ofelia's encounter with Antonio and with her own past, the sequence invites contemplation as a triptych, and it can be read in at least two ways. Seen as a single, spatially divided unit, the panels highlight the volatile barrier between life and death, which are clearly distinct yet urgently adjacent. Scanned left to right, the panels cue us to an understanding of our own reading as enacting the burning; the reader is identified as a participant. In the lower corners of the first panel, there are two shadows, each indicating the head of an unseen witness present for the burning. These elements rhyme visually with the head of the match that ignites the fuel in the second panel, suggesting that the reader is the one who, by reading, sets off the event being witnessed. Whether the reader is dispensing

6.12. *Gilbert Hernandez, page 181 panels 4–6 of* "Poison River," *1989–1993, collected in* Love & Rockets Library *edition, 2007.*

justice, enacting revenge, or simply committing a crime is unclear, but in McCloud's terms, reading the panels sequentially prompts us to enact closure as combustion.[11]

Here, autoclasm manifests as an oscillation between two opposed modes of apprehension—one a clarion call to witness, the other a radically ambivalent invitation to violence—that cannot be adjudicated or reconciled. At the moment of their destruction, the three victims are passive (unlike Israel and Tonantzín), but they bear the ambivalent dynamics of oppression and victimhood that animate both the micronarrative of Ofelia (herself the violent abuser of Luba) and the macronarrative of political conflict between left and right. Gilbert incorporates these ambivalences into the act of reading; the unresolved conflicts in the plot of "Poison River" resonate with self-opposed alternatives for consuming its images. In creating parallels between autoclasm at the level of form and the dynamics of violence at the level of content, Gilbert simultaneously displays comics as a medium struggling with the conditions of its own existence and makes this struggle a powerful means of expression for personal and historical tragedy.

As Gilbert has revealed through interviews, "Poison River" was a turning point in his career as a comics creator. The arc's length and labyrinthine complexity drew criticism even from readers who valued the richness of *L&R* as a whole. This poor reception and an accompanying drop in sales were certainly factors in the brothers' decision to end

L&R after fifty issues, and to work separately on their own titles for a few years.[12] In Gilbert's titles from this period, and in newer *Love and Rockets* work for which the brothers have reunited—*Volume* 2, a shorter run of stapled issues published from 2000 to 2007, and an annual square-bound series, *New Stories*, currently ongoing—the Palomar characters have appeared continuously.[13] However, their portrayal has been markedly different in a number of ways. The influence of readers' criticisms of "Poison River" is already detectable in the final issues of *L&R*. Gilbert creates more free-standing short stories that can be read on their own while also constituting a larger, more complex narrative if read as a group.[14] In subsequent work, this technique is used frequently, along with other, more decisive changes. Autoclastic elements are much less prominent, and in place of narratives of destruction, Gilbert has increasingly written stories that seem designed to avoid it.

This change is most readily visible in Gilbert's portrayal of Luba's niece Venus, whose adventures contrast markedly with those of older emigrants from Palomar. Growing up in the midst of a tangle of erotic and social conflicts, she emerges unscathed from various brushes with sex and violence—and with violent, sexy comics, which she reads indiscriminately alongside other old and new titles, enjoying a young adulthood that is, so far, free from trauma. For Venus, the world of comics is very much like what Gilbert knew as a child—though whether it will remain so is not clear—and her future seems potentially much brighter than the past of her ancestors from Palomar. And when serious violence arrives among adults in the Palomar timeline at present, it is now frequently displaced and contained as tragic closure, such as death, illness or accident, and it usually is not expressed through autoclasm.

What might it mean to the creator himself that he has muted the thematic and aesthetic elements that both typified his early work and connect him to the other creators considered in this study? The stakes of the change are revealed most clearly in the character of Rosalba Martinez, aka Fritz, who has arguably become the central figure in Gilbert's later Palomar work. Fritz first appeared in *Birdland*, a stand-alone pornographic miniseries Gilbert published when he was still in the middle of "Poison River"; he has testified that he made it as a relief from the difficulty of completing this arc (Gaiman interview 106–107). For the characters of this freewheeling series, which moves with comic rapidity from one sexual encounter to another, no amount of promiscuity produces any harm. In a 1995 interview, Gilbert states that *Birdland* is a "different world where there's no AIDS, there's no rubbers"—in short, a world without trauma, in which ejaculation (absurdly copious and frequent) seems to take the place of bloodshed (Gaiman interview 107). *Birdland* is, in fact, a world without any narrative consequences in the usual sense. The story features a heart pendant, apparently of alien origin, that seems to have the power to stop the narrative and begin it afresh, redistributing the characters into new configurations. In place of the broken heart icon that frequently concludes the Palomar stories in *L&R*, Gilbert puts an image of an undamaged heart that is also an inexhaustible source of ret-conning; this object seems able to erase and rework any story in which it appears.

Having introduced Fritz in this context, Gilbert has subsequently kept her connected to a set of conditional fictions that do not have real-world consequences. Together with her sister Petra, Fritz has been spliced into the Palomar universe; both characters are recast as Luba's half-sisters. For Fritz, however, entry into the Palomar universe has not resulted in any stable grounding in Palomar's tragic realities. Gilbert has turned her into a B-movie actress and has published various comics—some stand-alone graphic novels, some short stories or snippets within other stories—purporting to be adaptations of the films in which she appears. Thus far, they do include traumatic plot elements and a few moments of autoclasm (particularly the graphic novel *A Chance in Hell* [2007]), but these are now situated in a larger framework that announces its own fictionality. Irrevocable marks on characters, on our sense of what it means to read them, or on the medium itself are nowhere present. Even when the "films" in which Fritz performs are violent, her very appearance in each one is a reminder that they are mere fantasies; thus, both as character and as image, she seems to hold the promise of pleasurably inexhaustible consumption.

Here we can glimpse how, far from abandoning his early interest in problems of cultural division, Gilbert is approaching them in a newly canny and self-reflexive way. In one sense, the Fritz stories might appear to be a turn to the kind of self-enclosed, politically unproductive comics Gilbert condemns through the figure of Pedro in "Poison River." If the Fritz "films" are, sometimes rather implicitly, progressive in their political orientation (certainly few of them would meet the approval of right-ist ideologues like Garza), their contingent quality might seem to render their political content moot. In a sense, they protect readers from any sense of consequentiality as thoroughly as *Birdland*; even if Fritz should die, Gilbert can simply fabricate films made prior to her death as the basis for more comics. Yet this narrative self-enclosure is implicitly political insofar as it becomes a way for the creator to open new dialogues among narratives and genres often kept separate, in the world of comics as in other realms of culture.

Such opening has, interestingly enough, prompted quite a different kind of criticism from what Gilbert received for "Poison River." In a recent interview, Gilbert answers this criticism, attacking what he sees as an exclusionary tendency in today's independent comics, a kind of reverse snobbery that dismisses work based in popular genres or mass cultural traditions. While understanding that many readers gravitate toward independent comics because they are more likely to find cultural authenticity, free of commodified identities and stereotypes, Gilbert expresses irritation that he meets with disapproval when creating "any deviation from that, like what I'm doing with the Fritz books and some things in *Love and Rockets*." He indicts what he sees as a "subtle kind of fascism" in independent comics culture, "a kind of ghetto to me, I hate to say. There's this attitude people have where it's like, 'this is what a real comic is supposed to be about, and that icky Britney Spears stuff doesn't exist'" (Sobel interview 146–147). The B-movie comics of Fritz are, in many ways, a far cry from the realm of mass-cultural pop icons, but Gilbert obviously sees them as being on a continuum. And submerging Fritz in one stereotypical, generically determined narrative situation after another is, for him, a way to explore her possible meanings and expand, rather than restrict, the cultural facets of Palomar.

Yet—and here the full complexity of the arc of Gilbert's career becomes visible—this expansion has, in its turn, referred back again and again to the tragic realities of the earlier Palomar stories. One of Fritz's films, presented in the story "Proof That the Devil Loves You," is based on some of the earliest instances of tragic violence in Palomar, and the strangely awkward, even absurd, quality of the retelling is obviously intended to make it impossible to categorize. Gilbert presents his comic-book version of the film so as to make it unclear whether its repetition of violent and traumatic moments is supposed to exorcise their power or to amplify their ongoing resonance. The story in which this film appears also shows Fritz's grandniece Dora, aka Rocky, visiting Palomar in order to rethink her own career as an actress. Rocky's tour of Palomar is haunted by reminders of Luba's time in Palomar—and, indirectly, by earlier incidents in Luba's life as recorded in "Poison River." When Rocky announces that Palomar "doesn't feel haunted; it feels comfortable and safe," a longtime resident asks "Like a graveyard?"—a question that, like the strange tone of Fritz's film, makes it difficult to know whether Gilbert's current work is "haunted" by what has come before ("Proof" 56.5). Perhaps the unquiet dead of Palomar are finally being laid to rest for good, or perhaps they will continue to haunt future stories and future generations descended from the town's residents.

As of this writing, Gilbert has published the first volume of *Maria M.* (a second volume will follow), a comic "film" in which Fritz plays her and Luba's mother, Maria, filling in more of the early timeline alluded to in "Poison River." Not surprisingly, this retelling seems at once to displace the tragic history of this arc by rendering it newly available as a source of intrigue, action and sex, and to multiply the tragic elements, revealing more fully than before how marked Luba's family is by personal and political violence. "Proof That the Devil Loves You" and *Maria M.* are filled with in-jokes concerning the Palomar stories themselves, critics' reactions to Gilbert's work, and questions of how pornography and other low genres are valued. Yet even as these metafictional aspects of the new stories unfold, so, too, does a painful awareness of the realities of politics, sex, gender and culture that have long been Gilbert's central concerns. Thus, despite a seeming reversal of priorities, the new work is best understood as a series of attempts to explore the same tensions that animate the earlier Palomar stories.

Gilbert has remarked of his recent work: "I'm really concerned about the reader absorbing my stuff pretty quickly, because in the past I've made myself muddy, and it was a struggle to get through my work. I've known that for years. I don't even read my old stuff anymore. . . . *Poison River* [and other work from that period] . . . [i]t all became so dense I don't even want to look at it. . . . But now I'm much more conscious about making it easy to absorb" (Sobel interview 140). I confess I find it difficult fully to reconcile these sentiments with what I see in the recent stories. Admittedly, much of Gilbert's contemporary work clearly announces the way a given story is situated in an overarching plot, after which there are opportunities to make larger connections, should readers decide to follow a given story into the vast Palomar universe. What this tactic allows for, as Gilbert has deployed it more and more confidently, is a dense and variegated layering of themes and tones. Each new addition to the Palomar universe can be taken as an enjoyable fragment, but the more thoroughly a reader can map it onto the whole of which it is a part, the more clearly it reveals new possibilities that make each story just as dense as the early work Gilbert claims he cannot read anymore.

At any rate, the democratic vision of culture Gilbert possessed as a child has, thus far in his career, proved difficult to reconcile with the realities of cultural division he has continually confronted as a comics creator. And while the new work may be "easy to absorb" in some ways, it remains tied to, and haunted by, his earliest innovations. Well before Gilbert had to confront a resistant readership—a readership that initially found his work too dense and now finds it, if anything, too populist—he was already manifesting the struggle most central to his work by making comics that bled, and burned. Whether this autoclastic energy will continue to resonate throughout the rest of his career probably depends on whether the high-low divide that has impinged upon his work, and that of so many other comics creators, finally becomes a thing of the past.

Conclusion

ON BECOMING A COMICS SCHOLAR

The four figures I have examined all bear witness to the ongoing problem of cultural illegitimacy, which affects them in the process of creation just as much as it shapes the medium's reception in mainstream culture. In comics from the era of the graphic novel, autoclasm takes widely different forms and its thematic emphasis is variable. Yet a tendency to express the illegitimacy of the medium through self-opposition is frequent, as is skepticism toward any simple story of upward mobility. Many great works of the era of the graphic novel are best understood not as newly literary comics that break away from the medium's supposedly childish roots, but as complex struggles against the still-prevalent notion of literary maturity that condemns comics as childish in the first place. Seeing more clearly the conditions that even acclaimed creators confront, and taking seriously the way these conditions press upon their ambitions, we gain new appreciation and respect for the counterintuitive genius of their achievements.

We also gain a deeper understanding of why comics readers, casual or otherwise, would do well to follow the lead of these creators and be wary of the quasi legitimation comics have been granted. In *Comics Versus Art*, Bart Beaty characterizes the contemporary state of relations between comics and the fine arts thusly:

> It seems possible that we are witnessing a landmark shift . . . in the make-up of the audience for "serious" culture, producing an audience that has unprecedented openness to traditionally marginalized cultural forms. At the same time, it seems possible that the change resides not so much with the public but with the form itself. Could it be as simple as the fact that comics have, belatedly, grown up? That they are,

as so many newspaper and magazine headlines have suggested, "not just for kids anymore"? In the simplest terms, it can be noted that over time either cultural institutions evolve to accommodate new forms or those forms adapt to the demands of the institutions. . . . [I]n the case of comics in the art world, both these tendencies have played a role in changing the relationship between fields. (13)

Given the fact that Beaty focuses on the fine arts, his vision of the medium's shift in status makes some sense. His study describes some of the changes taking place in museum culture that have made at least a little room for comics. Beaty also shows how some sectors of comics culture are now increasingly privileging aesthetic values that overlap with fine arts appreciation. Yet, as Beaty's reluctant capitulation to the terms of the *Bildungsroman* discourse reminds us, powerful lines of force still affect the cultural disposition of comics. Upon close examination, the rhetoric of developmental legitimacy ("not just for kids anymore") is less a sign of a "landmark shift" in cultural priorities than a hegemonic enforcement of values that have regulated the status of comics for more than half a century.

In the course of this regulatory work, the *Bildungsroman* discourse has conferred better status on a handful of graphic novels. However, they are often valued through a kind of misrecognition not accounted for by Beaty's either-or logic. It is possible for critics to grant legitimacy to a comic without budging from their literary attachments, simply by not perceiving how that comic's creator espouses medium-centered values at odds with the critics' priorities (exactly this kind of misreading has gathered around Bechdel's *Fun Home*). In the era of the graphic novel, comics have undoubtedly changed in a number of ways that affect matters as diverse as publication format and creative scope. But in the case studies I have considered, creators have participated in such changes without bending toward the literary values that are often ascribed to them. To read such comics responsibly is to deal with the difficulties of an uncertain present, when the terms of legitimation begin to work in tokenistic fashion at the very moment they seem to be granting fair access to improved status. The era in which "comics aren't just for kids anymore" may, from the perspective of some future state of affairs, look like one necessary stage of a journey to legitimation. It will not, however, look like an end point, and the fate of comics is undecided for now. The antidevelopmental, autoclastic tendencies of contemporary comics are a vivid witness to the medium's uncertain destiny, and grappling with autoclasm is, I believe, a productive way to keep faith with comics as they are rather than as we might wish them to be.

While completing this study, however, I have occasionally wondered whether claiming that comics creators deserve respect for their struggle against the idea of growing up is really so different from an argument for respect on the basis of literary maturity. The position espoused in this study has, I think, the better evidentiary claim, but legitimacy of some kind is still its likely end product. I hope it will be a more dynamic legitimacy, better for comics readers and creators and truer to their history, than the uneven status associated with the current mainstream narrative. But what will such legitimacy look like? Exactly how can we tell the difference between fruitful legitimation and yet another Faustian bargain that, as Art Spiegelman argues, has long been the portion of comics? Can the scholar—avatar of institutional acceptance and adult normativity—really be on the side of comics, so long excluded from cultural acceptance, and often so wary of any notion of legitimacy?

To address these questions, however imperfectly, I want to look backward rather than forward, and ask where the urge to read comics at all— as a fan, a student, a teacher or a scholar—comes from, and what it has to do with the way of reading comics I have expounded. My immediate motivation for this project was deductive: I simply wanted to follow the clues I found on the pages of contemporary comics. Seeing repeated instances of self-thwarting signification and wariness toward ideas of progress and respectability, I felt compelled to understand what might give rise to these patterns. This led to a more careful reading of the *Bildungsroman* discourse, which I began to see as evidence of persistent status problems. But my attention to what I now call autoclasm was prompted by a cast of mind that predated any attempt to talk about comics as a scholar. I developed much of the critical stance worked out in this book in my childhood, by reading *MAD* magazine.

MAD is something like an urtext for the satirical wariness that flavors much of our social and political discourse. As a young reader, I made no conscious connection between the way *MAD* encouraged critical suspicion of practically everything about contemporary life and the fact that it was a comic. Nevertheless, I grasped its pages as laying out a distinct view of the world (however much diluted versions of it were expressed in the books, films and television programs that, unbeknownst to me, *MAD* had influenced). What was unusual about *MAD* had to do with the relationship between its intrinsically self-opposed quality and its status in culture. Relentless in its search for new cultural and political phenomena to mock, MAD constantly admitted that its relationship to the legitimate world was essentially parasitic. It existed only because the things it attacked existed, and the magazine attacked itself as harshly as it did the official objects of its critique. This complicit stance was also adopted by a great deal of the culture to which I was exposed in childhood, but politically oriented editorial writing, talk radio and television never mocked themselves, or admitted their implicated positionality, as clearly as MAD did. And though I could not have articulated this thought in full, I understood that the most rigorously and consistently self-critical publication I read was also the one least likely to be taken seriously by the adults around me (and most likely to lead to disapproval if I brought it home or to school).

The curious power of MAD resided, for me, in the link between its self-critical rigor and its contemptible status. To understand that eventually one stopped reading MAD and moved on to more respectable publications was to understand something about how cultural legitimation really worked—and it was not necessarily by encouraging critical self-awareness. Perhaps, in fact, legitimation required investment in an unexamined status quo. The awareness MAD encouraged was operating when I began to ask why there was a gap between the developmental language used to describe contemporary comics and the counterdevelopmental images I saw in comics themselves. Why, exactly, I wanted to know, did contemporary comics seem so MAD-aligned, while journalists, teachers and some critics talked as if they were pursuing a scheme of literary legitimation? This line of questioning was not the awakening of a new suspicion; it was the recollection of an old critical skill. From skeptical child to skeptical adult—this is the line my own comics reading has followed.

In mainstream culture and comics scholarship both, childhood comics reading is usually not connected to adult thought in this way. The kid who reads comics is imagined as innocent, unaware of cultural norms or concerns of status. The adult comics reader can look back on this self with longing, but also with mature awareness. In a 1998 lecture on the subject of comics and cultural illegitimacy, Thierry Groensteen claimed: "Comics still have a privileged relationship with childhood because it is in childhood that each of us discovered them and learnt to love them. . . . [M]any adults have forgotten or rejected childhood pleasures in favor of more sophisticated, supposedly more noble, pleasures. . . . [W]hy not admit it? All of us here in Copenhagen, delivering our clever papers, are probably doing nothing more than holding out our hands to the kids we used to be" ("Why Are Comics" 40–41). I cannot recognize myself in this description of the "clever" adult, burdened by sophistication and the need for respect, trying to recover a naïve, prelapsarian self. For me, at least, to realize the importance of status problems in contemporary US comics was to perceive a set of conditions that, in however inchoate a fashion, I had been seeing for a long time.

In asking how comics studies might develop in a way that is most helpful to the medium, I have pushed further into the entanglement I am attempting to address; I have asked how the comics critic grows up. In my own case, at least, the critic does so paradoxically: by refusing to accept developmental norms. As a genesis for comics scholarship, this model of growth raises problems different from the ones raised by Groensteen's nostalgic confession. One confronts not the pleasurable embarrassment of admitting a longing for childhood—the stigma of which is quickly dispelled by the act of admission—but the intellectual challenge of justifying a self-conscious critical leaning (as opposed to an innocent cultural preference) that one has felt from the first. The attitudes I am describing here are still my own, and in the present, rather than at a convenient and unthreatening distance. I remain suspicious of developmental discourses of legitimation, and I oppose the idea that such suspicion is an immature youthful habit rather than a useful and often necessary critical practice.

The responsible comics scholar must measure this suspicion against cultural realities that may change in the coming decades. Hopefully, comics' dubious "coming of age" will not last another thirty years, and we will see the arrival of substantial legitimacy. Should this kind of change come to pass, it will be followed by deconstructive and other discourses that will allow us to remain critically aware of all the ways such legitimation is never self-evident. But these discourses, as they are usually understood and deployed with respect to established languages, cultures, genres and media, cannot fully come into being until legitimation has taken place. As yet there is no deconstruction (as the term is usually understood) of comics as a medium—not so long as there is a struggle for legitimacy.

This struggle certainly has its paradoxes. Recall Joe Hill's deliberately immature, hostile declaration: "I don't want comics to be respectable. . . . I want the act of reading comics to feel dirty and unhealthy and transgressive" (Introduction n. pag.). As a critic, I find it no easy task to be responsible with regard to Hill's intentions and yet to insist that one does, in fact, want comics to be legitimate (not quite the same, I think, as what Hill means by "respectable"). It is as if we were trying to outgrow a restrictive paradigm of development, to mature beyond the concept of maturity. The risks of this attempt are numerous—and it may prove impossible, in the short term at least, to escape the *Bildungsroman* discourse that, as Art Spiegelman has frequently noted, is the Faustian bargain offered to comics.

At a moment when the very idea that comics have come of age works against the medium's full legitimation, how can we set a standard for more substantial improvement of comics' status? What will be the evidence that the paradoxes of the *Bildungsroman* discourse are resolved? Perhaps the clearest proof of definitive legitimation will be the arrival of adult readers to whom these kinds of paradoxes are alien, because they have no idea that there is anything culturally suspect about comics. Graphic novels of all kinds are now more available to young readers than ever before, and sheer quantitative exposure may produce more readers who would no sooner stop reading comics than they would give up any other mode of literacy they possess. Today, many librarians and teachers still believe that comics should be understood as a stepping-stone to other kinds of reading, and many of my own students claim that in their youth, they were given the message that comics are not fully legitimate. Pedagogical priorities may change further, and meanwhile, the material presence of comics in bookstores and libraries may speak louder than the way comics reading is institutionally framed. Perhaps a coming generation will truly see comics reading as coextensive with all other literacies. Should this generation emerge in force, the critical suspicion that has inspired this book will at last become a dated attitude, and comics scholars and teachers will see in their students not a window—nostalgic or otherwise—into their own pasts, but the sign of a genuinely different future.

Notes

INTRODUCTION

1. For Eisner's thoughts on the early days of the comics industry, and his own participation in the factory system, see *Eisner/Miller* chapters 16–17 and 20–21.

2. For Eisner's thoughts on the comics code and the events leading up to it, see *Eisner/Miller* chapter 11.

3. For Spiegelman's most recent thoughts on the perils and promises of cultural legitimation, see "Public Conversation."

4. For an alternate reading of this doodle, see Mitchell, "Comics as Media" 259. Mitchell interprets it as an exploration of creative possibility in a vein more attuned, I would suggest, to the dynamics of creative influence in legitimate media, such as literature and the fine arts.

5. See Pizzino, "Autoclastic Icons."

6. For a recent critique of this tendency in comics studies, see Kashtan. For definitions of comics as sequential art, see Eisner, *Comics and Sequential Art*, in particular, chapters 1, 3 and 4, and McCloud chapter 1.

7. For theories derived from semiotics, see Groensteen, *System* and *Comics and Narration*. For critical discussion of comics as a language, see Cohn's "Limits of Time" and *Visual Language*. It should be noted that Cohn would certainly not agree that his own work and Groensteen's converge on a single view of comics (see "Limits" 128–129 and *Language* 67); nevertheless, for both theorists, comics are most essentially a mental form whose physical manifestations, while perhaps important to the formation of a given work, are nevertheless incidental for comics as such. For a recent challenge to Cohn within the discipline of linguistics, see Bateman and Wildfeuer.

8. *Action Philosophers!*, by Fred Van Lente and Ryan Dunlavey, is one obvious exception; see chapter 2 for a brief further discussion of comics as an academic medium, and of the emergent category of the "metacomic."

CHAPTER 1

1. See Derrida.

2. For Wertham's manner of distinguishing comic books from comic strips, see *Seduction of the Innocent* 14, 266–267. For Wertham's account of the violence of comic books and their tendency to promote illiteracy, see *Seduction* chapters 4 and 5.

3. For an insightful analysis of postwar anxieties concerning endangered youth, see Rasula.

4. For accounts of the circumstances leading up to the formation of the comics code and of its aftermath, see Gilbert; Nyberg, *Seal of Approval*; Beaty, *Fredric Wertham* chapter 4; Gabilliet chapter 14; and Lopes chapter 2. See Nyberg, in particular, for a detailed account of the various comics codes and their strictures. While I believe the strictures of the comics code speak for themselves and clearly constitute censorship by any reasonable definition, there is some scholarly disagreement about the code's meaning and effects. For an alternate view, see Beaty 206–207.

5. For Wertham's rather dim view of the effects of the code, see "It's Still Murder."

6. The 1954 comics code is widely available in a number of print and online sources, but several of these sources do not include the preamble. I have made use of the reprint in the appendix of Gabilliet, which currently provides the only complete print version of which I am aware.

7. For useful accounts of this development, see Hatfield, *Alternative Comics* 35–36, and Nyberg, "How Librarians Learned" 30–38. The latter, though focusing more narrowly on librarians' attitudes toward comics, nevertheless provides the most thorough and up-to-date summary of the current place of comics in secondary schools.

8. For representative examples, see Lucas, Williams and Wilson, and Bakjian. For a more general overview of perspectives favorable to comics in diverse fields, including education, psychology and criminology, during the 1940s, see Gardner, *Projections* 78–79. In this decade, it should be noted, attacks on comics as the enemy of literacy, if not of civilization, were still common.

9. See, for instance, Stainbrook, Schwarz, and Hammond.

10. A typical example from 2009: "Kids love comics. Any frustrated teacher who has repeatedly reprimanded students for reading comic books in class can attest to this fact. Some teachers see comics as merely classroom distractions, but there's more to the genre than meets the eye. Despite resistance from teachers, administrators and parents, some educators strongly support incorporating graphic texts into teaching and learning. . . . Taking advantage of students' interests will stimulate learning and help them to connect to academic lessons in a new way. . . . [E]ducators can tap into dozens of ideas for integrating graphic texts into classroom or after-school activities and help students bridge the gap between entertainment

and achievement" (Sloan 1+). Although its tone conveys enthusiasm for new ped-agogical possibilities, this argument does not imply that the teacher who has repri-manded students for reading comics is to be reprimanded in turn. No shift in peda-gogical priorities is suggested here; what is recommended is merely a shift in tactics. Delinquent behavior can be turned to the purpose of training in order to "bridge the gap between entertainment and achievement," which is to say, between com-ics and literacy. It is striking how little this approach to comics deviates from the earliest attempts to understand how the medium might work for teachers. A typi-cal example from 1946: "The comic book may be used constructively as a stepping stone to a lasting interest in reading good literature. . . . In my own teaching I have been plagued for a long time by comic-book enthusiasts in my classroom. There are many boys and girls who surreptitiously carry copies of comic books between the covers of legitimate textbooks. . . . I found myself doing so much missionary work among my comic-book heathens that I began to make a list of books that might be offered as antidotes to, or stepping-stones from, comic publications. . . . [A] comic book is a challenge to our ingenuity as teachers and . . . it can be used constructively as a stimulus to wider and more profitable reading interests" (Dias 142–145). While there is more concern with public morality and cultural hygiene in the rhetoric of the 1940s than in that of the new century, the underlying project is the same: reme-diate literacy through pedagogical reform. Such reform envisions the comics reader as potentially delinquent and imagines that a student's proper development in liter-acy will eventually move away from comics and toward print.

11. There is, unfortunately, no indication that this way of viewing comics is at present yielding to more progressive, multimodal approaches. While the latter approaches have a definite and ongoing presence in educational research on com-ics, they constitute a minority position. An informal survey of research on com-ics and literacy suggests that teachers and scholars taking the "stepping-stone" ap-proach outnumber the more progressive voices by about four to one; this ratio has not varied significantly since 2010. Thanks to my research assistant Kaitlyn Smith for her work on this point.

12. There is no current, comprehensive account of the transmedial relation-ship of comics to other visual media. For a useful summary of changes in creators' rights, see Gabilliet chapter 12.

13. In what follows, it should be noted, I identify broad trends without giv-ing attention to the waxing and waning of the status of comics at various moments since the late 1970s and early 1980s. Useful accounts of the vagaries of the medium's cultural position can be found in Gabilliet chapters 8–9 and 14–17, and in Lopes chapters 4–6.

14. The term "graphic novel" obviously implies a new kind of producer, the "graphic novelist," who might reasonably be perceived with a new level of cultural respect. However, as I trust my account of the *Bildungsroman* discourse makes clear, the graphic novel itself is the lynchpin of legitimation; in rather paradoxi-

cal fashion, it is this ostensibly new form that confers respect on its creators rather than the reverse. This is not to say that there is no room for the idea of auteurist in mainstream perceptions of comics, but even now, the respected comics creator is subject to a number of limiting stereotypes: "As most graphic novelists themselves will gladly tell you, you have to be a bit of a weirdo to pursue this odd and solitary art form" (McGrath 30). This is not the kind of observation one finds literary journalists making about novelists or poets, whose art form is no less solitary. It should be noted that in recent years, academic discourse on comics has also made use of "graphic narrative," a term successfully put into circulation by Hillary Chute. This term has the advantage of improved accuracy, since it does not privilege fiction over nonfiction; Chute specifies that this is one of her primary motivations for introducing the term, which she intends to denote "a book-length work in the medium of comics" ("Comics as Literature?" 453). W. J. T. Mitchell subsequently declared that "the emergence of a strong tradition of nonfiction autobiographical comics has displaced the formerly fashionable graphic novel as the moniker for comics with the more general term *graphic narrative*" ("Comics as Media" 263). However, while it is certainly the case that "graphic narrative" has some currency in scholarship, it has not yet challenged the ascendancy of the "graphic novel" in other places, including bookstores, comics shops and mainstream journalism; indeed, with the exception of a few blogs, "graphic narrative" has no presence outside of academic discourse as yet. Additionally, within comics scholarship, the term "graphic novel" is still much more common than "graphic narrative"—though "comics" remains the preferred term above either. My thanks to Kaitlyn Smith for research assistance on this last point.

15. On the limits of legitimation provided by mainstream accounts of comics having "come of age," see Sabin 178–179.

16. To cite only one signal instance: on a panel held at the 1985 San Diego Comic Convention, when Frank Miller, Alan Moore and Marv Wolfman protested the way Marvel Comics had treated illustrator Jack Kirby, audience member Jim Shooter, Marvel's editor-in-chief, publicly scolded them for talking out of turn and asserted, in veiled but chilling terms, a corporate right to the exploitation of illustrators (Heintjes). This incident was shortly followed by a clash in which Moore, Miller, Wolfman and Howard Chaykin publicly protested the decision at DC Comics to plan a ratings system without consulting writers and artists. This protest was published in an issue of *Comics Buyer's Guide* that also featured an editorial by Moore ("Four Creators"). For another brief discussion of this incident, see chapter 3.

17. Also of note is that *Watchmen* is widely perceived as a crowning instance of the graphic novel, with very little journalistic acknowledgment that it remains, in Moore's view, an ongoing instance of abuse of creators' rights. For an overview of Moore's perspective on this subject, see Khoury 123–127. The controversy over rights to *Watchmen* has, admittedly, had a limited presence in the mainstream press; see Itzkoff.

18. Implied here is an opposition of literary realism to something like the romance as defined by Frye; see *The Secular Scripture*. For an analysis of the romance elements of the traditional superhero serial, see Eco's "The Myth of Superman" and "Innovation and Repetition." For an account of some of the ways that more contemporary superhero narratives have departed from romance conventions, see Klock.

19. See Cohn, "Limits of Time" and *Visual Language*.

20. Hatfield notes that while the original impetus behind the graphic novel was a desire to break into mainstream book publishing, it has also become an accepted term and a valued format among regular comics consumers; see *Alternative Comics* 29.

21. For a summary of this list, see "Top 100 Comics" 108.

22. Within the pages of the *Journal*, this stance has, over time, led to the risk of defeatism as regards the medium's future. Comics readers can now point to a considerable body of strong work in various genres and formats, and this work has no doubt contributed to the diversification of comics readership. Nevertheless, that readership remains quite small, and while the consistently excellent achievements of a handful of creators are evidence of a kind of *enrichment*, the skill and discrimination needed to see their greatness (for beginning comics readers, needed even to understand the plots of their stories) hold little promise for an *expansion* of comics literacy. Thus Gary Groth, editor of the *Journal*, has often seesawed between attacks on mainstream comics for their juvenile mediocrity and condemnations of the public in general for an unwillingness to be challenged by better work, or to spend the time necessary for an appreciation of the best in comics writing and cartooning. Further, while the *Journal* has certainly been the single most articulate advocate of creators' rights, it has made even this priority secondary to that of aesthetic quality; on occasion, Groth has said quite seriously that if a comic itself is worthless, the right of the creator to own it is not worth contesting. See his interview with Neil Gaiman 88.

23. See Koike and Kojima 19–20.

24. See Lopes's Introduction and Gabilliet chapters 15–17.

CHAPTER 2

1. For a full articulation of Mitchell's central question, see *What Do Pictures Want?* Preface and chapter 2.

2. For a fuller look at Mitchell's discussion of iconophobia, see *Iconology* Introduction and chapter 4.

3. When I first coined this term, I was unaware that "autoclastic" already existed as a scientific term in the field of geology.

4. Spiegelman has returned to this notion of a Faustian bargain in many discussions of the medium's fate; most recently, see "Public Conversation" (2014).

5. On the subject of racial difference and diversity in mainstream comics, see Brown, *Black Superheroes*; Nama; and Howard and Jackson, eds.

6. This is not to say that metacomics, to modify Mitchell's term, are impossible or nonexistent; the very existence of McCloud's work testifies to the contrary. However, in the United States, such works have been rare. Other metacomics have occasionally contributed to critical discussion since McCloud, not least a short critique of *Understanding Comics* by James Sturm and Art Baxter, "Build a Beach Head," as well as Van Lente and Dunlavey's recent history of US comics in comic book form, *The Comic Book History of Comics*. See also the comics interludes by William Kuskin and Matthew Slade in the 2008 *ELN* special issue "Graphia." For a brief summary of the growth of academic metacomics, as well as academic comics of other kinds, see Sousanis, "Varoom." If Mitchell is correct, metapictures can theorize images without having explicitly academic intent, and certainly there are narrative metacomics aimed at comics readers in general. See, for instance, Alan Moore and J. H. Williams's *Promethea*.

7. On the concept of phrase regimens and their significance, see Lyotard 28–29, 84–85, 140, 181.

8. See Cohn, "Limits of Time" and *Visual Language*.

9. On the practice and limits of erasure, see Spivak xiii–xx.

10. See Pizzino, "Autoclastic Icons."

11. See Hill, *Guide to the Known Keys*.

CHAPTER 3

1. For Miller's views on the need for broader readership, see Borax interview 43. For his championing of pulp mythologies and popular genres, see Borax interview 45 and "Good Old Days" 72–73, 85. These two impulses in Miller's work are often in tension, productive or otherwise, with one another, and this tension is usually visible when Miller seeks to articulate his own priorities as a creator; see "Return of the Dark Knight" 60–62.

2. For Miller's views on the code, see interview with Groth (1987) 76 and *Eisner/Miller* chapter 11.

3. *DKR* initially appeared as four square-bound single issues published in the first half of 1986. Each of the four issues bore its own title: *The Dark Knight Returns*, *The Dark Knight Triumphant*, *Hunt the Dark Knight* and *The Dark Knight Falls*. *The Dark Knight Returns* became the title for the collected graphic novel that followed later the same year. All page numbers refer to the 10th Anniversary Edition, first published in 1997 and currently in print.

4. See Pearson and Uricchio, eds., and two volumes by Brooker, *Batman Unmasked* and *Hunting the Dark Knight*.

5. A full (if rather hagiographic and *Bildungsroman*-discourse-influenced) ac-

count of the origins of *DKR* is "Masterpiece," a supplement included with the video release of Warner Bros.' 2012 animated adaptation of the comic.

6. Even Will Brooker, who emphasizes the variety of roles Batman has played as a pop culture icon, notes that his longevity has something to do with the essential and unchanging elements of the core mythology; see *Batman Unmasked* chapter 1.

7. I here follow Scott McCloud's basic categories for the sequential grammar of comics; see chapter 3.

8. On the initial fame of *DKR*, see Sabin 176.

9. For Miller's views on comics and politics from around the time of *DKR*, see Borax interview 41–48.

10. On the prevalence of action-to-action transitions in comics, see McCloud chapter 3.

11. On general "arthrology," see Groensteen, *System* chapter 3.

12. While *DKR* excoriates the aggressive US foreign policies of the Reagan era, Miller's recent post-9/11 work *Holy Terror* is unapologetic propaganda for the Bush doctrine. For a reading of *DKR* that aligns it with masculinist, Reaganite conservatism, see Iadonisi.

13. See, for instance, Schott; Pellitteri; Whaley; and Ditmer. Particularly symptomatic is Yockey, whose claims concerning the ideological function of superhero comics are in direct conflict with his passing acknowledgment of their suppressed status. Some critics have taken questions of cultural status into account much more successfully; see, especially, Brooker, "Hero of the Beach." There are doubtless many instances where the political import of comics can usefully be considered without any reference to the medium's status in the United States; see Dorfman and Mattelart.

14. See Delany, "Inside and Outside" and "Politics."

15. See Miller's editorial cartoon, published in tandem with an editorial essay by Alan Moore, in the pages of *Comics Buyer's Guide* in 1987. For Miller's thoughts on the attempt to create a ratings system at the time of *DKR*, see Groth interview. As recently as 1998, Miller observed of this moment in comics history: "We were close, it seemed, to repeating the mistake—no, the *crime* against the artform, and against the whole publishing industry—that the Comics Code had been" ("Good Old Days" 80).

16. On the subject of complicitous critique, see my earlier discussion in chapter 2.

17. On the role of US comics in World War II, see Murray. Not all scholars see G.I. Joe as politically multivalent; see Nordlund.

18. See "Neil Gaiman, Frank Miller."

19. For an overview of these aspects of book theory, see Cormac and Mazzio, the introduction in particular. My speculations on comics and "theory of the book" are indirectly indebted to Thierry Groensteen; see *System* 29–31, 91–102.

20. This state of affairs, now the norm for print works in any genre, with the

exception of poetry, took some time to stabilize, and it is important to recall that the conventions of print have always been subject to change; see McKitterick. Nevertheless, the idea that typesetting and page arrangement were typically beyond the purview of the writer—and also of little concern to the reader—was a commonplace by the time the conventions of realism were established.

21. For a discussion of Miller's treatment of Lichtensteinian pop art in *Sin City*, see Pizzino, "Art That Goes BOOM."

22. See Doris chapter 3.

23. On the growth of a comics art market, see Beaty, *Comics Versus Art* chapter 7.

CHAPTER 4

1. See Rubenstein interview 166 and "Across Borders" 169.

2. See, particularly, Muller; Cvetkovich; Pearl; Watson; and Freedman.

3. Bechdel continues to self-identify as a cartoonist as of this writing. She recently won a MacArthur "genius grant" and journalistic attention to this event, and to Bechdel's self-designation, has been accompanied by a certain curiosity and fastidiousness whose relation to anti-comics stigma is plain.

4. For a more extensive discussion of the question of mainstreaming lesbian culture in *Dykes to Watch Out For*, see Beirne chapter 6.

5. On the role of "Foul Play" in the Senate subcommittee hearings, see Wright 144.

6. It should be noted that Bechdel has had her own struggles with censorship, particularly since the publication of *Fun Home*. For Bechdel's thoughts on *Fun Home*'s being banned in Marshall, Missouri, see "Life Drawing" 39. A more recent, and widely publicized, incident of attempted suppression occurred at the College of Charleston; for a summary of this incident, see McCammon.

7. Obviously, illustrated children's books can also be categorized as comics; the distinction here is Bechdel's, not my own. See Rubenstein interview 114.

8. In the case of Baetens's discussion of *Fun Home*, this oversight is especially striking, because the framing of this discussion evinces a clear understanding of the cultural stakes of the term "graphic novel"; see 206–208. The fact that some of Bechdel's most obvious engagements with medium- and status-specific issues seem not to be visible, even to critics who are aware of these issues in general, indicates that we are not yet in the habit of expecting status problems to turn up on the comics page—when, for reasons this study has attempted to articulate, this is a place they are likely to appear.

9. For the provisions of the code obviously aimed at EC horror comics, see the reprint of the code in the appendix of Gabilliet (315), in particular "General Standards—Part B."

10. On comics as spatio-topia, see Groensteen, *System* chapter 1.

CHAPTER 5

1. For an account of the time Burns spent in Europe and a discussion of his reception there, see Sullivan interview 59–61, 88.

2. See Sullivan interview 61–63, 72.

3. One perceptive critic understood this satirical intent of mid-century horror comics immediately; see Lukács 47.

4. See Sullivan interview 56.

5. For praise of Hefner as a cartooning editor, see Feiffer interview (n. pag.) and Wilson 54–57. Even Harvey Kurtzman, whose relationship with Hefner is reputed to have been tendentious, complimented him on occasion; see Kurtzman.

6. See Sullivan interview 78.

7. See McCloud 28–53.

8. See the pictorial vocabulary diagram in McCloud 52–53. McCloud himself, working from a sense of the comics Burns published prior to *Black Hole*, maps his style somewhat differently; note figure 29 of the diagram.

9. *Black Hole* is not paginated, but for the purpose of this discussion, and for the sake of future scholarly and classroom work on Burns, I have created pagination, markers of which are provided here. The first chapter heading, "Biology 101," is page 3. The chapter heading "Racing Towards Something" is page 37. "Cut" is page 75. "Cook Out" is page 119. "Windowpane" is page 147. "Under Open Skies" is page 175. "Lizard Queen" is page 203. "Summer Vacation" is page 231. "Driving South" is page 299.

10. Again, see McCloud 52–53.

11. Mitchell, it should be noted, does not believe that abstract painting is nearly as pure as this description might suggest; he believes in fact that it is "a pictorial code requiring a verbal apologetics as elaborate as that of any traditional mode of painting" (*Iconology* 41–42). For a fuller version of Mitchell's take on this subject, see *Picture Theory* chapter 7.

12. Burns himself is an admirer of Lichtenstein, however; see Sullivan interview 85.

13. In 2001, as *Black Hole* was (in relative terms) nearing completion, Burns observed: "Despite all the limitations, I like comics as objects: separate, self-contained books that you can hold in your hand and read again and again. . . . I also like the fact that I have total control over the final product: designing the book, breaking down the story and not censoring myself in any way when it comes to the content. Even though I was writing the stories I wanted to in the weekly comic I was doing, there was still subject matter that I was starting to get interested in that wouldn't fit into the all-ages papers that were publishing them" ("Six Guys" 68).

14. See Champion interview. Burns was also thinking in general terms about AIDS when he made "Teen Plague"; see Sullivan interview 65.

15. See Sontag 112–121.

16. Again, see Sontag.

17. See Moretti, in particular, chapter 1.

18. Particular thanks to Jasmine Morrisette for noting this resemblance.

19. See Rust 48.

CHAPTER 6

1. As readers familiar with the story of Fantagraphics are well aware, the economics of its publishing model have been considerably more fraught than my brief summary might imply. Even popular titles, such as L&R, did not allow Fantagraphics as a whole to break even financially, and over the course of the 1990s the company became solvent only by developing Eros, a line of pornographic comics. Gilbert's *Birdland*, discussed later in this chapter, was a successful Eros title. For a useful summary of these matters in the context of L&R, see Marc Sobel's interview of Gary Groth in *The Love & Rockets Companion*.

2. The publication of underground "comix" in the 1960s, which offered R. Crumb a measure of prosperity, can arguably be seen as an earlier example of such a system. However, the distribution network offered by direct market comics shops, and the option for at least some limited chain bookstore distribution, were not in place until after the heyday of the underground.

3. "Frida" first appeared in L&R issue 28 (Dec. 1988). Citations for this story and, unless otherwise noted, all other citations in this chapter are taken from the Love & Rockets Library volumes released from 2007 to the present.

4. For Crumb's recent thoughts on the Hernandez brothers' mastery of figure drawing, see "Genesis" 25.

5. My thanks to Pedro Morán-Palma for pointing me to this antecedent.

6. For the purposes of describing Gilbert's aesthetics, I have kept my focus on Jaime, regular co-contributor to *Love & Rockets*, without reference to the more intermittent contributions of Mario, whose style differs greatly from that of his brothers. While they differ in their portrayals of violence, Gilbert and Jaime both tend toward a synthesis of the realistic and the iconic (see McCloud's charting of their work on 52–53 of *Understanding Comics*). Mario deploys a style that, in contrast to the work of his brothers, is at once more realistic in terms of detail and shading and more loose and expressive as regards perspective, proportion and line.

7. See McCloud chapter 2, particularly 27–39.

8. The precise scope of comics burning at mid-century is not known. What is known, however, is that while some burnings targeted certain (very broadly defined) kinds of comics, it was the fact that they were comics in the first place that made their burning acceptable. For accounts of some specific, well-documented instances, see Hajdu chapter 14.

9. For the brothers' early thoughts on the question of Latina/o identity and representation in their work, see "Pleased," in which both Jaime and Gilbert—the

latter, in particular—repeatedly express their ambitions to create both a new kind of comics and a new representation of Latina/o culture for a US audience. For the brothers' more recent recollections on this question, see Sobel interview 123.

10. Though Hatfield persuasively argues that Pedro has a polysemic function in "Poison River," I see Pedro as being more strongly identified with right-wing ideologies (101).

11. On the dynamics of closure in comics reading, see McCloud chapter 3, particularly the discussion of reader involvement on 63–68.

12. Charles Hatfield, assembling evidence from existing interviews along with new conversations with the artist, has best established the impact of "Poison River" on Gilbert's career; see *Alternative Comics* 102–107.

13. Gilbert has made clear that his and Jaime's motivation for reviving the *Love and Rockets* moniker was economic: "When we started to do comics that weren't called *Love and Rockets*, they weren't selling. . . . During that time between the two versions of *Love and Rockets*, we actually did more comics than we ever have, but they went almost unnoticed" (Aldama interview 173).

14. For example, see the three stories "Bread, Love and Maria" (issue 45), "The Gorgo Wheel" (issue 47), and "Luba Conquers the World" (issue 48).

Works Cited

Arnold, Andrew D. "The Graphic Novel Silver Anniversary." Time.com. 14 Nov. 2003. N. pag. Web. 14 July 2012.

Baetens, Jan. "*Fun Home*: Ithaca, Pennsylvania." *Modernism Today*. Ed. Sjef Houppermans, Peter Liebregts, Jan Baetens and Otto Boele. Amsterdam: Rodopi, 2013. 205–218. Print.

Bakjian, Mardie Jay. "Kern Ave. Junior High Uses Comics as a Bridge." *Library Journal* 70.1 (1945): 291–292. Print.

Ball, David M. "Comics Against Themselves: Chris Ware's Graphic Narratives as Literature." *The Rise of the American Comics Artist: Creators and Contexts*. Ed. Paul Williams and James Lyons. Jackson: U of Mississippi P, 2010. 103–123. Print.

Bateman, John A., and Janina Wildfeuer. "Defining Units of Analysis for the Systematic Analysis of Comics: A Discourse-Based Approach." *Studies in Comics* 5.2 (2014): 373–403. Print.

Beaty, Bart. *Comics Versus Art*. Toronto: U of Toronto P, 2012. Print.

———. *Fredric Wertham and the Critique of Mass Culture*. Jackson: U of Mississippi P, 2005. Print.

Bechdel, Alison. *Are You My Mother? A Comic Drama*. Boston: Houghton Mifflin, 2012. Print.

———. "Comics and Cartoons Across Borders: Alison Bechdel." *Columbia* 27 (Winter 1996–1997): 169. Print.

———. *The Essential Dykes to Watch Out For*. Boston: Houghton Mifflin Harcourt, 2008. Print.

———. *Fun Home: A Family Tragicomic*. New York: Mariner, 2006. Print.

———. *The Indelible Alison Bechdel: Confessions, Comix, and Miscellaneous Dykes to Watch Out For*. Ithaca, NY: Firebrand Books, 1998. Print.

———. "An Interview with Alison Bechdel." Interview with Hillary Chute. *Modern Fiction Studies* 52.4 (2006): 1004–1013. Print.

———. Interview with Anne Rubenstein. *The Comics Journal* 179 (August 1995): 112–121. Print.

———. Introduction. *Dykes and Sundry Other Carbon-Based Life Forms to Watch Out For*. Los Angeles: Alyson Books, 2003. N. pag. Print.

———. "Life Drawing: An Interview with Alison Bechdel." Interview with Lynn Emmert. *The Comics Journal* 282 (2007): 34–52. Print.

Beirne, Rebecca. *Lesbians in Television and Text After the Millennium*. New York: Palgrave Macmillan, 2008. Print.

Blumenberg, Hans. *The Legitimacy of the Modern Age*. 1996. Trans. Robert Wallace. Cambridge, MA: MIT P, 1985. Print.

Brooker, Will. *Batman Unmasked: Analyzing a Cultural Icon*. New York: Continuum, 2000. Print.

———. "Hero of the Beach: Flex Mentallo at the End of the Worlds." *Journal of Graphic Novels and Comics* 2.1 (2011): 25–37. Print.

———. *Hunting the Dark Knight: Twenty-First Century Batman*. London: I. B. Tauris, 2012. Print.

Brown, Chester. "Chester Brown: From the Sacred to the Scatological." Interview with Scott Grammel. *The Comics Journal* 135 (April 1990): 66–90. Print.

———. Untitled comic. *New York Times Magazine* 11 July 2004: cover, 25. Print.

Brown, Jeffrey A. *Black Superheroes, Milestone Comics, and Their Fans*. Jackson: UP of Mississippi, 2000. Print.

Brown, Jonathan Rikard. "I Am Robin: The Reader's Gateway into the World of *The Dark Knight Returns*." *International Journal of Comic Art* 13.1 (2011): 644–653. Print.

Burns, Charles. *Black Hole*. 1995–2004. New York: Pantheon, 2005. Print.

———. "Curse of the Molemen." 1980. *Big Baby*. Seattle: Fantagraphics, 2007. 9–40. Print.

———. *The Hive*. New York: Pantheon, 2012. Print.

———. Interview with Bryan Hood. *Anthem* 10 Mar. 2008. N. pag. Web. 6 Feb. 2009.

———. Interview with Darcy Sullivan. *The Comics Journal* 148 (February 1992): 52–88. Print.

———. Interview with Edward Champion. *The Bat Segundo Show* episode 177. 10 Feb. 2008. Web. 15 Feb. 2009.

———. Interview with Hillary Chute. *The Believer* 50 (January 2008): 47–64. Print.

———. Self-portrait. *The Comics Journal* 148 (February 1992): cover. Print.

———. *Sugar Skull*. New York: Pantheon, 2014. Print.

———. "Teen Plague." 1980. *Big Baby*. Seattle: Fantagraphics, 2007. 41–62. Print.

———. *X'ed Out*. New York: Pantheon, 2010. Print.

Caruth, Cathy. *Unclaimed Experience: Trauma, Narrative, and History*. Baltimore: Johns Hopkins UP, 1996. Print.

Castle, Gregory. *Reading the Modernist Bildungsroman*. Gainesville: UP of Florida, 2006. Print.

Chute, Hillary. "Comics as Literature? Reading Graphic Narrative." *PMLA* 123.2 (2008): 452–465. Print.

———. *Graphic Women: Life Narrative & Contemporary Comics.* New York: Columbia UP, 2010. Print.

———. "Secret Labor." *Poetry* 202.4 (2013): 379–381. Print.

Cohn, Neil. "The Limits of Time and Transitions: Challenges to Theories of Sequential Image Comprehension." *Studies in Comics* 1.1 (2010): 127–147. Print.

———. *The Visual Language of Comics: Introduction to the Structure and Cognition of Visual Images.* London: Bloomsbury, 2013. Print.

Comics Magazine Association of America Comics Code. 1954. Appendix. *Of Comics and Men: A Cultural History of American Comic Books* by Jean-Paul Gabilliet. 2005, trans. 2010. 313–336. Print.

"Comics Not Just for Kids Anymore, Reports 85,000th Mainstream News Story." *The Onion* 48.28 (12 July 2012): 1. Print.

Cormack, Bradin, and Carla Mazzio. *Book Use, Book Theory: 1500–1700.* Chicago: U of Chicago P, 2005. Print.

Crumb, R. "The Genesis Interview." Interview with Gary Groth. *The Comics Journal* 301 (February 2011): 20–69. Print.

Cvetkovich, Ann. "Drawing the Archive in Alison Bechdel's *Fun Home*." *Women's Studies Quarterly* 36.1–2 (2008): 111–128. Print.

Cwiklik, Greg. "What's Wrong with Comics Today? A Completely Personal Overview." *The Comics Journal Special Edition* 1 (Winter 2002): 37–46. Print.

Delany, Samuel R. "Inside and Outside the Canon: The *Para*doxa* Interview." 1995. *Shorter Views: Queer Thoughts & The Politics of the Paraliterary.* Hanover, CT: Wesleyan UP, 1999. 186–217. Print.

———. "The Politics of Paraliterary Criticism." 1996. *Shorter Views: Queer Thoughts & The Politics of the Paraliterary.* Hanover, CT: Wesleyan UP, 1999. 218–270. Print.

Derrida, Jacques. "The Law of Genre." 1980. Trans. Avital Ronell. *Critical Inquiry* 7.1 (1980): 55–81. Print.

Dias, Earl J. "Comic Books—A Challenge to the English Teacher." *English Journal* 35.3 (1946): 142–145. *JSTOR Arts & Sciences IV.* 4 Oct. 2012. Web.

Díaz, Junot. *The Brief Wondrous Life of Oscar Wao.* New York: Riverhead, 2007. Print.

Ditmer, Jason. "Captain America in the News: Changing Mediascapes and the Appropriation of a Superhero." *Journal of Graphic Novels and Comics* 3.2 (2012): 143–157. Print.

Dorfman, Ariel, and Armand Mattelart. *How to Read Donald Duck: Imperialist Ideology in the Disney Comic.* 1971. Trans. David Kunzle. 2nd ed. New York: International General, 1984. Print.

Doris, Sara. *Pop Art and the Contest over American Culture.* Cambridge: Cambridge UP, 2007. Print.

Eco, Umberto. "Innovation and Repetition: Between Modern and Postmodern Aesthetics." *Daedalus* 114.4 (1985): 161–184. Print.

———. "The Myth of Superman." Trans. Natalie Chilton. *Diacritics* 2.1 (1972): 14–22. Print.

Edidin, Rachel. "Four-Color Invasion: How Comics Crashed the Canon." *Gulf Coast* 20.2 (2008): 295–302. Print.

Eisner, Will. *Comics and Sequential Art.* 1985. New York: Norton, 2008. Print.

———. *A Contract with God.* New York: Norton, 2006. Print.

Eisner, Will, and Frank Miller. *Eisner/Miller: A One-on-One Interview Conducted by Charles Brownstein.* Ed. Diana Schutz and Charles Brownstein. Milwaukie, OR: Dark Horse Books, 2005. Print.

Elder, Will. "Damn You, Larry Storch: The Will Elder Interview." Interview with Gary Groth. *The Comics Journal* 254 (July 2003): 78–135. Print.

Erickson, Steve. "Dreamland: When Neil Gaiman Writes the Last Chapter of 'The Sandman' This Fall, the Greatest Epic in the History of Comic Books—Seven Years and 2,000 Pages—Will Come to a Close." *Los Angeles Times* 3 Sept. 1995. N. pag. Web. 1 July 2013.

Feiffer, Jules. Interview with Paul Morton. N. pag. *Bookslut.* Apr. 2009. Web. 5 June 2015.

Fiedler, Leslie. "The Middle Against Both Ends." *Encounter* 5.2 (1955): 16–23. Print.

"Four Creators Refuse to Work on Rated Comics." *Comics Buyer's Guide* 691 (13 Feb. 1987): 1+. Print.

Freedman, Ariela. "Drawing on Modernism in Alison Bechdel's *Fun Home.*" *Journal of Modern Literature* 32.4 (2009): 125–140. Print.

Frye, Northrop. *The Secular Scripture: A Study of the Structure of Romance.* Cambridge, MA: Harvard UP, 1976. Print.

Gabilliet, Jean-Paul. *Of Comics and Men: A Cultural History of American Comic Books.* 2005. Trans. Bart Beaty and Nick Nguyen. Jackson: U of Mississippi P, 2010. Print.

Gaiman, Neil. Interview with Gary Groth. *The Comics Journal* 169 (July 1994): 54–108. Print.

Gardner, Jared. *Projections: Comics and the History of Twenty-First-Century Storytelling.* Stanford, CA: Stanford UP, 2012. Print.

———. "Storylines." *SubStance* 124/40.1 (2011): 53–69. Print.

Gilbert, James. *A Cycle of Outrage: America's Reaction to the Juvenile Delinquent in the 1950s.* New York: Oxford UP, 1986. Print.

Gombrich, E. H. *Art and Illusion: A Study in the Psychology of Pictorial Representation.* Princeton, NJ: Princeton UP, 2000. Print.

Groensteen, Thierry. *Comics and Narration.* 2010. Trans. Ann Miller. Jackson: U of Mississippi P, 2013. Print.

———. *The System of Comics.* 1999. Trans. Bart Beaty and Nick Nguyen. Jackson: U of Mississippi P, 2010. Print.

———. "Why Are Comics Still in Search of Cultural Legitimization?" *Comics &*

Culture: Analytical and Theoretical Approaches to Comics. Copenhagen: Museum Tusculam Press, 2000. 29–41. Print.

Grossman, Lev. "All-TIME 100 Novels: Watchmen." Time.com. 11 Jan. 2010. N. pag. Web. 22 July 2013.

Groth, Gary. Interview with Marc Sobel. *The Love and Rockets Companion: 30 Years (And Counting).* Ed. Marc Sobel and Kristy Valenti. Seattle: Fantagraphics, 2013. 160–177. Print.

———. "Just Six Guys in a Hotel Room: The Industry's Most Influential Creators Talk Art and Craft with Gary Groth." Interview with Charles Burns, Kim Deitch, Bill Griffith, Joe Sacco, and Seth. *The Comics Journal* 234 (2001): 60–76. Print.

Guillory, John. "Genesis of the Media Concept." *Critical Inquiry* 36.2 (2010): 321–362. Print.

Hajdu, David. *The Ten-Cent Plague: The Great Comic-Book Scare and How It Changed America.* 2008. New York: Picador, 2009. Print.

Hammond, Heidi. "Graphic Novels and Multimodal Literacy: A Reader Response Study." Diss. University of Minnesota, 2009. University of Minnesota Digital Conservancy. Web. 17 July 2012.

Harris, Charlie. Letter. *Love and Rockets* 31 (1989): 33. Print.

Harrison, Sylvia. *Pop Art and the Origins of Postmodernism.* Cambridge: Cambridge UP, 2001. Print.

Hatfield, Charles. *Alternative Comics: An Emerging Literature.* Jackson: U of Mississippi P, 2005. Print.

———. "Defining Comics in the Classroom; or, the Pros and Cons of Unfixability." *Teaching the Graphic Novel.* Ed. Stephen E. Tabachnick. New York: Modern Language Association, 2009. 19–27. Print.

———. "Thoughts on *Understanding Comics*." *The Comics Journal* 211 (April 1999): 87–91. Print.

Hays, Matthew. "Of Maus and Man: Art Spiegelman Revisits His Holocaust Classic." *Globe and Mail* 8 Oct. 2001. N. pag. Web. 11 Feb. 2014.

Heer, Jeet, and Kent Worcester. "Early Twentieth Century Voices." *Arguing Comics: Literary Masters on a Popular Medium.* Ed. Jeet Heer and Kent Worcester. Jackson: U of Mississippi P, 2004. 1–3. Print.

———. Introduction. *Arguing Comics: Literary Masters on a Popular Medium.* Ed. Jeet Heer and Kent Worcester. Jackson: U of Mississippi P, 2004. vii–xxiii. Print.

Heintjes, Tom. "Shooter Speaks Out on Kirby Art." *The Comics Journal* 104 (January 1986): 9–11. Print.

Hernandez, Gilbert. "An American in Palomar." 1985. *Love & Rockets Library: Heartbreak Soup.* Ed. Kim Thompson. Seattle: Fantagraphics, 2007. 169–192. Print.

———. *Birdland.* Seattle: Eros Comix, October 1990–July 1991. Print.

———. "Bullnecks and Bracelets." 1987. *Love & Rockets Library: Heartbreak Soup.* Ed. Kim Thompson. Seattle: Fantagraphics, 2007. 268–287. Print.

———. *A Chance in Hell.* Seattle: Fantagraphics, 2007. Print.

———. "Farewell My Palomar." 1993. *Love & Rockets Library: Human Diastrophism.* Ed. Kim Thompson. Seattle: Fantagraphics, 2007. 124–139. Print.

———. "Frida." 1988. *Love & Rockets Library: Amor Y Cohetes.* Ed. Kim Thompson. Seattle: Fantagraphics, 2008. 175–186. Print.

———. "Holidays in the Sun." 1986. *Love & Rockets Library: Heartbreak Soup.* Ed. Kim Thompson. Seattle: Fantagraphics, 2007. 199–212. Print.

———. "Human Diastrophism." 1987–1988. *Love & Rockets Library: Human Diastrophism.* Ed. Kim Thompson. Seattle: Fantagraphics, 2007. 17–122. Print.

———. "Human Diastrophism Part 3." *Love and Rockets* issue 23 (1987): 1–17. Print.

———. Interview with Frederick Luis Aldama. *Your Brain on Latino Comics* by Frederick Luis Aldama. Austin: U of Texas P, 2009. 171–181. Print.

———. "The Laughing Sun." 1984. *Love & Rockets Library: Heartbreak Soup.* Ed. Kim Thompson. Seattle: Fantagraphics, 2007. 117–128. Print.

———. *Maria M. Book 1.* Seattle: Fantagraphics, 2013. Print.

———. "Poison River." 1989–1993. *Love & Rockets Library: Beyond Palomar.* Ed. Kim Thompson. Seattle: Fantagraphics, 2007. 7–189. Print.

———. "Proof That the Devil Loves You." *Love and Rockets: New Stories* no. 5. Seattle: Fantagraphics, 2012. 15–62. Print.

———. Reply to letter of Charlie Harris. *Love and Rockets* 31 (1989): 33. Print.

———. "The Reticent Heart." 1985. *Love & Rockets Library: Heartbreak Soup.* Ed. Kim Thompson. Seattle: Fantagraphics, 2007. 153–163. Print.

———. "Venus Tells It Like It Is!" 1997. *Love & Rockets Library: Luba and Her Family.* Ed. Eric Reynolds and Kristy Valenti. Seattle: Fantagraphics, 2014. 222. Print.

Hernandez, Gilbert, and Jaime Hernandez. Interview with Neil Gaiman. *The Comics Journal* 178 (1995): 91–123. Print.

Hernandez, Gilbert, Jaime Hernandez, and Mario Hernandez. "Pleased to Meet Them . . ." Interview with Gary Groth, Robert Fiore and Thom Powers. *The Comics Journal* 126 (1989): 60–113. Print.

———. Interview with Marc Sobel. *The Love and Rockets Companion: 30 Years (And Counting).* Ed. Marc Sobel and Kristy Valenti. Seattle: Fantagraphics, 2013. 120–159. Print.

Hernandez, Jaime. "Mechanics Part 6." 1983. *Love & Rockets Library: Maggie the Mechanic.* Ed. Kim Thompson. Seattle: Fantagraphics, 2007. 61–70. Print.

Hill, Joe. Introduction. *Incognito: Bad Influences.* Written by Ed Brubaker and illustrated by Sean Phillips. New York: Icon, 2011. N. pag. Print.

Hill, Joe, writer. "Freddy Wertham Goes to Hell." Illustrated by Seth Fisher and Langdon Foss. *Grave Tales* 3.2/6 (2009). Forest Hill, MD: Cemetery Dance Publications. N. pag. Print.

———. *Locke & Key: Guide to the Known Keys* one-shot. Illustrated by Gabriel Rodriguez. Oct. 2011. San Diego: IDW. Print.

———. *Locke and Key Volume 1: Welcome to Lovecraft* issue 2. Illustrated by Gabriel Rodriguez. Mar. 2008. San Diego: IDW. Print.

————. Script. *Locke and Key Volume 1: Welcome to Lovecraft Special Edition*. San Diego: IDW, 2011. 181–294. Print.

Howard, Sheena C., and Ronald L. Jackson II, eds. *Black Comics: Politics of Race and Representation*. New York: Bloomsbury Academic, 2013. Print.

Hutcheon, Linda. *The Politics of Postmodernism*. 1989. 2nd ed. London: Routledge, 2002. Print.

Huyssen, Andreas. *After the Great Divide: Modernism, Mass Culture, Postmodernism*. Bloomington: U of Indiana P, 1986. Print.

Iadonisi, Richard. "'A Man Has Risen': Hard Bodies, Reaganism and *The Dark Knight Returns*." *International Journal of Comic Art* 14.1 (2012): 543–553. Print.

Itzkoff, Dave. "The Vendetta Behind 'V for Vendetta.'" *New York Times* 12 Mar. 2006. Web. 5 Nov. 2013.

Kashtan, Aaron. "My Mother Was a Typewriter: *Fun Home* and the Importance of Materiality in Comics." *Journal of Graphic Novels and Comics* 4.1 (June 2013): 92–116. Print.

Khoury, George. *The Extraordinary Works of Alan Moore*. 2003. Ed. George Khoury. Raleigh, NC: TwoMorrows Publishing, 2008. Print.

Kidd, Chip. "Graphic Novels Panel Discussion." Interview with Charles Burns, Kim Deitch, Kaz, Richard McGuire, Art Spiegelman and Chris Ware. *The Comics Journal* 243 (May 2002): 33–44. Print.

Klock, Geoff. *How to Read Superhero Comics and Why*. New York: Continuum, 2003. Print.

Koike, Kazuo, and Goseki Kojima. Interview with Frank Miller. *Comics Interview* 52 (1987): 16–21. Print.

Kunitz, Stanley J. "Libraries, to Arms!" *Wilson Library Bulletin* 15.8 (1941): 670–671. Print.

Kupperman, Michael. "Are Comics Serious Literature?" *Tales Designed to Thrizzle* 1 (2005): 32. Print.

————. Interview. *The Onion*. 21 July 2009. Web. 30 Mar. 2014.

Kurtzman, Harvey. Interview with Don Swaim. Audio. 28 June 1985. *Wired for Books*. Web. 5 June 2015.

Kuskin, William, and Matthew Slade. "Preface: Talking About Comics"; "Into the Book"; "Pilgrimage to the MLA"; "Slugging It Out with the Mainstream Serial"; "Epilogue." *English Language Notes* 46.2 (2008): 3–4, 17–21, 73–75, 153, 213. Print.

Lemberg, Jennifer. "Closing the Gap in Alison Bechdel's *Fun Home*." *Women's Studies Quarterly* 36.1–2 (2008): 129–140. Print.

Lindauer, Margaret A. *Devouring Frida: The Art History and Popular Celebrity of Frida Kahlo*. Hanover, CT: Wesleyan UP, 1999. Print.

Lopes, Paul. *Demanding Respect: The Evolution of the American Comic Book*. Philadelphia: Temple UP, 2009. Print.

Lucas, Mary R. "Our Friendly Enemy? The Library Looks at the Comics." *Library Journal* 66.22 (1941): 824–827. Print.

Lukács, Georg. *Realism in Our Time: Literature and the Class Struggle*. 1964. Trans. John and Necke Mander. New York: Harper & Row, 1971. Print.

Lyotard, Jean-François. *The Differend: Phrases in Dispute*. 1983. Trans. Georges Van Den Abbeele. Minneapolis: U of Minnesota P, 1998. Print.

"Masterpiece: Frank Miller's *The Dark Knight Returns*." Supplementary feature. *Batman: The Dark Knight Returns*. Warner Bros., 2012. Video.

McCammon, Sarah. "Books with Gay Themes Put S.C. Colleges' Funding at Risk." *NPR.org*. 9 May 2014. Web. 1 Jan. 2014.

McCloud, Scott. *Understanding Comics: The Invisible Art*. New York: Harper-Collins, 1993. Print.

McGrath, Charles. "Not Funnies." *New York Times Magazine* 11 July 2004: 24+. Print.

McKitterick, David. *Print, Manuscript and the Search for Order, 1450–1830*. Cambridge: Cambridge UP, 2003. Print.

Miller, Frank, writer and illustrator. Lynn Varley, colorist. Klaus Janson, inks. *The Dark Knight Returns*. 1986–1987. 10th Anniversary Edition. New York: DC Comics, 1997. Print.

———. *The Dark Knight Strikes Again*. 2001–2002. New York: DC Comics, 2002. Print.

———. Editorial cartoon. *Comics Buyer's Guide* 691 (13 Feb. 1987): 4. Print.

———. "Frank Miller: Return of the Dark Knight." Interview with Kim Thompson. *The Comics Journal* 101 (August 1985): 58–79. Print.

———. "The Good Old Days . . . and Now." Interview with Gary Groth. *The Comics Journal* 209 (December 1998): 72–90. Print.

———. *Holy Terror*. Burbank, CA: Legendary, 2011. Print.

———. Interview with Dwight R. Decker. *The Comics Journal* 70 (January 1982): 68–93. Print.

———. Interview with Elvis Mitchell. 22. Feb. 2002. *KCRW's The Treatment*, National Public Radio. *KCRW.com*. Audio. Web. 30 June 2008.

———. Interview with Gary Groth. *The Comics Journal* 118 (December 1987): 74–83. Print.

———. Interview with Mark Borax. *Comics Interview* 31 (1986): 38–53. Print.

Miller, Frank, Denny O'Neil, Louise Jones and Roy Thomas. "Relevancy in Comics." Panel Discussion, San Diego Comicon. 1981. *The Comics Journal* 68 (November 1981): 52–59. Print.

Mitchell, W. J. T. "Comics as Media: Afterward." *Critical Inquiry* (Spring 2014): 255–265. Print.

———. *Iconology: Image, Text, Ideology*. Chicago: U of Chicago P, 1986. Print.

———. *Picture Theory*. Chicago: U of Chicago P, 1994. Print.

———. *What Do Pictures Want? The Lives and Loves of Images*. Chicago: U of Chicago P, 2005. Print.

Moore, Alan. Editorial. *Comics Buyer's Guide* 691 (13 Feb. 1987): 4+. Print.

Moore, Alan, and J. H. Williams. *Promethea*. 1999–2005. America's Best Comics. Print.

Moore, Anne Elizabeth. Editorial. *The Comics Journal* 235 (July 2001): 3–8. Print.

Moretti, Franco. *The Way of the World: The Bildungsroman in European Culture*. London: Verso, 1987. Print.

Mowatt, Raoul V. "Batman Gathers Fellow Heroes to Set Things Right in DK2." *Chicago Tribune* 21 Aug. 2002. N. pag. Web. 22 June 2012.

Muller, Agnes. "Image as Paratext in Alison Bechdel's *Fun Home*." *GRAAT* 1 (March 2007): n. pag. Web. 7 May 2008.

Murray, Chris. "*Pop*aganda: Superhero Comics and Propaganda in World War II." *Comics & Culture: Analytical and Theoretical Approaches to Comics*. Copenhagen: Museum Tusculam Press, 2000. 141–155. Print.

Nama, Adilifu. *Super Black: American Pop Culture and Black Superheroes*. Austin: U of Texas P, 2011. Print.

"Neil Gaiman, Frank Miller, Jim Lee and More Join CBLDF Advisory Board." *Comic Book Resources*. 5 Apr. 2013. Web. 20 June 2013.

Nericcio, William Anthony. "A Decidedly 'Mexican' and 'American' Semi[er]otic Transferrence: Frida Kahlo in the Eyes of Gilbert Hernandez." *Latino/a Popular Culture*. Ed. Michelle Habell-Pallán and Mary Romero. New York: New York UP, 2002. 190–207. Print.

Nordlund, Christopher. "Imagining Terrorists Before Sept. 11: Marvel's G.I. Joe Comic Books, 1982–1994." *ImageTexT* 3.1 (2006). Web. 3 Aug. 2011.

North, Sterling. "A National Disgrace." *Chicago Daily News* 8 May 1940: 21. Print.

Nyberg, Amy Kiste. "How Librarians Learned to Love the Graphic Novel." *Graphic Novels and Comics in Libraries and Archives: Essays on Readers, Research, History and Cataloguing*. Ed. Robert G. Weiner. Jefferson, NC: McFarland, 2010. 26–40. Print.

———. *Seal of Approval: The History of the Comics Code*. Jackson: U of Mississippi P, 1998. Print.

Orbán, Katalin. "A Language of Scratches and Stitches: The Graphic Novel Between Hyperrreading and Print." *Critical Inquiry* (Spring 2014): 169–181. Print.

Pearl, Monica B. "Graphic Language: Redrawing the Family (Romance) in Alison Bechdel's *Fun Home*." *Prose Studies* 30.3 (2008): 287–304. Print.

Pearson, Roberta E., and William Urrichio, eds. *The Many Lives of the Batman: Critical Approaches to a Superhero and His Media*. London: Routledge, 1991. Print.

Pellitteri, Marco. "Alan Moore, Watchmen and Some Notes on the Ideology of Superhero Comics." *Studies in Comics* 2.1 (2011): 81–91. Print.

Pizzino, Christopher. "Art That Goes BOOM: Genre and Aesthetics in Frank Miller's *Sin City*." *ELN* 46.2 (2008): 115–128. Print.

———. "Autoclastic Icons: Bloodletting and Burning in Gilbert Hernandez's *Palomar*." *ImageTexT* 7.1 (2013). N. pag. Web. 2 Feb. 2014.

Pynchon, Thomas. *Gravity's Rainbow*. New York: Viking, 1973. Print.

Raeburn, Daniel. *Chris Ware*. New Haven, CT: Yale UP, 2004. Print.

Rasula, Jed. "Nietzsche in the Nursery: Naive Classics and Surrogate Parents in Postwar American Cultural Debates." *Representations* 29 (1990): 50–77. Print.

Reynolds, Eric, Sergio Aragonés, Donna Barr and Devon DeLapp. Cover illustration. Composed by Carrie Whitney. *The Comics Journal* 235 (July 2001). Print.

Rust, David. "No. 75: *Black Hole*." Top 100 Comics of the Century. *The Comics Journal* 210 (February 1999): 34–108. Print.

Sabin, Roger. *Adult Comics*. London: Routledge, 1993. Print.

Sandifer, Philip. "Amazing Fantasies: Trauma, Affect and Superheroes." *English Language Notes* 46.2 (2008): 175–192. Print.

Schott, Gareth. "From Fan Appropriation to Industry Re-appropriation: The Sexual Identity of Comic Superheroes." *Journal of Graphic Novels and Comics* 1.1 (2010): 17–29. Print.

Schwarz, Gretchen. "Expanding Literacies Through Graphic Novels." *English Journal* 95.6 (2006): 58–64. Print.

Seda, Dori. "Fuck Story." 1986. *Dori Stories: The Complete Dori Seda*. Ed. Don Donahue and Kate Kane. San Francisco: Last Gasp, 1999. 86–90. Print.

———. "How My Family Encouraged Me to Become an Artist!" 1987. *Dori Stories: The Complete Dori Seda*. Ed. Don Donahue and Kate Kane. San Francisco: Last Gasp, 1999. 136–137. Print.

Simmons, David. "'Nothing Too Heavy or Too Light': Negotiating Moore's *Tom Strong* and the Academic Establishment." *Studies in Comics* 2.1 (2011): 57–67. Print.

Slaughter, Joseph. *Human Rights Inc.: The World Novel, Narrative Form and International Law*. New York: Fordham UP, 2007. Print.

Sloan, Willona M. "No Laughing Matter: Comic Books Have Serious Educational Value." *Education Update* 51.10 (2009): 1–7. *Education Research Complete*. 29 Sept. 2012. Web.

Sontag, Susan. *Illness as Metaphor and AIDS and Its Metaphors*. New York: Picador, 2001. Print.

Sousanis, Walter Nickell. "Varoom, Drawing and Comics Research Roundup." *Spin Weave and Cut*. 31 Oct. 2013. N. pag. Web. 6 Dec. 2013.

Spiegelman, Art. Interview with Gary Groth. Part 1 of 2. *The Comics Journal* 180 (September 1995): 52–106. Print.

———. Untitled sketch dated 24 Mar. 2007. *Be a Nose! Three Sketchbooks*. San Francisco: McSweeney's, 2009. N. pag. Print.

Spiegelman, Art, and W. J. T. Mitchell. "Public Conversation: What the %$#! Happened to Comics?" *Critical Inquiry* (Spring 2014): 20–35. Print.

Spivak, Gayatri Chakravorty. Translator's preface. 1976. *Of Grammatology* by Jacques Derrida. 1967. Trans. Gayatri Chakravorty Spivak. Baltimore: Johns Hopkins UP, 1997. ix–lxxxvii. Print.

Stainbrook, Eric. "Reading Comics: A Theoretical Analysis of Textuality and Discourse in the Comics Medium." Diss. Indiana University of Pennsylvania, 2003. Print.

Stewart, Garrett. "Bookwork as Demediation." *Critical Inquiry* 36.3 (Spring 2010): 410–457. Print.

Sturm, James, and Art Baxter. "Build a Beach Head: A Response to Chapter Nine." *The Comics Journal* 211 (April 1999): 100–103. Print.

Tabachnick, Stephen E. Introduction. *Teaching the Graphic Novel*. Ed. Stephen E. Tabachnick. New York: Modern Language Association, 2009. 1–15. Print.

Tarantino, Quentin, writer and director. *Inglourious Basterds*. Weinstein, 2009. Film.

"The Top 100 (English-Language) Comics of the Century." *The Comics Journal* 210 (February 1999): 34–108. Print.

Van Lente, Fred, and Ryan Dunlavey. *The Comic Book History of Comics*. San Diego: IDW, 2012. Print.

Watson, Julia. "Autographic Disclosures and Genealogies of Desire in Alison Bechdel's *Fun Home*." *Biography* 31.1 (Winter 2008): 27–58. Print.

Wertham, Fredric. "The Comics . . . Very Funny!" *Saturday Review of Literature* 29 May 1948: 6+. Print.

———. "It's Still Murder: What Parents Still Don't Know About Comic Books." *Saturday Review* 9 Apr. 1955: 11+. Print.

———. *Seduction of the Innocent*. New York: Rinehart and Co., 1954. Print.

Whaley, Deborah Elizabeth. "Black Cat Got Your Tongue?: Catwoman, Blackness, and the Alchemy of Postracialism." *Journal of Graphic Novels and Comics* 2.1 (2011): 3–23. Print.

Williams, Gweneira M., and Jane S. Wilson. "Why Not? Give Them What They Want!" *Publisher's Weekly* 141.16 (18 Apr. 1942): 1490–1496. Print.

Williams, Paul, and James Lyons. Introduction. *The Rise of the American Comics Artist: Creators and Contexts*. Ed. Paul Williams and James Lyons. Jackson: U of Mississippi P, 2010. xi–xxiv. Print.

Williams, Raymond. *Marxism and Literature*. Oxford: Oxford UP, 1977. Print.

Wilson, Gahan. Interview with Dennis Daniel. *The Comics Journal* 156 (Feb. 1993): 42–71. Print.

Witek, Joseph. *Comic Books as History: The Narrative Art of Jack Jackson, Art Spiegelman and Harvey Pekar*. Jackson: U of Mississippi P, 1989. Print.

———. "Seven Ways I Don't Teach Comics." *Teaching the Graphic Novel*. Ed. Stephen E. Tabachnick. New York: Modern Language Association, 2009. 217–222. Print.

Worden, Daniel. "The Shameful Art: *McSweeney's Quarterly Concern*, Comics, and the Politics of Affect." *Modern Fiction Studies* 52.4 (2006): 891–917. Print.

Wright, Bradford. *Comic Book Nation: The Transformation of Youth Culture in America*. Baltimore: Johns Hopkins UP, 2003. Print.

Yockey, Matt. "Retopia: The Dialectics of the Superhero Comic Book." *Studies in Comics* 3.2 (2012): 349–370. Print.

Index

Page numbers in italics indicate figures.

CPSIA information can be obtained
at www.ICGtesting.com
Printed in the USA
LVOW08*1514010217
522880LV00007B/134/P